ANCIENT LIVES

ANCIENT LIVES

THE STORY OF
THE PHARAOHS' TOMBMAKERS

John Romer

Weidenfeld & Nicolson
LONDON

ISBN 0 297 78500 1

George Weidenfeld & Nicolson Limited
91 Clapham High Street, London SW4 7TA

Maps by Line and Line

Filmset by Butler & Tanner Ltd
Colour separations by Newsele Litho Ltd
Printed and bound in Great Britain by
Butler & Tanner Ltd, Frome and London

CONTENTS

LIST OF COLOUR PLATES   vii

LIST OF DRAWINGS   ix

LIST OF MAPS   x

FOREWORD   xi

PART ONE: **Ambience**

1	Thebes	3
2	Earthly Powers	6
3	The Great Place	13
4	The Village	19
5	Scribe Kenhirkhopeshef	32
6	Royal Tomb	40
7	Festival	48

PART TWO: **Orbit**

8	Four Kings	57
9	Foreman Paneb	60
10	Dreams	68
11	Kenhirkhopeshef II	73
12	Paneb II	79
13	The Foreman's Brother	88
14	Fragments	94
15	Oracle	100
16	Scribe Amennakht	106
17	Strike	116
18	Vizier and High Priest	124
19	Painters	135

CONTENTS

PART THREE: Ending

    20   Tomb-Robbers   145
    21   Scribe Harshire   156
    22   Thebes II   163
    23   Renaissance   177
    24   Kings and Wadis   191

EPILOGUE: Deir el Medina   202

MAPS   211
CHRONOLOGY   217
TIME-CHART   218
BIBLIOGRAPHY   220
DOCUMENTS CITED   224
ACKNOWLEDGEMENTS   229
THE FILMING OF 'ANCIENT LIVES'   230
INDEX   231

COLOUR PLATES

(The photographs were taken by John Romer. References are given in brackets; for an explanation of abbreviations see page 224.)

Between pages 20 and 21

1 View of western Thebes
2 The tombmakers' village and cemetery
Paintings from the tomb of Ipy (TT 217):
    3 Washermen
    4 Goat herders
    5 Fishermen
    6 Villagers making funeral equipment
    7 Villagers working on ritual furniture
    8 Villagers making a shrine
9 Portrait of Osiris, rear wall, burial chamber of Ramesses I
10 The Valley of the Kings, looking west
11 The tombmakers' village, looking east

Between pages 84 and 85

12 Wooden statue of an unknown villager (Turin Museum 3049)
13 Wooden statue of workman Penbuy (Turin Museum 3048)
14 Wooden statue of an unknown villager (Turin Museum 3106)
15 Pyramidion of Scribe Ramose (Turin Museum 1603)
16 Detail of a door-frame showing Foreman Neferhotep (Turin Museum 1464)
17 Detail from the ceiling of the tomb of Seti II
18 The rising sun, south wall of the first corridor, tomb of Seti II
19 The 'chariot battle' ostracon (Cairo Museum 25125)
20 Interior of the Amun temple of Ramesses II at Deir el Medina
21 Head of a statue of Amenhotep I (Turin Museum 1372)
22 Ramesside cartouches in the Wadi Hammamat

COLOUR PLATES

Between pages 116 and 117

23 The Ramesseum
24 Foreman Anhirkawi and his family, from his burial vault (TT 359)
25 West end of burial chamber ceiling, tomb of Ramesses VI
26 Ceiling detail, tomb of Ramesses VI (soffit between room H and lower corridor)
27 Painting from the tomb of Nakhtamun (north wall of burial chamber C, TT 335)
28 Detail of an astronomical ceiling, tomb of Ramesses VI
29 Detail of the south wall, tomb of Ramesses IX
30 Detail of the south wall, tomb of Prince Montuhirkhopeshef

Between pages 148 and 149

31 Detail of a scene over the entrance to the tomb of Ramesses XI
32 The river Nile and western Thebes
33 The tombmakers' village, looking north
34 Head of the coffin of an unknown Ramesside prince (Cairo Museum 49549)
35 Detail from the funeral papyrus of Nebhepet (Pap. Turin Museum 1786)
36 The compound of Ramesses III's temple at Medinet Habu
37 Scribe Butehamun's house at Medinet Habu
38 Wadi Sikkat el Agala, looking south
39 Scribe Butehamun, detail from his outer coffin (Turin Museum 2236)

DRAWINGS

(The drawings are by Elizabeth Romer. Sources and reference numbers are given in brackets; for full bibliographical details and an explanation of abbreviations see pages 220–4)

	page
Hieroglyph: the standard of the Egyptian Nome (Davies 1958, pl. x, no. 14)	3
Hieroglyph: the scribal kit (Davies 1958, pl. VIII, no. 6)	12
Hieroglyph: an official or a noble (Davies 1958, pl. I, no. 5)	18
Scribe Ramose's appointment graffito in the Valley of the Queens (Černý 1956; TG 1406)	24
Scribe Ramose offering to the mummies of five ladies of his household (Bruyère 1927; TT 250)	31
Hieroglyph: a ripple of water (Griffith 1898, pl. II, no. 12)	39
'The sitting-place of Scribe Kenhirkhopeshef' (Černý 1956; TG 1400)	42
A lute player (Brunner-Traut 1956, no. 59)	54
A scribe painting a panel (Baud 1935, fig. 7; TT A18)	59
The Seth animal (Brunner-Traut 1979, no. 29)	67
A hippopotamus (Moss 1968, pl. XXVI)	72
'Get back Shehakek. . . .' Sketch of a pottery village charm, similar to Scribe Kenhirkhopeshef's, that was hung around the neck (Brunner-Traut 1956, no. 48)	75
A typical bronze bowl	78
Aapahte praying to Seth (Bierbrier 1982, fig. 21; BM EA 35630)	87
Paneb at prayer (Bruyère 1952; TT 211)	88
Detail from the Turin Erotic Papyrus (Omlin 1973)	93
Neferabu praying to a serpent-headed sphinx (Černý 1956; TG 1082)	94
A hippopotamus and a blackbird fig-picking (Omlin 1973)	97
An animal orchestra (Omlin 1973)	98
Detail from the Turin Erotic Papyrus (Omlin 1973)	99
'Will they mention me to the Vizier?' An inscribed potsherd that was presented to the village oracle (Černý 1942, no. 30)	102
The goddess Meretseger, from Neferabu's prayer-stela (Tosi 1972)	105

	page
Scribe Amennakht and two of his sons, Amenemopet and Pentaweret (Hayes 1959; stela MMA 21.1.6)	115
Pack donkey and driver (Capart 1926, fig. 195)	123
Three sons of Ramesses III (Epigraphic Survey 1957)	134
Painter Amenhotep at the funeral of Priest Keneben, possibly a self-portrait (Wilkinson 1837–78, pl. 86; TT 113, destroyed)	137
Scribe Hay from the tomb of Anhirkawi (Brunner-Traut 1956, no. 41; TT 339)	142
Hieroglyph: a roll of papyrus (Davies 1958, pl. VIII, no. 9)	155
King Ramesses IX rises with the sun (Guilmant 1907; KV 6 b.ch south wall)	162
A tomb-painter's sketch designs for the cartouches of Ramesses X (Petrie 1925)	167
A barge being pulled along a canal (Davies 1926; TT 40)	176
Anukis, a goddess of the southern border at Elephantine, drawn by a tombmaker (Peterson 1973, no. 29)	190
'Year 1 [of the new reign] Scribe Butehamun ...' From a graffito in a southern wadi (Černý 1956; TG 1301a, first line)	196
Limestone fragments, inscribed by the villagers, found above the Wadi Gharbi (from a photograph by John Romer, 1976)	198
Herihor and his wife Mutnedjmet, from her funeral papyrus (Budge 1899, pl. X, vol II)	201
Hieroglyph (Davies 1958, pl. X, no. 5)	210

MAPS
Ancient Egypt showing places mentioned in the text	212
The tombmakers' village and its monuments	213
Thebes in the time of the tombmakers	214–15

FOREWORD

This is the biography of a 3000-year-old village – a village whose life is preserved in rich and often eccentric details. Of one of its people, for example, there might remain a comb with some hair around it, a fragment of a letter, a receipt or two; of another, a legal document, a small library and so on. By setting such minutiae against the grandeur of ancient Thebes, I have aimed to make these ancient villagers walk through their own landscape once again. Nothing of the merely typical has been loaded upon an individual back: these villagers are *real* people. My descriptions of their homes, their belongings and their lives, the Theban temples and tombs, the Nile's floods, the sunsets and breezes of a Theban evening, are drawn from a mixture of scientific research and my own experience of the places where they lived and the work that they did there.

The most rewarding discovery during my research was that the villagers' stories were more than mere anecdotes of people in a daily round. For these villagers – the artists and craftsmen that made the Pharaohs' own tombs – were bound to the kings and their courts in a most direct way. History came up the track to the desert village with the food and water, and it affected the villagers not only by making them richer or poorer but also by changing their attitudes to their gods, their relationships to one another. Alone, perhaps, in all the ancient world, in this village you may observe the course of national history directly affecting the lives in individual families through generations.

If such fine stories as remain to us may ever flow in their telling, they must avoid the sweet diversions of scholarship; the information at the end of the book will usually show the manner by which I have arrived at my conclusions. Inevitably, my broad vision of the village and the framework of individual lives inside it rests heavily upon the work of the late Jaroslav Černý, Professor of Egyptology at Oxford, who spent much of his life studying these ancient people.

It should be noted that although many egyptologists refer to the tombmakers' village as having a lifespan of some five hundred years, the documentation of the first two hundred (the xviiith dynasty) is so slight as to not even allow the inhabitants the title of royal tombmakers. As the ancient villagers themselves never once referred to any of the first seventeen dynasties of Egyptian history, it seemed pointless to encumber the kings who founded their village with the title of the xviiith dynasty. To the villagers, these kings were an almost legendary line of monarchs that had long since gone. Consequently, I refer to them as the old dynasty and to their successors - our xixth and xxth dynasties, the tombmakers' own epoch - as the new dynasty. I have also employed translations of the ancient names for many of the places that the villagers knew: Thebes, the Southern City as it was known, is now partly covered by the modern town of Luxor; King Ramesses iii's fortress-temple is today called Medinet Habu; the Great Place, the Valley of the Kings; the Place of Beauty, the Valley of the Queens; and the village, with its little world of shrines, temples, houses and tombs clustered all around it, is known nowadays as Deir el Medina.

JOHN ROMER
Aiola, Tuscany, 1984

Note on the quoted passages:
... *indicates a break in the original text*
— *indicates an omission of part of the original text*

PART ONE
AMBIENCE

1

THEBES

Thebes stands as an altar between the sky's arc and the earth's curve, in a landscape so large that you can never comprehend it all, yet so small that you may walk across it in an hour. The river on its axis shines as straight as quicksilver in a glass, its broad valley etched across the barren desert as are the canals on the surface of Mars. The living city stood on the east bank, a dull Nile-silty city of enormous enclosures and packed suburbs. A sullen city of tight houses, wide processional avenues, dark shaded temples and squared lakes. On the west bank, waterways as symmetrical as the veins in a casting field irrigated the fields of black alluvium brought down by the river's flood. Along the edge of the fields, all plastered and painted and with pennants flying as if gathered for a fair, stood a row of temples. Behind them, and behind the bright green crops, a desert strip desiccated the Theban dead laid in deep-cut burial chambers, done up in death in fine white linens.

Above the rim of the valley's western cliffs is a plain of salty limestone, the edge of the Sahara. Primeval floods tore across this desert plateau, cutting a maze of valleys at its edge and dropping fans of sand and stone on their way to the river. The ancient Egyptians used these little deserts in the valley as the sites of royal temples and, at the southern end of Thebes, for the foundations of a sprawl of brick palaces. These same primeval deluges also sent colossal slabs of limestone, small hills, slipping down off the plateau into the river valley, and these gently eroded hillocks were later used by the Thebans for their cemeteries. The Thebans held that, as the evening sun dropped down behind these cliffs, the dead came up from their funerary vaults to stand by their tomb chapels and look back over the river to the living city, still illuminated in the dusk of the eastern bank. If today, you stand with the ancient dead in this slanting yellow light, you can still feel, as their prayers describe, the river's wind blowing gently down its wide-spanned valley, you can still smell the sweet-damp scent of flowering crops, the aromas of the evening meal, still hear the textured sounds of a living city and, beyond it all, the silence of the desert hissing in the evening

3

air. Three and a half thousand years ago, this same mellow bowl, this warm valley, held within it the capital of an international empire.

> What do they say every day in their hearts,
> those who are far from Thebes?
> They spend their day blinking at its name,
> if only we had it, they say —
> The bread there is tastier than cakes made with goose fat,
> its water is sweeter than honey,
> one drinks of it till one gets drunk.
> Oh! that is how one lives at Thebes.

So wrote a metropolitan scribe, memorializing his visions of the living city, whilst other writers give broader views: telling that the first sights to be seen as you approached the city's harbour in your river boat were the golden tips of hundreds of temple flagpoles flashing like crystals in the distance; then, as you drew closer, myriad linen pennants glittering against the purple cliffs.

Consider these temples of the Nile and why they stand. Why kings living in mud brick rooms attended gods in huge chambers made of fine hard stone. These temples were conduits between heaven and earth, they were the lenses pulling the universe into focus, the guy ropes of heaven, and they studded the capital with mystic interconnections. At Thebes there were two types of temple, and these were separated by the wide river. On the east bank, to the north of the living city, were the vast houses of the state gods, still among the largest religious buildings in the world. On the west bank, stretching in a single row along the edge of the fields, were the temples of the kings, gods amongst these other gods. As their priests were numbered in thousands, so the temples' servants were numbered in tens of thousands and their high priests ranked amongst the most powerful people in the state. All the temples had straight processional ways marching through their centres, through successive pairs of high gateways and sun bright courts, their pylons, monumental gateways, holding high pinewood masts, tips sheathed in gold and silver alloys, their doors as elephantine as an aircraft hangar's, built of logs plated with shining metals and chased with amulitic designs. Many of the temple walls that were close to human contact were similarly clad in bright metals, and glistened with lustrous stones and inlaid glazes.

At the temples' centres stood airless complexes of sunless rooms, chambers that only the ritually pure could enter, surrounding the small central shrines. In these dark sanctuaries elaborate rituals were celebrated through days and nights: rites that spanned years, decades and centuries, communions with eternity, the designs of numberless lives absorbed in deep pieties, built upon the impulses that sustained life in the Nile valley: the tremendous power of the gods, the daily passage of the sun over the river valley, the river's annual flood and the liquefaction of its fields, the germination of seed, the ripening of the crop. The endless rhythms of the ancient state. And on every day of every year, in shadowed chambers of a precise and alien elegance, at the temples' cores, underneath hieratic poses of war and ritual that covered the walls in long rhythmical registers, priests administered the offices of the cult.

2

EARTHLY POWERS

Each one of the west bank temples was surrounded by a hive of buildings, all enclosed by huge rectangular walls. These compounds held within them ceremonial palaces to accommodate the living king and the homes of the priests and scribes who administered the temples' estates. But by far the greatest number of buildings inside the walls were storerooms, acres upon acres of them, the store-cities of the Bible, the granaries of Pharaoh that Joseph had opened for the people in the time of famine. Long, echoing, barrel-vaulted warehouses that held not only the booty of the empire, skins and ivory, lapis lazuli and bright metals, but also the grains and livestock levied from Egypt's own farms. From the cool columned courtyards alongside these dark warehouses, the temples' scribes disbursed their vast stocks in the name of the king.

In 1275 BC, in the fourth year of the reign of King Ramesses II, a young scribe named Ramose was working, so he tells us, in one of the royal temples, counting and listing the herds of cattle sent from estates up and down the Nile valley. Unusually for Thebes, where inheritance of profession was usual, Ramose had not followed his father Amenemheb in his profession as a messenger carrying instructions and reports between the state officials at Thebes, though it must have been Amenemheb's constant attendance upon the bureaucrats that had first brought his son to the notice of one of the scribes. These men were the counters and recorders of the state, and as the grinders of gods' wheels, the millers rather than the grist of their society, they formed an astute middle class. One of these men, then, took the messenger's boy into the scribal schools that many such officials ran and there taught him the skills of writing and accountancy. The young Ramose was shown the use of the equipment that made up a scribe's kit and which was also the honoured badge of that profession: the small slates on which the raw pigments for the inks were ground; the circular dishes in which the fine-ground pigments were mixed with their binders to make the inks; the smoothing stones with which the papyrus writing sheets were burnished to allow the brushes a smooth progress; the method of preparing the reeds that served as brushes by carefully chewing their ends to separate their stiff fibres enabling them to hold the ink; the rectangular wooden palettes, with places for small cakes of ink and a central slot to hold a dozen brushes; and the special knotting that was used to tie all these pieces together with a cord to make a single portable kit. Ramose was also taught the prayers that all scribes recited before they started work, along with the gentle ritual of sprinkling drops of water in honour of the spirits of the profession's patrons. He had to memorize the 700-odd hieroglyphic signs and their flamboyant cursive equivalents used in the records of the royal administration. And finally, by the hypnotic process of repetition, the boy was filled with the elaborate repertoire of form and phrase that made up the literary language of the state.

These scribes' schools were hard, their morality, the backbone of the state, strict and straight. Later in his life, one scribe recalled that his training had consisted of having his back beaten to allow words to enter his ear. Certainly such training did little to cultivate originality. What it did produce, however, were generations of stolid men set for lifetimes in the state machine – pleasant lives engrossed in bureaucracy and the care of large households. If such training filled the scribes with arduous virtues, these were usually leavened in the individual by a fine wit and an awareness of the dignity of life appropriate to a nation of good farmers. There was a genuine social tenderness in Egypt which had, at its root, an instinctual piety. From the whores and drunks of the Theban beerhalls to the highest officials in the land, everybody lived in a world inhabited by mortals and gods alike. And just as Ramose and his friends understood the sanctity of the structure of this carefully ordered state, so they appreciated their role within it. They also understood that, like the gods and kings, as a part of this intricate coalition of men and gods, they too might live for ever.

Yet with all their yearnings for immortality, few people ever consciously attempted to preserve that most precious of modern conceptions: personality. Scribe Ramose for example, has memorialized himself, his wife, his concubines and his farmhands on dozens of monuments. In the course of a long life he built three chapels, supported a large household and died a well-to-do and respected leader of his community. Yet a careful sifting of the detritus of all this activity will reveal, with but a few moving exceptions, only the public face of the man. But this too is important, for this is the vision that a Theban scribe held of himself – one indeed which he has handed down to us with great care – and its themes and preoccupations provide a yardstick for the public aspirations of the people of Thebes. It also forms a backcloth against which the stories of the real personalities of the ancient city, the few individuals of whom record has survived, can be told.

Several of Ramose's monuments recall that as a young man he worked in the temple of a long-dead king of the old dynasty, the House of Tuth-mosis IV, where, throughout his early twenties, he was awarded a whole string of titles by the temple hierarchy: Scribe of the Temple Treasury, Scribe Accountant of the Cattle of the God Amun, Chief of the Adminis-tration in the House of the Seal Bearer. Ramose always remembered his connection with this ancient King with some pride, for he had ruled at a time when Egypt's power was still waxing in Asia and Africa and the nation's wealth was accumulating beyond all previous ambition, when the kings were secure in their royal bloodline and sure of their divine ancestry; an age that in Ramose's day was regarded as being of a heroic splendour.

In his mid-twenties Ramose was appointed to work in another temple, one built to house the cult of a courtier of King Amenhotep III, a man who, like Ramose, had started his career as a junior scribe but who had ended his days, a hard-worked prince, round-shouldered and hollow-cheeked, the supervisor of the King's building projects and the most powerful official in the country. The temple of the scribe, the Mansion of Amenhotep the son of Hapu, stood meekly behind the enormous walls of his King's temple. Beyond its two modest pylons a courtyard held a pretty pool reflecting the grove of trees planted around its edge; it was an elegant and sophisticated monument designed and decorated by the craftsmen of a stylish court.

Some sixty years before Ramose had gone to work in the little temple, the King had called a gathering of senior Theban officials in its outer courtyard to deliver a solemn homily to them. For he was intent upon ensuring the survival of the spirit of his most valued servant. A decree was issued forbidding the destruction of the foundation that would support the temple's modest ceremonies and offerings to the spirit of the scribe – a most sensible precaution as many older temples had been stripped of their assets by successive kings, some being plundered even of their stone. A royal curse was pronounced upon anyone who took the temple's serfs from their work in the fields or who stole directly from the temple and its warehouses. The royal snake, the fire-spitter sitting on the head of the King, would devour them, the edict proclaimed; they would burn in holy flames and their bodies would be engulfed by the sea and hidden from decent burial. Never again would they hear the voice of their King, the nobles would not visit their houses; their sons would not succeed to posts at court; their wives would be raped before their eyes. And if those who had been gathered to hear the decree should break its commands, then these curses would touch them especially, for such people were enemies and should hunger and die.

By calling up such fears King Amenhotep's malediction reached to the core of the national nightmare: the horror of loneliness; of the death of the spirit; of the breaking of family succession; and the act of rape which denied the very legitimacy of the miscreant's children. Oblivion in this world, in the next, and for all eternity. On the other hand, the second half of the royal proclamation offered rewards for aiding the spirit of his faithful scribe which were the precise opposite of the curse: the traditional blessing of a life of a 110 years, the promise of family succession to official appointments, the boon of a fine tomb whose mortuary cult would have its offerings and rituals doubled by special royal donation. Security in this world, in the next world, and for all eternity. This royal decree, a bureaucracy of promises to encourage Ramose and all his fellows, was engraved in hieroglyphs upon a large stela (an inscribed stone).

The government in which Ramose served was headed by two viziers who, apart from the King, were the highest civil authority in the land. For thousands of years there had been only one vizier in Egypt, but with the rise of the empire the job had been split into two halves: one vizier governing Lower Egypt from the city of Memphis at the apex of the Nile delta, the other governing Upper Egypt from Thebes. Under these two officials came all the myriad functionaries of the state administration, tax officers, city mayors and all the rest. The vizier also kept close contact with the high priests, the commanders of the army and the chancellor controlling the royal household. At the time of Ramose's transfer to the temple of the King's Scribe Amenhotep, the Vizierate of Upper Egypt was administered by Paser, shown by his statues as a sleekly confident man, whose father was the High Priest of Amun and whose mother was the head of that god's harem. Paser held the title of 'Hereditary Prince' and was also 'Count and Overseer of Thebes, the Southern City', and it was there, on the west bank, that he held his daily court: sitting on a dais on a throne-like cushioned chair at the end of a large pillared hall, a carpet at his feet, a baton of state in his hands and the written laws of Egypt open before the attending scribes. All around him, just as statues stood around the gods' shrines in the halls of the temples, stood the officers of administration and the ministers of state. And each man would step forward to tell his part of the business of Upper Egypt. There were also private petitioners at the court, each seeking a personal judgement or a special benefit from the Vizier. All the business of this daily court was recounted by the Vizier in his regular interviews with the King.

Paser had gained office under King Seti i. He served a nervous dynasty of hard conservatives who had risen from a line of scribes to take the throne after the bloodline of the old dynasty had ignominiously failed. Though of a secular regality the new kings were filled with an earnest patriotism and they built temples throughout Egypt on a grander scale than ever before. In the desert of sacred Abydos, north of Thebes, Seti i had made a granite tomb to house his spirit, as the kings 2,000 years earlier had done. Above this ponderous cenotaph he built a massive temple with seven shrines to house the major gods of Egypt, and established immense estates for the support of his temple and its staff of priests and servants. At Heliopolis, close to Memphis, he dedicated another huge temple to the god Ptah, after Amun of Thebes the most revered of all the state gods. At Thebes, on the west bank, a new temple was built for the spirit of the King and his short-lived father, and a vast mysterious hall – the 'Great Hypostyle Hall' – was added to the front of Amun's temple, the holiest of all Egypt's shrines. Other temples all over Egypt had also been enriched by the pious new kings and much of this work had been directed by the two viziers, who also took active roles in the ceremonials of state. At Memphis, along with the King and the Crown Prince, Vizier Paser had officiated at the burial of the Apis Bull when it was ceremoniously entombed in a vast granite sarcophagus. At Thebes, he directed the annual festival of Amun, the first holiday in the state calendar, when the statue of the god was taken in elaborate procession to visit other gods in the sanctuaries of their own temples.

The viziers were also responsible for the supervision of the west bank at Thebes, the domain of the royal funerary temples and the cemetaries of the nobles and the kings, the 'Place of Truth'. Paser was the man 'to whom the west of Thebes was entrusted', the Vizier who knew all 'the secrets of the work of Anubis' (the slim black jackal-god who oversaw the embalming of the dead). There it was that Vizier Paser ordered the excavation of a grand tomb for himself in the cemetery of the nobles under the western cliffs, with elaborate columned halls decorated with statues and wall reliefs. Deep underneath this chapel a burial chamber was excavated to hold both himself and his wife Tiy and here the Vizier planned to lie in a coffin of red granite that had been given to him by King Seti I as a special mark of royal favour. Texts inscribed in the tomb prayed that the Vizier might rest in his burial vault for ever and that Paser, who had stood at the very side of the King, whose ears were filled with truth and had heard the teachings of Amun, would receive offerings in the chapel above to sustain his spirit for all eternity.

And, in fact, Vizier Paser survived King Seti I, who died after a reign of eleven years to be succeeded by his son, a twenty-two-year-old prince named Ramesses after his grandfather. Paser now served this new king and, as the most senior advisor of the young ruler, he was given the titles Beloved of the God (i.e. the King, Ramesses II) and God's Father. Now the Vizier's first task of the new reign was to be the supervision of the burial of King Seti I, and indeed he had been responsible for the work in the royal tomb for several years already. King Seti's tomb had been excavated like those of his predecessors in the desolate desert valley that lay behind the screen of cliffs forming the western horizon of Thebes: the Valley of the Kings, the 'Great Place'. Most of the kings of the old dynasty had been buried in this same valley, the 'great field that sinners do not enter', each one in a burial chamber set deep into the cliffs at the end of a long system of rooms and corridors, and the kings of the new dynasty followed them. But whereas the tombs of the kings of the old dynasty had been simple and elegant affairs with sacred texts drawn quickly on to the walls at the time of the funeral, the new kings wanted grander and more complex architecture: the walls carved and painted with elaborate scenes and long hieroglyphic texts like the decoration in the state temples.

Not surprisingly many practical problems had arisen, for the men who made the royal tombs had never attempted work on such a scale. The first king whose tomb had been planned in the new style, King Horemheb, had been buried in a half-finished vault amidst piles of stone chippings left over from work still underway at the time of his funeral. True, some of the colourful scenes of the tomb's outer corridors had been finished and, indeed, rank as individual masterpieces, but the illustrated texts, a brand-new theological guide to the King's afterlife, which were to cover the walls of the deep-cut burial chamber, had barely been begun, whilst the walls awaited even the first sketches of the master draughtsman. And this was after a reign of some thirteen years. A similarly ambitious plan for the second of the new-style tombs, one intended for Seti's father, had fared even worse, for the old King had died after just two years in office, while his tomb was still being cut from the rock. Instead of lying at the centre of an elaborately decorated burial chamber, the splendid climax of a grand processional way of rooms and corridors running deep in the Theban hills, the King was interred in an unfinished sarcophagus standing in a rough room, quickly cut from the bottom of what had originally been intended to be the tomb's first corridor. Obviously an urgent reorganization of the work plan of the royal tomb was needed if the similarly ambitious scheme for King Seti's tomb was ever to be finished in time for his funeral.

In the days of the old dynasty the work of making the royal tombs had been overseen by the office of the Mayor of Thebes, one of many similarly ranked officials of Paser's court. Now the gangs of men that made the kings' tombs were placed under the direct control of the Vizier. Paser himself directed the last stages of the work in King Seti's tomb and for the first time the tombmakers became an independent department in the government, truly the king's own men. So proud were they of their new affinity with the throne that the scribes amongst them now privately described themselves as 'King's Scribes' though in reality the title described an elevated position at the royal court. As a part of his reorganization of the tombmakers the Vizier increased the wealth, the standing and the size of their gangs, almost doubling their numbers, in fact, if the increase in the numbers of their houses may be said to stand as a reliable indication. And now for the first time the tombmakers' work was concentrated solely upon the royal tombs, where it was decided that in order to allow any future premature royal dead the elegance of at least a half-finished funeral vault, the upper sections of the kings' tombs should be completely finished before the elaborate lower parts were even quarried out of the cliff. As a further part of this reorganization, all the tools and materials, as well as the tombmakers' own food rations and other supplies, were put under the control of a special group of scribes, who were also charged with keeping a daily record of the work at the royal tomb. Previously such accounting as there was had been made by junior scribes; now Paser had given it over to scribes who were directly responsible to the office of the vizier and who held equal status with the workmen's foremen.

Thus from the time of Paser's reorganization during the reign of King Seti, the written records of the tombmakers' lives and work, previously so spare and disjointed, were composed regularly and in great quantities. One consequence of all this was that King Seti was buried in a vast and beautifully made tomb that held more fine art than all the earlier royal tombs of the Great Place combined. Another was that Scribe Ramose was taken away from his duties at the House of Tuthmosis iv and the temple of Amenhotep the Scribe and sent to the Great Place as one of the new administrators of the work at the royal tomb.

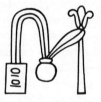

3

THE GREAT PLACE

Ramose worked for some forty years in the Valley of the Kings, an arid intractable place where no plant would ever grow, yet the seeds that he helped to place there in the dry rock were very fruitful, for they were the dead kings of Egypt, a vital element in the bargain that the Egyptians had struck with their gods: a contract between ordered civilization and natural forces. Held amidst of the ceremonial of life and death, the kings of Egypt were the earthly representatives of the divine order, orchestrators of the marvellous balance struck between the fruitful rhythms of nature and the regular ordering of society. The death of a king was a potentially destructive event for the state, a random brutal happening that had to be methodically joined, carefully subsumed, into that same fruitful order of nature.

Dying and decay were made into a rite: the royal corpse was mummified, changed from a naturally-decaying body into a man-made object. First the viscera were removed, the king's body being split open with a flint, and the priest who performed this 'killing' ritually fled after his cutting was completed, to escape the forces of the state. Then, after long ceremonies of wrapping and encoffining, the royal cadaver, now dried out, re-sewn, re-shaped, half man, half statue, was taken to the Great Place where the tombmakers had excavated the elaborate theatre which would house the last act of the drama: the entry of the king into the underworld.

The royal burial was a mass of rites so old, so densely packed with twisting metaphors of the universal order and royal destiny that not even the officiating priests understood their full significance. What was readily appreciated, however, was that all the elaborate ritual of the burial established the dead king, who had abdicated his earthly powers, as a god; it was the essential act which alone could establish the legitimacy of the new king as the true son of a god. So the dead king was sent to join the immortal gods, where his tremendous power would strengthen the forces of nature which they maintained. The king's individuality had been overtaken at his death by his office and his role in the state; a subtle expression of the idea that man loses his identity within the machinery of government. Similarly, there were many animal gods, species rather than individual beasts, who straddled the same gulf between nature and the state, between men and the endless power of the gods as did the king. A hawk-headed human deity, Horus, flew with the sun, and the kings flew with him; Thoth, another bird, a wise ibis, was the god of writing and mathematics; Osiris, the mummy-king of the underworld who took the dead king into himself, controlled hordes of frightful flesh-eating animals; and the dead king was daily pushed to one of his resurrections by another little animal, a beetle who rolled him out on to the horizon each morning with the sun to leave his mummy, shell-like, back in the underworld of the royal tomb.

Thus the ancient Egyptians recognized a profound connection between dying and renewal, between evening and morning, winter and spring, death and the forces of fertility. And whilst the royal tombs that Ramose and the gangs made contain nothing about the personalities of the kings that they hold, they teem with life: humans, animals and monsters swarm over their walls. Here, deep in the earth, in the 'interior' as the gangs sometimes called the Great Place, the dead kings put their power at the service of the world, joined all the processes of recreation and renewal; the vaults that the tomb-makers excavated were designed to hold within them the essence of creation. And as the tombs held the life force within them, so there was an inevitable connection there with the sexual, the erotic. The royal tomb was also a womb set in the mother of mothers, Hathor of the Western Mountain, and the dead king was her ritual lover, his sarcophagus the couch on which creation was sparked. All around the head of the valley of the Great Place, deep under the enfolding cliffs of the Western Mountain, the dead kings lay in silent conclave, each in pitch-dark chambers filled with the images of a multitude of gods.

Priests had performed rituals upon these figures and brought them to life, and so real were they to the tomb artists who had made them that they offered prayers to them. One carpenter, a man of the work gangs who had made wooden figures of the gods, called himself 'a maker of god's image', whilst the gods sculpted in relief on the walls of the kings' tombs were called the 'gods and goddesses of the Tomb'. And just as the deep sanctity of these icons was easily appreciated by the workmen, so they also understood that the royal tombs they had cut under the western horizon were the underworld, and called them the 'Horizons of Eternity'.

When Scribe Ramose first went to work in the Great Place the floor of its valley was much lower than it is today, a network of water-cut v-shaped channels partly choked with flints and stones which had rolled down from the slopes above. In the sides of these channels stood the doorways of the tombs of the new dynasty kings, surrounded by fresh piles of white stone chippings that stood like blobs of cream on the gold-crusty patina of the desert valley. In between the tombs, white paths passed in and out of the dry channels and up and down the hills and screes at the valley's head. Water jars were set up at intervals in the valley and they dripped as their porous clay allowed a gradual surface evaporation, cooling their contents. In the valley's centre stood a conglomeration of huts and store-houses that served the needs of the workmen. Apart from the visiting commissions of nobles, a vizier and even, occasionally, the King himself, the valley usually held about 100 men and, as they worked, lived and slept there, the noise and bustle of them all must have been much like that of any small village; but this was a community of quarrymen, stonemasons and artists, even occasionally a scholar priest sent to set out and correct the sacred texts of the royal underworld, and they worked with the calm authority of experts.

Ramesses II's tomb was sited, like its predecessors, low down in the valley, its entrance running off the main channel of the ancient watercourse. Inside, the corridors were so steep that the procession of labourers who carried the leather baskets of excavated chips away from the rock face had to struggle hard to bring their loads up to the sunlight. There it was that Ramose had started his work in the Great Place, and there it was that he spent the greater part of his working life, deep in the shadowed corridors of the long tomb, filled with the scent of fresh-cut stone. By the time the scribe came to the Great Place, in the fifth year of the King's reign, the first frenzy of work at the tomb had died down and was already replaced by a more deliberate progress through the rock. After all, the King was young and in good health. Clearly he would reign for a long while. Decades came and went and whilst the King oversaw a prospering and peaceful country, little by little his huge tomb was brought nearer to completion.

The living rock from which the tomb's architecture was cut came away in large flat slabs that followed the grain of the rock. The limestone of the Great Place is so soft when it is freshly cut that you can mark it with your fingernail, yet, after it has been exposed to the desert air, it shrinks slightly and becomes as hard and as brittle as brick. Apart from the salt with which it is impregnated, which dries and cracks the skin, it is an easy rock to cut, a fine medium for a sculptor. The quarrymen worked the rock in stepped excavations with copper chisels, discarded one after another as their shanks first tempered, then split with fatigue, or their soft points bent on the flints that ran in straight seams through the cliffs. There was a constant industry concerned with keeping both the quarrymen and, later on in the work, the relief sculptors, in sharpened chisels. Coppersmiths resmelted the worn tools, then beat them into their final shapes by hand: single-pointed spikes for the quarrymen and a wide range of smaller flat-tipped wooden-handled chisels for the sculptors.

The blocks cut from the cliff were often very large and had first to be split up before they could be taken out of the tomb and dumped round its doorway. At the front of the tomb stood two walls which the tombmakers called 'the corridor that is in the way of free air'; they rose low off the valley floor and reached up on either side of the entrance to prevent sharp stones falling back into the tomb. These two outside walls were a recent innovation. The kings of the old dynasty all lay in hidden tombs whose doorways were modestly placed in clefts in the valley's cliffs. Even the tell-tale heaps of excavated debris were carried far from these hidden doorways, and their entrances, covered over with sand and stone after the funerals, had been quite obliterated by the action of the floodwater that passed harmlessly over them on its infrequent passage through the valley. But the new kings had moved their tombs down into the centre of the valley and, by Ramose's day, four of them stood confidently in the golden valley, marked indelibly in the landscape by their two walls and the high white heaps of fresh-cut stone.

It was from these huge mounds of chippings, lying in such profusion throughout the Great Place, that Scribe Ramose and his colleagues selected the limestone flakes on which they wrote the majority of their notes and checklists, records of the day-to-day affairs of the work at the King's tomb. Some of these stones, shaped oval like a hand, were smaller than a postcard. Others, of similar proportions were more than two feet long and weighed seven or eight pounds. All were smooth, creamy-white and so brittle that they rang like roof tiles when they were struck. In the harsh desert environment they were a near perfect medium for the scribes' field notes and on them we may still discover all the minutiae of the tombmakers' enterprise. 'There was no doorkeeper here [today] except Psarpot, for Sanehem slept and the doorkeeper Sunero came only at noon,' notes one scribe on his stony staff-register, a small happening perhaps but one worth recording; for the doorkeepers, the guardians of the tomb in which the gangs were working, were a part of the careful security system operating throughout the royal valley. With such a wealth of kings lying in the Great Place, the valley's vulnerability was a constant preoccupation.

Like most of the world's royal burial grounds from Westminster Abbey to the tombs of the Ming Emperors, the security of the Great Place and its rich graves ultimately depended more upon the reverence in which the kings' tombs were held by their subjects than on cunning architectural subterfuge or an army of perpetual guards. But for all that the Great Place had been well chosen for its immediate security, for although it was quite close to the river it could be approached easily by only two routes, one of which the workmen used regularly, walking over the cliffs along the edge of western Thebes. And as this path dropped down from the western horizon to enter the royal valley three stone steps in the track marked the exact boundary of the Great Place, the demarcation between living Thebes and the realms of the dead, and these steps were bounded on one side by a wall and on the other by a guardpost. This in all probability was the main guardpost, the 'fortress' of the scribes' records. The other approach to the Great Place was along the arduous winding track running up the wadi cut by the ancient rainwaters as they drained down through the Great Place to the riverside plain. The Great Place, the wadi's head, was on a higher stratum of limestone than the long wadi and could only be reached by climbing through a narrow crevice in the terrace separating the two. As it passed through this, the track narrowed to allow the passage of only one or two people at a time. Close by stood a small guard hut. Several smaller tracks ran down into the Great Place from the high desert but these approaches were exposed and could easily be observed from the ring of little guard huts standing on the cliffs above the royal tombs.

The royal tombs were not the only things that the guard huts protected. There were also warehouses in the valley holding much of value: supplies of food for the workmen; material and pigments used by the artists and sculptors in their work; and large supplies of oil and wicks, used to light the interior of the deep tombs. There were storerooms too for copper chisels, the optimum tools of the day, which the quarrymen used in large numbers. On the open market just ten of the large copper points used by the quarrymen were worth a year's grain ration for a workman and his household. These warehouses and their valuable contents were the responsibility of the storekeepers, working under the orders of the scribes.

Ultimately, however, everything in the Valley of the Kings was protected and guarded by its own police force drawn from the medjay, the corps of men who were the traditional policemen of Thebes, a legacy of the old custom of using foreign mercenaries in the service of the state. In the days of the old dynasty, the medjay had been recruited from Nubia, south of Egypt, and some of their rhythmic names - Psuro, Psaro, Karoya, Kasaya - hinted at their foreign origins. At the Great Place they manned the fortress on the workmen's path and the ring of guard huts. From such observation posts the medjay could not only see all the activity in the valley below but they could hear the slightest noises as they echoed, amplified, around the encircling cliffs. The guards heard the murmurings of the workmen as they rested in their small settlement of huts at the valley's centre, their calls and conversations as they walked to and from the royal tomb and dealt with the scribes and storekeepers; they heard the footfalls of visitors approaching, perhaps a party of inspectors with a high priest, a vizier or the superintendent of the royal works, or a train of donkeys carrying supplies and braying as their minders goaded them up the long wadi; they heard, too, the singing and dancing of the workmen's festivals when the statue of their patron king was carried down the path into the royal valley; even, perhaps, the sharp words and the chisellings of would-be robbers – for sounds gather and rise up in the Great Place like whispers hovering around a cathedral dome.

4

THE VILLAGE

The tombmakers and their families lived in an isolated desert village on the west bank. To go home from the Great Place they had to climb the path running past the medjay's fortress with its three steps, out on to the horizon of Thebes with its sweeping view of the river valley, then turn southwards along a rim of cliffs, the western horizon of Thebes. Their village was set under these cliffs, isolated from the rest of Thebes, by a walk of some two miles along paths that swung round the sheltering desert hills, squeezed past the white walls of the royal temples, then went straight over the flat fields on a high silty causeway to the ferry-landing where they could cross to the city on the eastern bank.

Scribe Ramose had gone to live in this unique community when he began work in the royal tomb, and the change in his life was dramatic. Most Thebans, after all, lived a noisy communal life, largely out of doors. Now Ramose had left all that and moved to the quiet valley of the royal tombs and a remote yet tight-packed village filled with expert craftsmen: distinctive and unusual people, men of special knowledge and careful values, men who made the figures of the gods. Most Thebans lived in simple dusty houses with whitewashed walls and a few rough furnishings; a world of limited colour and texture. Of Ramose's possessions only his scribal kit, the emblem of his profession, would have been well made and of elegant proportions. The luxurious trappings of the court and the temples, elegant and ethereal objects, were magical symbols of status and rank, remote emblems of power. And every one of these strange things was unique, glowing with the touch of the craftsmen who made it, men whose lives were saturated in deep colours, absorbed in the careful values of their hybrid art. Ramose had joined a community of such people, a hot-house isolated from the bustling farmers and peasants who made up the bulk of Egyptian society.

He took a house in the oldest part of the village, close to and on the same side of the street as the gang foreman, Kaha. Just as the work at the tomb was divided by tradition between two gangs, each under its own foreman, so the village was split into two halves, east and west, by a street so narrow

19

that you could stretch out your arms and touch the walls on either side. When Ramose came there were about seventy houses in the village, each similar in its design, with four ill-lit rooms running behind one another; two large family rooms of some five yards by four yards being followed by a smaller kitchen and storeroom. A stair gave access to the roof where the family would sleep in the hot summer nights. Though modest by modern standards, about the same size as a small terraced house of the last century, Ramose's village house probably held larger rooms than any he had lived in before. All the village houses were of a more regular, more compact, design than the usual dwellings in Thebes and many of them had ovens and cellars, cut from the desert rock. Dark, but with whitewashed walls reflecting the sunlight which fell from small slots in the roof, their public rooms held cushioned couches, neat wooden chairs and cabinets of rush and wood, all set on simple matting. On one of the walls there was a family shrine containing a little stela with a prayer carved on it and with busts, perhaps, of the ancestors standing close by. The largest room was probably reserved for gatherings of friends, for there was no square, no open ground, near the village where people could meet in the evenings. So we may imagine villagers seated in a parlour, bright beams of light holding in them the smoke from the ovens and dust hovering in the air. The white wooden door is open to the street, old friends make music together, play games or simply sit and talk, and children run in and out and all around.

When Ramose arrived at the village it was entirely contained inside long rectangular walls, with only one doorway, on its northern side, which opened into the central lane, the village high street. The village plan was like a fish skeleton, its spines the walls that partitioned the houses one from another, its backbone the narrow high street. The fish lay with its mouth, the gate, pointing up the valley to the north, and its tail some 140 yards away at the lowest point. As the high street was probably roofed over, from a distance the whole settlement would have had the appearance of a single low dusty-brown building with one small doorway, entirely filling the bottom of the desert valley.

Outside the village's north wall, on the high ground, was a group of temples, small versions of the huge stone temples of the state gods, some of which were already hundreds of years old in Ramose's time. Outside the south wall, the village rubbish was dumped so that it flowed further down the valley floor. The hillsides around the village were peppered with tomb shafts and covered with small mud-brick chapels and miniature pyramids, rows and rows of small white buildings with bright painted doorways. The main cemetery was on the western hillside, running down a slope from the little cliff at its top and almost touching the village wall. A network of paths and ramps, serving both as processional ways for funerals and to give access

1 The desert cemeteries of Thebes, from the fields. The columns are part of the mortuary temple of Ramesses II.

Overleaf 2 The tombmakers' village with its hillside cemetery. The white path leads over the mountains to the Valley of the Kings.

Six paintings from the
tomb of sculptor Ipy:

3 Servants washing
linen. With water
rationed at their desert
village, the tombmakers
clothing was laundered
at the riverside.

4 Village servants
herding goats. A man
churns milk in two
skins slung from a yoke.
A woman offers round
cheeses at a local
market.

5 In a lotus marsh by
the river bank village
fishermen are working
from their fleet of small
boats. Above, a man
mends his nets while
another fillets and racks
the catch to dry it in the
sun.

Villagers making
ieral equipment –
: work of their spare
ie. A scribe paints a
ffin while a man holds
ipright for him; a
ilptor works upon a
immy mask.

Villagers working on
arge piece of ritual
niture; they are using
: balloon-headed
llets still favoured by
lptors today, one of
ich has been dropped
a carpenter's foot.
ove, a sleepy
rkman is being
ken by a friend.

'illagers making a
ine for King
enhotep I. The wall's
d plaster – the dun-
ured ground that
:s Ipy's paintings
ir brilliance – is left
osed, indicating
haps that, like the
itself, the shrine is
inished.

9 Osiris, the great green-skinned god who took the dead kings to himself. This fine portrait of the ruler of the underworld was made by the villagers in the tomb of Ramesses I.

Opposite 10 The Great Place – the Valley of the Kings – where the villagers made the royal underworlds. The tombs, cut into the foot of the cliffs and the low hills, extend for hundreds of yards into the mountain.

11 The tombmakers' village, looking east across the Nile to Thebes; the contrast between field and desert, life and death, is absolute. Their village's situation in the dead-preserving desert was exceptional: most were in the damp, living fields.

to the chapels containing the cults of the village ancestors, ran right through the cemetery, and on feast days the villagers would go to their family chapels to share their meals with their ancestors and make offerings to them at the family altars. Statues and pictures of the dead stood in the chapels and in the houses of the living. The spirits of the dead mingled freely with the living at the little village: Scribe Ramose started to make a tomb and chapel for himself in the cemetery even before he had found a wife.

Although the sturdy little curved wall that surrounded the oldest houses of the village had been built in the old dynasty, during the reign of King Tuthmosis I, tradition held that it had been this King's father, King Amenhotep I, who had founded the community; some two and a half centuries later Vizier Paser's administration considered King Amenhotep, now a god, to be the owner of the village and its houses. With his wife, Queen Nefertari, the dead King was the revered patron of the village, with his shrine at the heart of the village temples. At times of festival the King's statue was taken from its shrine and carried through the village, and served as a popular oracle. In deference to their founder, the King's name, though common enough amongst ordinary Thebans, was seldom used in the families of the tombmakers.

In fact, even before King Amenhotep's time, there had been a group of houses in the valley. They had grown up on either side of the desert track which later became the village high street. The well-ordered village that King Tuthmosis had girded with his wall had been built above some of these more open-planned houses, and consisted of a dozen or so dwellings on each side of the path, all with the number and size of rooms and installations which became the standard pattern for the later houses in the village. In all probability, these houses had held tombmakers and craftsmen too, since they were situated in the heart of the Theban cemeteries; though these early villagers also seem to have worked upon temples and royal building projects and nobles' tombs in every capacity from stonemasons to artists and architects. At all events, their community had thrived sufficiently by the end of the dynasty to have seen another dozen houses added on to the outside of the western wall.

Then the troubles that accompanied the end of the old dynasty affected the village, and it seems that the tombmakers were taken away from Thebes to live in a new town in the middle of Egypt that the heretic King Akhenaten had founded as the centre of his new state. There they performed the same tasks as at Thebes, and in the process learnt many of the vivid artistic mannerisms of that eccentric period as well as its special skills of carving relief in stone and plaster. Their return to their old, now ruined, village came with the rise of the new dynasty under King Horemheb as a part of the restoration of the ancient state religion at Thebes. It was now that the

Mayor of Thebes began the reform of the village and the work in the royal tomb that was to be so brilliantly concluded by Vizier Paser. Written news of the village at this time is almost non-existent; fortunately a litigant in a legal dispute of a much later date inadvertently recorded the beginning of the enlargement of the gangs and the further spread of the village in a deposition concerning the ownership of a tomb in the village cemetery:

> [In] year seven of King Horemheb [1313 BC], on the day of induction of my father Hay [i.e. on the day he joined the village], the Mayor of Thebes, Djutmose, apportioned the places that were in the village cemetery to the workmen — and he gave the tomb of Amenmose to Hay, my father — as my mother, Hel, was — [Amenmose's] daughter and he had no male child.

Vizier Paser's reorganization of the village was far more comprehensive than Mayor Djutmose's had been. When Ramose arrived the village houses had more than doubled in number, some twenty dwellings being added to each side of the high street and others built beyond the village entrance in the north wall. The southern end of the high street was extended across an open patch of ground, which had provided stabling for the village's cows and donkeys, by cutting through the old wall of Tuthmosis I. The new housing plots laid out on either side of it were generally larger than the older houses in the village and had been taken over by the longer-established village families, who later extended their domains southwards into other unoccupied plots as their succeeding generations needed houses of their own. At this time many of the village houses were given limestone doorposts engraved with the names of their occupants. As with villages everywhere, many of the houses would later be known by these names long after their original inhabitants had died.

While all this activity took place at the village, the Vizier's office had to be told of the progress of the work. One of the junior scribes, a man whose real employment was to paint the texts on the walls of the royal tomb, happily reported to him:

> The Scribe Nebre salutes his Lord, the Fan Bearer on the right side of the King Re, Chief of the gangs in the Place of Truth, Seal Bearer, Chief Priest of the Gods, Lord of Upper Egypt, City Overseer and Vizier, giver of justice. Paser, in life prosperity and health! This letter is to inform my Lord that the village — which is under the authority of your Lordship, is in excellent condition, all the enclosing walls being intact, the servants of the King living there —

The two village foremen had both set up house in the new southern extension, but one of them, Neferhotep, had so many sons that they could not all be accommodated either at the village or in the work gangs at the royal tomb. While the eldest, Nebnefer, eventually succeeded his father at

22

the royal tomb, another left the village to serve as an army scribe and become an 'officer of his majesty', a third entered the civil administration and prospered, and a fourth went to work as a doorkeeper at the massive mortuary temple of King Ramesses II. This, under the supervision of Vizier Paser, was being built nearby in the plain between the village and the river. The two foremen, Neferhotep and Baki, had between them supervised the quarrying and decoration of King Seti's tomb; a beautiful monument that would remain as one of the villagers' finest works. But for his own memorial Baki chose a simpler style than that of the huge tomb in which he had worked all his life. In the carefully made texts of a small round-topped stela which bore a modest picture of him worshipping Amun, Baki prayed that, like Vizier Paser, in his tomb, he too would have the truth in his mouth and see the festivals of the gods forever before his eyes. While Neferhotep lived on into the next reign to supervise the work in the upper corridors of young King Ramesses II's tomb, Baki died in the fullness of his years and was buried in the village cemetery in a fine vaulted tomb chamber built and decorated by him and his friends: a small brilliantly coloured room made by the finest of the royal tombs' painters.

As well as making their own tombs, some of the villagers still made chapels and vaults in the Theban cemeteries. The villager Poy, on the other hand, a most experienced draughtsman who had worked in all the royal tombs of the new dynasty up to that of King Ramesses II, painted nobles' coffins with traditional scenes and patterns. Other villagers had special knowledge of the elaborate rituals which had to be performed upon such coffins to enable them to come alive and become living receptacles for the mummies which fitted so tightly inside them. Many of the tombmakers worked in this lucrative cottage-industry, supplying tomb furnishings to wealthy Thebans. Providing a wide variety of such esoteric talents, and with a ready market amongst the multitudes of priests and bureaucrats in the capital, the village flourished. Following Paser's reorganization, the village households, around eighty at their maximum, held some twenty-five interrelated families, and many of their members had, like Poy, served for generations in the royal tombs. All these people, the families of the scribes, the foremen and the men of the two gangs, were bound together by strong feelings of loyalty and pride.

Ramose was about thirty-five when he moved into this exclusive community. In his neat hand, he recorded the exact date on a flake of limestone: 'Made scribe in the Place of Truth in year five, third month of the season of inundation, day ten [13 September 1275 BC] of the King of Upper and Lower Egypt, Usermaatre Setepenre, Son of Re, Ramesses Beloved-of-Amun.' In a state where official appointments normally passed down through families it is an unusual record, for such an announcement would have been an inadvertent notice of a father's death and hardly a cause for celebration. Ramose's words, however, reflected a pride in his promotion, the most important event in his life. So proud, indeed, was Ramose of his new job that he also celebrated it high on the rocks of a nearby desert valley, the Place of Beauty where many queens and princes were buried. There, at the valley's head, the scribe scrambled up the cliffs high above the doorway of an unfinished tomb and, using the red ochre of his scribe's palette, he drew a picture of himself kneeling at prayer and, once again wrote his name, his new title and the date of his appointment.

At his new job, Ramose checked and listed, measured and registered just as he had done in the storerooms of the temple of the King's Scribe Amenhotep; and not only with regard to the work at the tomb, as the scribes also kept records of the rations of food and supplies sent to their village. Lacking both soil and water, the village's needs were entirely supplied from outside: they were either sent from the warehouses of the royal temples or by the retainers working directly for the tombmakers and their families. Labourers tended a continuous line of donkeys that carried earthenware jars filled with water out across the desert to the bone-dry village and all the village's grains, vegetables, meats and fish arrived by the same route. Everything indeed, except the honey that the villagers collected from their own desert hives, was sent up to them from the fertile valley. And Ramose the scribe oversaw and checked these deliveries and reported upon them to the office of the vizier: 'The wages of the necropolis have been delivered, being absolutely complete, without any arrears. '

These provisions were delivered in bulk to the village and scribes divided them into rations which reflected the status of each householder in his work at the tomb. As a scribe, Ramose's grain ration – grain and emmer (a species of wheat) for bread; barley for beer; the two village staples – was on a par with that of the foremen, and about a third more than the amounts issued to the workmen's families. Ramose's grain ration was about four hundredweight a month, which would amply support a household of twelve or fourteen people. By village reckoning this was worth the equivalent of a little over one and a half pounds of copper - eight *deben*, the abstract measure used as a standard when bartering goods and services. The grain ration, sent directly from the warehouses of the royal temples, was the pith of the village economy.

Many of the other supplies to the village, such as fresh fish and vegetables, were provided by the village auxiliary servants. River fishermen brought their catch straight from the village's own Nile fishing-boats, gardeners brought bunches of vegetables from their fields, potters supplied the village households with domestic utensils, woodcutters brought fuel for cooking and heating. Sometimes when extra hands were needed at the royal tomb, these village servants would be called in to help.

By Ramesses II's fifth year, when Ramose arrived to work in the Great Place, the upper corridor of the King's tomb had been finished, its walls sculpted with traditional religious scenes and texts. So quick off the mark had the tombmakers been at the beginning of the reign that the scribes who had laid out the religious texts on the tomb's walls had spelt the royal name incorrectly and the sculptor had had to plaster over their mistake. When Ramose arrived the gangs were already quarrying away deep down in lower sections of the tomb, and one of his jobs was to collect the blunted quarrying chisels and ensure that their precious metal was returned to the royal workshops for recasting.

Ramose's superior in the work at the Great Place was Scribe Huy, a member of an old village family. Huy's father had been a quarryman and had worked in the tomb of King Seti I as well as on the Theban temples, dressing the rough blocks of sandstone sent by barge to the city from quarries upstream. Such stoneworkers were specialists and his name, Thothmaktef - 'Thoth protects him' - links him with the god who was the patron of order and mathematics, an accurate affiliation for a man whose life was concerned with numeration and precision. Huy had no children of his own to continue in the family's tradition, indeed, this had probably been the reason for Ramose's appointment to the village. Happily the relationship between the two scribes was a good one and Huy virtually adopted Ramose as his son. Scenes in Huy's funeral chapel at the village cemetery, which traditionally would have pictured the spirits of the tomb's occupants being presented with offerings by their eldest son, show Scribe Huy and his wife Nofretke sitting before their offering table whilst young Ramose offers them perfume and pastries. Other members of Huy's family were friendly to the newcomer too, and commissioned Ramose to decorate some of the furniture they planned to take with them into their funerary vaults. For Huy's brother and his wife, Ramose drew scenes upon a box that would hold little models of the servants the couple wanted to take with them into the afterlife, called *ushabtis*; for this work they paid him goods that were the equivalent of two *deben* of copper, a week's grain ration.

Apparently Ramose had arrived in the village a single man, for he married a village woman named Mutemwia, whom he called, in affectionate abbreviation, 'Wia'. Their household held many of Wia's relatives as well as several of the female servants allotted to each of the village households for chores such as grinding the grain ration into flour and making bread and beer. Usually such village servants were required to work in rotation in different village households, and it was possible for individual villagers to sell their household's share in this work ration. One of Ramose's close neighbours recorded exactly such a bargain. 'Third month of the summer season, day twenty-one, the day when the mistress — gave the day of her servant to the workman Any; being ten days each month, 120 days per year, [and for four years] 480 days. [Here is] the list of silver which Any gave her.' The list that follows makes it clear that these servants' labours were worth very little; another of Ramose's neighbours swapped his share of a woman's working time in his house for a wickerwork sieve and a small basket.

For the most part, it was the handful of scribes in the village who wrote these humble records of village life, for along with their official duties at the royal tomb and the village they also acted as the villagers' own scribes. Sometimes they composed petitions for them: prayers to the gods or pleas to the office of the vizier for the redress of earthly wrongs. 'I am the aged servant of my Lord since the seventh year of King Horemheb — I acted as medjay of the west of Thebes guarding the walls of the Great Place and I was appointed chief of the medjay, an excellent reward, because of my good behaviour — ' begins a petition to the Vizier composed by one of Huy's scribes on behalf of Mininuiy who, at the time of the petition, had guarded the Great Place and its workers for more than fifty years.

By transforming the villagers' spoken words into formal written documents the scribes imbued their simple declarations with a gravity beyond speech, a metamorphosis that must have received tangible corroboration from the very bulk of the stone flakes and the sherds of pottery - both called ostraca - on which much of the village business was recorded. It is easy to imagine that such solid documents appeared to the villagers to be self-contained entities with a veracity of their own, powerful abstractions which gave a special gravity to the day-to-day affairs of their small community. As the creators of such marvellous things, Huy, Ramose and the other scribes of the village were especially important people.

In the high summer of Ramesses II's long reign all the villagers were flourishing as never before and their prosperity found expression not only in their tombs, which they made more colourful, more magnificent, than ever, but in the village's shrines and temples, many of which were enlarged and enriched. With the participation of Vizier Paser, probably the village's greatest single benefactor, new temples were built to stand alongside the old, and Ramose supervised the construction of some of them: 'I made a sanctuary [for the god] — and this statue of my Lord [the King] rests in it,' he proudly announced in an inscription cut upon the base of a grand doorway in the new temple of Hathor, one of many such texts from the village temples linking the scribe, the Vizier and the King. Despite their generally modest appearance - for these temples were built, like the village houses, of rough stones set in mud mortar with stone doorways and floors - some of them would be used as sacred buildings for a thousand years and more: the houses for the village gods and the temples for the dead kings in whose tombs the villagers had worked. In them the workmen and their families placed thousands of small monuments, multitudes of little stelae and fine statues of themselves made of polished wood and fine white stone. Ramose and Wia were especially well-represented.

Good Thebans both, Ramose and Wia worshipped the King of the Gods Amun, his wife Mut and their son the moon-god Khonsu, and had their prayers engraved on stelae and set up inside the little temples. Mut the mother was often worshipped with singing and dancing and the rattling of a sistrum, a simple instrument whose tinkling metal discs, like those of a tambourine, provided a medium as sympathetic as incense for communion with the goddess. 'Giving praise to Mut, Lady of Heaven, Mistress of the House of Amun, with beautiful hands carrying the sistra, sweet of voice. Singers be content with all she says, [for it is] pleasing to your hearts,' prayed the scribe in the text of a little stela he set up in a village temple.

The wide choice of gods that the couple worship on their stelae, all carefully selected from the myriad deities of the ancient world, shows a discrimination, an erudition, that is also apparent in one of Ramose's prayers to Amun Re, that is Amun of Thebes joined to Re of Heliopolis to make a composite national god, for when the scribe had the prayer copied on to a stone stela it was already more than a century old:

Adoration of Amun Re — the chief of all the gods, the good god, beloved one, who gives life to all warm-blooded creatures and all beautiful animals. Hail to you, Amun Re, Lord of the Thrones of the Two Lands, foremost in Thebes, bull of his mother, foremost of his fields, wide of stride, foremost in Nubia, Lord of the Medjay, Ruler of Punt, most ancient in heaven and eldest in all the world, who dwells in all things.

Ramose and Wia, the 'Lady of the House, whom he loves', also prayed for children, for the gods looked well on those who raised large families, indeed it was the duty of all people to do so, to bring the powers of fecundity and the proper rhythms of family succession into village life. A household without children was considered to be a sure sign of its occupants' meanness, especially when the childless did not adopt children to take the place of those they had not engendered. Unhappily childlessness was not uncommon amongst the village families. In their predicament Ramose and Wia raised statues and stelae to a multiplicity of gods. They prayed to Hathor, the goddess of the Western Mountain, the mother who held the dead kings within her cliffs and prepared them for their daily rebirth with the sunrise. Ramose had supervised the construction of a village temple for the 'Golden Lady' who, as the mother of all the kings, was a prime deity of fertility and childbearing. There the scribe dedicated a limestone phallus to the goddess, a unique and most personal statement of Ramose's that brings us as close to the man as we may ever be. Along the side of the rough object he inscribed a touching plea for children as rewards, as compensations, for the pious works he had performed on the goddess's behalf. 'Hathor, remember the man at his burial. Grant a duration in your house as a reward for the scribe Ramose, O Golden One — let me receive a compensation of your house as one rewarded.' The Golden Lady did not hear his prayers, so Ramose set up stelae to foreign deities, to Reshef and Kadesh, Palestinian gods, and as well as these exotics, the couple also prayed and offered to the traditional gods of Egyptian households, to Thoeris and Min, the gods of childbirth and fertility and Shed, the saviour and helper of mankind. But none of the gods listened to them. Ramose and Wia lived on in their comfortable household and began to prepare for the afterworld. Village craftsmen made the couple all the paraphernalia of noble burial: fine coffins, bright-painted tomb furniture and delicately drawn books for the dead that would serve as passports and talismans in their journeys through the next world. Ramose and Wia also commissioned servant statues as Scribe Huy and his wife had done.

The small tomb chapel that Ramose constructed for himself before he married was cut high in a rocky bay at the top of the western cemetery. But this modest enterprise was superseded by another chapel decorated and inscribed with the names of both Ramose and Wia. The generous scribe also built a tomb for nine women of his household, a large monument set close to the village walls with three separate chapels and burial vaults beneath, large enough to accommodate, in silent groups of three, a whole harem of coffins. Five of the women were from Wia's family, the others probably house-servants and Ramose's concubines. Scenes painted on the wall of the central chapel show the women at a funeral banquet, being served by the living guests. Other paintings in the chapel show their funerals, the coffins up-ended and standing in rows outside the chapel while priests perform the ancient rites of vivification and purification. An offering table stands behind one of the priests and by its side a scribe consults a papyrus, to check that Ramose has supplied the correct amounts of offerings.

Scribe Ramose became one of the village's most prosperous sons, not only because of his own hard work and Paser's patronage, but also because he had kept control of some fields which he had overseen before he arrived in the community. For whilst the other villagers had lost all connection with the land, Ramose's fields were farmed for him by a peasant called Ptahsankh, who even appears in a scene in one of the scribe's tomb chapels, where he is drawn ploughing with 'West' and 'Beautiful Flood', his two fat cows. Ptahsankh serves his master here, in death, as he had done in life and, in return for this eternal servitude, is named in the accompanying inscription – one of the handful of ancient peasants whose names have survived. In a speech cut above the ploughing scene, Ptahsankh tells Ramose that 'the fields are in a good state and their grain will be excellent'. In village terms, Ramose the scribe was, with the exception of his childlessness, a hugely successful man. Such an opulence of public piety, such a multitude of monuments would not again be seen in the little community. The scribe from outside had become a figure to look up to, and he often appears with Wia alongside the figures of the King and the Vizier in scenes on the walls of the village chapels. With due modesty, however, Ramose described himself simply as an 'honest scribe' and had a stonemason write as much on the elegant pyramid-shaped cap-stone that topped one of his tomb chapels. This became a well-known landmark in the village cemetery, a monument for future generations, the public face of a rich age.

Towards the close of Ramose's career in the Great Place, in Ramesses ii's fortieth regnal year, the surviving attendance registers show that it was not unusual for the gangs of tombmakers to work just one day in four in the Great Place. Work at the royal tomb had slackened, the village's rations had been regularly delivered, decade after decade, and the skilled workmen of the royal tomb now had time to look to their own affairs. Like many of the long reigns of history, Ramesses ii's had provided his country with a cultural stability that still lends a special aura, a coherence, to his age: a state tempered by the years of an old man's inscrutable rule.

Workmen and, indeed, Scribe Ramose himself, had joined the work in the Great Place, and grown old without ever having worked on a new royal tomb. The old Foreman Neferhotep's son, Nebnefer, became in his turn foreman of the royal tomb for thirty years before he too died and handed his job to his son, named Neferhotep after his grandfather. In his time, Nebnefer had seen little that was new in the Great Place, except the numbers of the two gangs dwindling slowly to a third of their former strength. Some of the men were sent to work in the temples of Thebes as their fathers had been before them, while others were set to cutting tombs for favoured members of the King's family: princes and queens who were now dying before the long-lived monarch. Several of these tombs, large carefully made vaults often designed to hold more than one burial, were excavated in the Place of Beauty – the Valley of the Queens – the old royal cemetery behind the workmen's village where, early in the reign, Scribe Ramose had so proudly written his notice of appointment. Now the tomb-makers returned to this rocky valley, a traditional burying-ground of queens and princes, and excavated a half-dozen new tombs for the wives and daughters of Ramesses II. Of one of them, the tomb of Queen Nefertari, they made a minor masterpiece.

This famous Queen had married Ramesses in his youth and he regarded her so highly that when, early in his reign, he built a string of temples throughout Nubia to hold that subject nation in awe of Egypt's presence, his temple for the goddess Hathor – an expression of the fertility and generosity of Egypt and a balance to the other minacious monuments – was filled with images of her; its façade a congregation of bland deities and rounded figures of the Queen. In the Place of Beauty, Ramesses granted her a large tomb, and in lines that tremble like fresh-cut flowers the village artists, as fascinated apparently by the lady's beauty as was King Ramesses, drew her there, her face blushing in quiet awareness, golden on the gleaming walls. The King had also granted the Queen a splendid sarcophagus of pink granite and a full complement of gods and servants for the next world. She died young, when Ramesses had ruled thirty years, less than half the span of his reign. One of the texts on her sarcophagus begs the goddess Isis, a mourner at all royal funerals, to help her progress to the rebirth: 'May your arms be beside the Osiris, Queen Nefertari. Make her face shine brightly and open her eyes. '

The state coasted like a well-oiled machine, the glories of earlier ages – the temples, the statues, the obelisks, and all the images of the gods – being yearly equalled by the prodigious new monuments that were rising through-out the land. Some of the finest tombs ever made in the village cemetery were cut during these languid years. In the low cliff that ran along the top of the western hill, under the path leading to the Great Place, a whole line of tomb chapels were excavated and decorated for the families of the fore-men, scribes and senior men of the gangs. Scribe Ramose had his second tomb chapel excavated for himself and Wia beneath the north end of this imposing row, while Foreman Nebnefer had taken over a part of the chapel of his father Neferhotep to make a large joint tomb for the two of them and their family. Next door Nebnefer's son Neferhotep excavated another tomb chapel that would remain the largest in the cemetery, with two open courtyards and a wide ramp that ran from half-way down the hillside right up to its bright wooden doorways.

Young Neferhotep gathered together a fine cast of characters in his tomb chapel to honour him and his family after their deaths. On one wall, the august trio of Neferhotep and his father and grandfather were drawn in a line, and behind them Neferhotep's brother Amennakht and family friends. The open court outside held splendid examples of the opulent sculptural style which also decorated the walls of King Ramesses II's own tomb. But here the sculptures were in the round: life-sized figures of some of Neferhotep's family and that of his fellow-foreman, Kaha. All were carefully carved from huge blocks of limestone in a slightly archaic style; the women, full-stomached and round-thighed in the manner of the later years of the old dynasty, are especially beguiling in their billowing pleated gowns, each one carefully knotted under the right breast to show their full figures to advantage. Foreman Neferhotep appears as a young man, dressed in the heavily-starched robes worn at feasts and festivals. Under his sculpted chair sits a monkey and a little boy, a servant of the foreman's household, who feeds grapes to the family pet one by one.

Foreman Anhirkawi, Kaha's successor, made a large tomb for himself at the southern end of the main cemetery. As fascinated by the past and its styles as Foreman Neferhotep, he commissioned a strange stela for his tomb which was engraved with a prayer to Amun and a figure of Tuthmosis IV, a monarch who had then been dead some 150 years. Both the figure of the King and the prayer on the stela were copied from some of the old monuments in the village cemetery, just as Ramose had copied his. But Anhirkawi had gone further, even to the extent of making a cunning play of words in the text between his name and the name of a village architect who had lived in the days of the old dynasty. Such antiquarianism and the ability to work in many different styles was typical of the artistic sophistication of the village, now wealthy and filled with clever workmen. The two gangs were no longer merely tomb-cutters controlled by scribes, who scribbled sacred texts on the plaster walls of the royal tombs, but had become a body of skilled craftsmen containing some of Egypt's finest artists.

5

SCRIBE KENHIRKHOPESHEF

Vizier Paser eventually relinquished his post in the civil administration in the fourth decade of King Ramesses II's reign and succeeded to his father's post as High Priest of Amun. At about the same time, a new scribe was brought into the village from the outside since Scribe Ramose was now middle-aged and had no sons to succeed him. Just as Scribe Huy and his wife had adopted young Ramose a quarter of a century before, so now Ramose and Wia adopted this fifteen-year-old, Kenhirkhopeshef. The young man was a good choice: he proved a most competent scribe and performed all the duties expected of a village son. But Kenhirkhopeshef was of a very different metal from his predecessors and his particular combination of energy and curiosity has left individual traces.

Kenhirkhopeshef was fascinated by the past: sensitive to the culture and history of his country. In his loping hand he copied a famous old text written before he had been born, which recounted the story of a battle fought by young King Ramesses II in Syria. He had lists of the great King's sons and lists, all in order, of the kings whose mortuary temples stood together in a long row along the fields' edge at western Thebes, and he had many of the more illustrious of them engraved on a memorial for his own funeral chapel. He collected other texts too: medical diagnoses and prescriptions, spells, hymns, letters, poetry, tables of household hints, even interpretations of dreams. Perhaps more than anything else it is these remnants of Kenhirkhopeshef's library and personal writings that show us the scope of his intellect, for his surviving official documents present us with another, less attractive face.

We know little enough of the first years of Kenhirkhopeshef's career with the tombmakers. Certainly Ramose must have felt strong sympathy with him, for, as he watched over the beginnings of Kenhirkhopeshef's life at the village, he saw many of the circumstances of his own youth played out again before his eyes. Like Ramose, Kenhirkhopeshef had not been born of a family of scribes, his parents would have no memorials beyond their son's inscriptions, and he had not been born in the tombmakers' village. For ten years the two scribes worked together in the Great Place before Kenhirkhopeshef was appointed as a full scribe and then, upon Ramose's death a few years later, Kenhirkhopeshef succeeded to the position as the senior scribe of the tomb, a position he would hold with great authority for some thirty-five years.

The first task of Kenhirkhopeshef's majority, like the first office of a new king, was to officiate at his father's funeral and follow behind Ramose's coffin sledge with all the old scribe's household, friends and family, as it was dragged up through the stony cemetery to the tomb chapel. There, tightly packed inside three bright coffins of sweet cedar, Ramose's mummy was set up in the sun for the funeral rites which accompanied every villager into his burial vault. When Kenhirkhopeshef had finished the offerings to his father's spirit Ramose was lowered into the deep shaft that dropped down to his burial vault. There, so that Ramose's soul might live and his shadow prosper, Kenhirkhopeshef carefully counted, in the best scribal manner, all the magical aids to the afterlife that his adopted father had so carefully collected together in his lifetime and which now went with him into the warm darkness of his grave. We do not know whether Wia died before her husband and already lay there in the vault; certainly she would have joined her husband when she died. Then, with old Ramose set safely upon his journey into the next world, Kenhirkhopeshef walked back down through the cemetery to his village household. When the work in the Great Place started once again, he would carry the old scribe's records with him along the shadowed high street, past the doors of his neighbours' houses, out through the north gate into the sunlight and up, again, past the village tomb chapels, along the bright paths of the high desert, over the horizon of Thebes and down into the Great Place, there to continue the work of his village father, the honest Scribe Ramose.

On Kenhirkhopeshef's promotion, a junior scribe, Anupemheb, seems to have taken over many of his routine tasks: receiving and distributing the rations of grain, fish and wood and sending the broken chisels to the coppersmiths for recasting. Now when fellow-scribes record Kenhirkhopeshef's absences from the Great Place they are deferential to him: they seldom supply the same precision of detail as when they record the truancies of the workmen. As the senior scribe, Kenhirkhopeshef's status in the community had changed. Unfortunately, despite his long apprenticeship to the job, his attitude towards the tombmakers seems to have changed as well:

The draughtsman Prahotep salutes his superior, the scribe in the Place of Truth Kenhirkhopeshef: in life prosperity and health! What does this bad way mean in which you behave to me? I am like a donkey to you. If there is some work, bring the donkey, if there is some food, bring the ox. If there is some beer, you do not look for me, but if there is work you do look for me. By my head, if I am a man of bad behaviour with beer, do not look for me! — It is good if you have listened.

It was common practice among state officials to take subordinates from their official work and set them tasks on their own account, indeed, the tombmakers expected to work for the foremen and scribes as well as the King. They owed strong allegiance to their superiors, and such work affirmed their status as the associates of an influential person. But in return for such fidelity, the foremen and the scribes were expected to take care of their men – the two foremen representing them directly in dealings with the administration, and the scribes recording their legal and domestic affairs whenever written documents were needed. Prahotep's letter is indignant because he believed that some beer that was rightly his had not been given him – and since beer was not only a social drink but an important part of the village diet his letter accuses the scribe of neglecting the welfare of his subordinates. So strong is Prahotep's claim to be heard, that the man's words, just as they were dictated to the recording scribe, still seem high-pitched and not a little angry, for such a lack of sensibility offended the order of village society, where each person had responsibilities and obligations to others.

Just as the men of the two gangs were bound together in mutual responsibility with their foremen and scribes, so all the villagers were responsible for the quality and progress of the work in the Great Place, and the administration judged their performance very carefully. 'Be very, very, watchful in performing well all the commissions of the Great Place of Pharaoh,' the Vizier warned in a letter to Foreman Nebnefer, and as it was the foremen who controlled the work in the tomb but the scribes who reported to the Vizier on its progress, it is easy to see there was considerable room for friction between these various 'chiefs of the tomb'. None the less, despite the fact that the demarcation of responsibility between the foremen and the scribes was never precise, there were seldom serious disputes amongst them. So friendly was the relationship between the young Foreman Neferhotep and Kenhirkhopeshef, who had both been promoted at the same time, that Neferhotep even included him in a scene on the wall of his huge tomb chapel – the only time, indeed, that the fractious scribe appears in any of the village tomb chapels! But then, by the end of their careers, the two men had worked side by side in the Great Place for some forty-odd years.

The mores of the village matched those of the gods and of the King and his court: just as elderly monarchs sometimes chose to rule in co-regency with their crown princes, so, as we have seen, village elders or scribes took junior partners to work alongside them and eventually succeed them. Similarly, litigation was as common amongst the gods, where the rights and wrongs of their feuds, vast cosmic contests of life and death, were judged by tribunals of other gods, as amongst the villagers, whose disputes, debts, and petty transgressions were judged by a village court where the scribes, foremen and senior workmen sat in judgement. Despite all Vizier Paser's reforms, the old patterns of responsibility and authority did not change at the village; these were simply part of the natural order of the universe and of the state at its centre.

The middle years of Ramesses II's reign continued after Ramose's death, and as the work in the royal tomb inched forward year by year, the tomb-makers looked for ways to make their lives more comfortable in the Valley of the Kings. At the start of Ramesses' reign they inhabited a huddle of huts, little crude shelters of piled stones which they built in the centre of the valley. But these pens were scarcely comfortable at the best of times and, with the temperature fluctuating from that of a moon-bright January night when thin skins of ice might form across the tops of water jars to the summer months when the whole valley baked like a slow oven, they must have been unbearable for much of the year. So now the tombmakers built themselves new accommodation up by the fortress at the three steps, on the path joining their village to the Great Place, constructing three groups of huts in a little hamlet standing right at the saddle of the pass where the track from the village turns away from the Nile valley to run down into the Great Place. Here they could look over miles of the river-greened plain, right across the river, over the vast city on its east bank, over the temples of Amun and his family and beyond to the hills of the far eastern horizon. Above their new settlement hung the same mountain that loomed pyramid-like over the Great Place. The peak was known by the villagers to be a 'gate of heaven' inhabited by Meretseger, the sacred lady 'who loves silence', 'she who faces her lord' Amun, the king of the gods whose temple at Karnak lay far below them on the other side of the river. To one side of their huts the men built a small temple for the village's patron King Amen-hotep and close by it Kenhirkhopeshef scratched a sentence on the cliff honouring 'Amun of the good encounter', for the temple stood exactly at the point on the path where the tombmakers would first see Amun's vast temple on the east bank as they climbed up out of the Great Place. High above, on the slopes of Meretseger's mountain, some of the workmen made small personal shrines for the Theban gods whose temples they could just see faintly through the dusty air, their obelisks and pylon pennants flashing in the sunlight across the shimmering valley. Like the village, the settlement was divided into two main halves which stood on either side of a central street – here the path from the village to the Great Place. As the gangs walked up from their work in the royal tomb, they first passed by the low walls of the medjay's fortress with its three steps, and here they left the confines of the Great Place to rest in their settlement close by.

It was a strange village that the tombmakers built on the mountainside, with no accommodation for families or servants. And this seems all the more odd when it is understood that the men often spent their entire working week of up to eight days living in this settlement and working in the royal tomb without returning to their village. None the less, no ash or cooking charcoal has ever been found there. Food must have been brought up every day after its preparation in the village houses and, indeed, one note has survived, written by a workman, asking his daughter in the village to send extra bread and beans to him as her two brothers were helping their father in the work at the tomb. Usually such young men drew rations of their own when they worked in the royal tomb, for all the men who worked in the valley were provisioned from the storerooms in the Great Place; the arrival of the two brothers must have been unexpected.

So this little settlement was intended to house the tombmakers only during the time they worked in the Great Place. The huts had just two rooms, an inner, sleeping chamber and an antechamber with stone seats set along its walls so that groups of men might sit and talk together in the evening light and enjoy the fresh breezes rising from the wide valley below at sunset. These seats, each one U-shaped in careful imitation of the wooden seats of the furniture in the village houses, were made of blocks of limestone. Foreman Neferhotep had a chair in his hut inscribed for 'Chief of the Gang, Neferhotep'. Perhaps his wife Wabkhet used to visit him, for a woman of that name is mentioned briefly on a damaged chip of stone as being a lady 'of the settlement', whilst another hints that drinking parties for both men and women took place there as well. Scribe Kenhirkhopeshef also had a stone seat inscribed for him, this with a text that honoured his village father: 'King's Scribe in the Place of Truth, Ramose, his son who makes his name live, Kenhirkhopeshef'. He inhabited the largest, most centrally placed hut in the settlement, which unlike all the others had three rooms, each paved with slabs of limestone. In all probability, this was Kenhirkhopeshef's office, where he tended the records of the work at the royal tomb and composed his correspondence to the officers of the administration. With the settlement's fine view over the royal temples below in the Theban plain it was doubtless from here that Kenhirkhopeshef made his lists of their names. And here too, in his office, he probably compiled the collection of words that has survived in his handwriting, related to the general terms for 'chief' and 'overseer'; a list that shows an interest in words and their variations of meaning – the lexigraphic ruminations of an ancient Dr Johnson.

The settlement's two main groups of huts shared common roofs and in the evenings when the men came up from their work below the site must have resembled two beehives, busy and noisy as people moved from one doorway to another to sit in groups. And there, just as they did at the village, the men used this time at the settlement to strike bargains with each other, play games, make music or simply sit and talk.

Some of the men set up small workshops in the settlement where they made statues and the little *ushabtis* that people took with them into their tombs. Nebre, the same draughtsman scribe who had reported to the Vizier about the condition of the village during its reorganization, owned a slip of stone with a carefully drawn figure of one of these servant statues upon it, and it was covered with the precise texts with which such figures were traditionally inscribed: 'in truth, I am here and will come whenever you call me' says the little statue after a recital of its dead owner's name and title. On the reverse of this copying stone was a drawing of the special scarab placed over the heart of the eviscerated corpse during mummification. Nebre had a careful copy of the correct text for this amulet too, its spell precisely the same as it appears in the Book of the Dead: 'May nothing oppose me in the judgement in the presence of the Lord of the trial, Osiris. Let it be said of me, of what I have done, "his deeds are right and true", may nothing happen against me in the presence of the great god Osiris.' The prayer had been composed by Thoth, a god who, when Nebre made his copy, was at least 2000 years old and, for its full power to become manifest, it had to be carved in hieroglyphs on the flat underside of a large green-stone scarab set in gold.

Other workmen engraved stone stelae while they stayed in the little settlement, making scenes showing the villagers praying before their gods. Sometimes these were commissioned from an engraving sculptor by another workman in the gangs and were traded directly against other goods. A few of the small tablets were made on speculation, with spaces left blank in their inscriptions to be filled in later. Some of the men decorated their huts, fitting them with stone doorsills and plastering the walls with strawed mud, a workman called Nebenmaat engraving his name on a smooth block of stone set into his hut wall. Along with the names and titles carved upon the stone seats, such texts show more than a simple desire to advertise ownership, for they served to remind later generations that their predecessors still mingled with them, both in family life at the village and in the work at the Great Place. And, indeed, like the houses of the village, these little huts on the col were inhabited for hundreds of years by generation after generation of the same families, though always inscribed with the names of their first owners.

Even in this unchanging world, however, some individual events occurred

which, like the personalities of some of the tombmakers, still stand out
sharply after more than 3000 years. One happening of such drama and
devastation that it seemed to contain the struggles of the gods themselves,
occurred in the Great Place late in the reign of Ramesses II, at the end of
a hot spring day, while the workmen were sitting in their new settlement in
the evening, when the sun had set and left the desert to cool in its afterglow
and the air was still heavy with the day's heat. Then the tombmakers saw
bolts of pink lightning raining down from a mass of dark clouds miles away
to the south: an electric storm, playing down on the high desert like the
needle of a sewing-machine.

Suddenly there is a noise like a deep growl from the plateau above and
a bore of water bursts down the slope of Meretseger's mountain in a flood
of foam and rock. The valley's head seems to dissolve as the sky overhead
darkens, filling with hard plum-coloured clouds, blown in from the high
desert. The storm roars over the Great Place and forked lightning plays
down into the valley in neon stripes. Rain falls in huge dead drops and
hisses on the rocks as their dry stone sucks at the moisture. The air is
charged, the ground crackles. The high slopes above the Great Place, already soaked by the passage of the flash flood, turn into a mass of sludge
that flows like lava down through the bottom of the valley. Then the flood
stops as abruptly as it has begun, and the rain blows away in broad theatric
gestures, south down the Nile valley. An eerie light has come to the Great
Place, the old rocks seem tired and heavy. From start to finish the storm
has passed in just twenty minutes.

In the Nile's plain below, the floodwaters flowed in wide sheets across
the fields and into the river. Waterlogged houses slipped glutinously to the
ground, their bricks and mortar dissolved, returning to the river silt from
which they were made. Earlier, many houses were smashed by the flood's
first force, which took people and animals along with it, floating bloated
down the stream to the wide river. Temple officials and farmers were not
able to pass across the area for several days, and all the while the shining
water that lapped gently around the temples' walls was pouring down into
the nobles' burial vaults, soaking the contents, spinning them round and
turning them rotten. When, at last, the men of the two gangs dared to
venture down into the Great Place again they walked across a new landscape. At the valley's head, the cliff had been gouged away, undercut so
that some of its limestone had collapsed and been carried away down the
valley by the floodwater. Boulders ten and twelve feet high had been sent
rolling along in the flood like juggernauts, cutting deep channels in the
valley floor. Along with the gangs' storerooms, the old huts at the centre of
the valley had been smashed to pieces then buried under a slurry of rock
and sand. Their replacements would be built further down.

Standing high on a fresh scree of wet flood debris that sloped down from the top of the cliffs to the valley floor, the scribes and some of the workmen scratched their names and titles, along with those of King Ramesses II, on a rock face that before the flood had soared inaccessibly above their heads. Thirty feet beneath them some of the old tombs, excavated low down in the valley, lay deeply buried. Many had had their walls smashed and soaked by the flood, some were half-filled with rock, sand and water, and would soon collapse as the soft shale under the limestone cliffs expanded, then dissolved, transforming their precise architecture into ruined caverns. The floodwater stayed for hundreds of years in some of the tombs, escaping only by the slow process of evaporation through deep faults running through the cliffs. The simple tombs of the old dynasty nobles, cut lower in the valley than those of their royal masters, suffered the most, but several of the kings' own tombs, including that of Ramesses II, also stood full in the flood's path. By the time the desert valley had desiccated again and the tombmakers were back at work, the thick layer of flood debris had set as hard as cement over the buried tombs. Some of them, such as the makeshift chambers that held King Tutankhamun of the old dynasty were, as far as the tombmakers were concerned, lost for ever. The locations of other, more important tombs were, however, remembered by the men, and in later reigns when they were opened again it was found that the doors of many of them had stood firm against the flood.

But what of King Ramesses II's own tomb, which had stood open in the flood's path? It is almost certain that the huge monument in which Scribe Ramose and the tombmakers had spent a lifetime's work felt at least a trickle of water in it, as the flood's deep fingers ran down through its corridors. It is even possible that the great tomb was filled to its mouth with rocks and wet sand. Today the tomb is so badly destroyed by a succession of floods that only the most painstaking excavation could hope to give an answer. If Ramesses II's tomb was destroyed before he died, we should imagine that the two gangs were suddenly sent into furious action to excavate another tomb for the King and this, indeed, is what the surviving records hint at. At least one other huge tomb was built and decorated in the valley at this time and bears Ramesses II's names, though this too, is now so damaged, so filled with flood debris, that no archaeologist has ever been inside it. What is certain, however, is that the old King was finally put to rest in the Great Place.

6

ROYAL TOMB

Great Ramesses eventually died, of the ailments of an imperious old age, in 1212 BC, in the sixty-seventh year of his reign. No less than thirteen crown princes having died before their august father, the throne was now taken by Prince Merneptah, himself in creaking middle age after a lifetime in the civil administration. Disgruntled, perhaps by the lack of fortitude that his offspring had displayed, the old King had barely acknowledged the son who eventually succeeded him.

Whilst Ramesses underwent his mummification, the tombmakers assisted in laying out, in precise ritual order, the vast quantities of equipment that, together with the objects of the royal funeral procession, would surround King Ramesses in whichever of his tombs he lay. Then after the funeral, with Merneptah on the throne and Egypt with its earthly god again, the Vizier and a commission of courtiers came to the Great Place to search, as a later text describes, for 'a place of piercing' for the new King's tomb. It was, of course, the first expedition of its kind to take place in the commissioners' lifetimes and, in the wake of the flood, they were presented with a transformed landscape in which the tombs of the old dynasty lay buried deep around them. For all that, Merneptah's commissioners had only a limited number of sites to consider for the tomb. Much of the valley was periodically attacked by floodwater and was quite unsuitable. Further, the valley's head was not large and most of it had already been taken by older tombs. Ingeniously, the commission eventually settled upon a modest site that was quite unused: a small side valley running behind the tomb of Merneptah's illustrious father. Here, the doorway and entrance corridor could be cut through a massive slab of limestone that had slumped into the Great Place from the plateau above and lay like a low hill on the valley floor. A deep trench was cut from the front of the tomb to deflect flood-waters away from its entrance down into the centre of the valley. Eventually this trench became choked with stones and sand, but it successfully protected Merneptah's tomb throughout ancient history.

First the village's quarrymen cut the tomb's doorway into the rock, then they excavated a corridor, quarrying straight into the limestone hillock in a series of steps that ran down from the ceiling to the floor of the excavation like a giant stairway. The rough walls that they left behind were finished smooth by stonemasons, and cracks that had been exposed were plastered shut. The walls were then prepared for the drawings and relief sculptures which would cover them.

And so it was that first the doorway, then the entrance corridor, and then all the 'corridors of the sun's path' that led to the royal burial chamber, were cut into the limestone of the Great Place. For the first time in many years the villagers were excavating, and would soon start to decorate, a royal tomb. Now, however, they were making an underworld for a king who was in his fifties and stiffening with arthritis, and the tomb's commissioners had to make sure that it was sufficiently finished at all the stages of its manufacture to house a premature royal burial.

The rock of Merneptah's tomb was seeded with parallel rows of flints that ran like strings of pearls in lines sloping down to follow the strata of the limestone. With only their soft copper chisels to attack the intractable flint, it caused the quarrymen many delays. A typical entry in the scribes' journal reads: 'Year one, on the twelfth day of the first month of summer, the boulder of flint was found on the right', a happening that served to retard the usually fast-moving excavation.

Scribe Kenhirkhopeshef was in overall charge of the upkeep of the work-journal of the new tomb; after an apprenticeship of some thirty-five years in the Great Place, he was the best man for the job. On ostraca both large and small, he and his staff scribbled endless notes from which the log books would be compiled. For his own records Kenhirkhopeshef favoured the larger flakes of limestone and, before he started to write upon them, would blunt their edges to ensure that none of his text would be lost by the accidental fracture of a sliver of stone. Sometimes the scribes would use the physical weight of these ostraca as a record of the weight of another material, such as copper or even food; the receipt being written on the stone, so: 'weight of the chisel which has perished with [the workman] Iny; to be recast; [written] by the hand of the scribe Kenhirkhopeshef'. But not for Kenhirkhopeshef the elegantly turned forms and dense black characters of Ramose's writing! His is a large and scratchy hand, quick and functional, in short movements that barely stop to re-charge the frayed pen with fresh ink, chopping over the flat stones in letters so big that even the most poor-sighted of his scribes could read the script with ease. Verifying and listing over and over again, Kenhirkhopeshef left his stones ink-greyed with washed-out entries: recording the depth of a day's quarrying, listing the workmen present and absent, noting the number of wicks used in the tomb lamps. All was carefully checked and often marked with hurried red dots as his skipping pen went quickly through the lists.

41

'The Great Tomb of Baenre, Beloved of Amun, the Son of Re, Merneptah, Satisfied with Truth' was Kenhirkhopeshef's splendid title for the monument on which, at the age of fifty-one, he now started thirteen years of
work. Above the door of the tomb, under the valley's surrounding cliffs, he
had a niche cut in the rock where he could sit comfortably in the shade and
watch the comings and goings below. In his inimitable hand he scribbled

on the cliff beside his seat: 'Sitting place of the Scribe Kenhirkhopeshef'. Inside the new tomb, the foremen Neferhotep and Anhirkawi were
overseeing gangs that had been enlarged to about fifty men each. Despite
the near-frantic speed with which a new tomb was always begun, it had
proved pointless to employ larger numbers than this, for the size of the
rock face would only permit two or three men working side by side at any
one time. The artists and masons were equally limited in their working
time, not only by the space available to them but also by the fact that the
processes of quarrying and decoration could hardly take place at the same
time, for it was impossible for the draughtsmen and sculptors to work on
the walls of the narrow corridors whilst continuous lines of labourers carried baskets filled with chippings past them and clouds of dust rose from
excavations in the lower sections of the tomb. Thus the shifts of quarrymen
had to alternate with the tomb's decorators and, to ensure that at least a
part-finished tomb was always available for the royal burial at any time
during the reign, both these activities had to proceed simultaneously.

Neferhotep and Anhirkawi were responsible for this detailed planning
and they also oversaw the work of the quarrymen, sculptors, plasterers and
the supporting gangs of labourers, plastermakers and carpenting scaffold-
erectors. They were responsible, too, for the quality of the workmanship in
the tomb, from the laying-out of its architecture to the final delicate painting of the wall reliefs. The first major problem any foremen faced with a
new tomb was that of maintaining strict accuracy throughout the architecture. Unlike the laying-out of temples, which was done with ropes and posts

set into the ground, it was hardly possible to survey a tomb plan in the depths of the rock. The solution was a clever one. After the first rough quarrying of the doorway, a series of precise vertical cuts was made. It was from these fixed points that the dimensions of the next section of the tomb would be calculated. As the quarrymen worked further the system was repeated. It was these especially precise corners and edges that were the key to the accuracy of the tomb's architecture; they were also used as reference points for the lay-out of the tomb's decorations. Thus, using the simplest quarrying tools – hammers of hard stone bound into wooden hafts and copper adzes and spikes – the villagers were able to make tombs that were marvels of precision. The architecture of King Ramesses II's tomb, for example, was accurate to within a hundredth of an inch, and King Merneptah's was almost as fine: an absolute precision to last throughout eternity.

This exact architecture was carefully reproduced from reign to reign. Tradition determined the exact size, order and number of the rooms, pillars and corridors in the tombs and even the locations of the sacred texts, the stories of the royal progress through the underworld, carved on the tombs' walls. The rite of constructing a royal underworld allowed very little deviation from a primeval masterplan, the perfect original. But despite this enormous burden of precedent, there was also room for refinement and even, sometimes, for a little experimentation, for Egyptian architects liked nothing better than to improve and simplify the designs of their predecessors. One small change typical of many in Merneptah's tomb was the relocation of scenes traditionally placed just inside the doorway of the tomb. It had not passed unnoticed that as the two wooden doors of Ramesses II's tomb opened into the tomb they covered the splendid figures in the wall reliefs showing the King worshipping the gods on his arrival in the underworld. This unfortunate occurrence, the blocking-off of the royal presence, was carefully corrected in Merneptah's tomb by setting the two scenes further down the corridor walls by exactly the width of one door. Such refinement ensured that the making of a new tomb was never a mechanical rite, and by making each one a little smoother, a little closer to perfection, these thoughtful changes aided the progress of the dead king. By far the biggest innovation in Merneptah's tomb and one that broke with the most ancient traditions of royal tombmaking was the way the plan cut straight down from the doorway to the burial chamber, with no sudden turns to disorientate the funeral procession as it meandered through the royal underworld, no right-angles to block the daylight from the burial chamber. It became the normal pattern for all the later royal tombs in the Great Place.

By the second year of the reign, both gangs were making good progress in the tomb and Kenhirkhopeshef was able to send an optimistic report to the Vizier: 'A summary of the work done in the Great Place of Pharaoh'. The entrance stairway with its wide flat steps was finished, as were all the upper corridors of the tomb, where scenes and texts had been engraved and painted. Deep in the rock below, the quarrymen were now excavating the burial chamber. The scribe also reported that some plastermakers, carpenters and other craftsmen were being added to the gang, and that the gang's blunt chisels were being returned to the royal founderies for recasting and reforging.

In the following years, the records of Kenhirkhopeshef's that have survived deal mainly with the issuing of wicks used in the lamps lighting the parts of the royal tomb beyond the daylight. The workmen used small pottery lamps which filled the tombs with soft globes of yellow light and illuminated the huge paintings in flickering haloes. When the King and the courtiers visited the tomb they walked through mysterious conjunctions of corridors and rooms whose relationships they may have apprehended but which they never clearly saw; magically precise details of painting and architecture floating, lamplit, in high dark caverns. The lamp wicks that so occupied Kenhirkhopeshef were made of twisted rags soaked in tallow and laid on the sloping sides of the oil-filled lamps. You may see such lamps today, fuelled with olive oil, in the myriad shrines for the Virgin that exist throughout the Christian lands of the Mediterranean. If the oil is pure there is little cause for worry about the lamps' smoke sooting the rooms in which they burn.

The lamp oil was delivered, with the other supplies, from the storerooms of the royal temples, and the storekeepers of the Great Place issued them to the foremen, hour by hour, for use in the tomb. This oil, also used by the villagers for cooking and lighting their homes, was a valuable commodity, a continuous and heavy expense of the work at the tomb. Strict account was kept of the wicks and their fuel. 'First month of winter, day five, consumption of wicks made on that day: right six, left six, making twelve [for the morning]; right six, left five, making eleven [afternoon], total twenty-three', notes one industrious scribe. Kenhirkhopeshef's lengthy records of the rate at which these wicks were issued from the stores suggests that the morning and afternoon shifts at the tomb were both of the same length, probably four hours' duration. The records also show that after three years' work the painters and sculptors had still not reached the darkest, lowest, sections of the tomb where the wick consumption would have jumped to double the amounts recorded by the scribe.

Occasionally there were frustrating delays in the delivery of supplies, caused by the government bureaucracy. A letter sent by Kenhirkhopeshef direct to Vizier Panhesi reports that the absence of the court from Thebes has caused the administration to clog and that neither the officials at the royal warehouses nor the storekeepers in the Great Place are distributing the stocks that they hold. He urgently asks the Vizier for fresh supplies of chisels and plaster as well as the leather baskets that were used to carry quarried stone from the tomb. But despite this bottleneck the scribe reassuringly observes that: 'The Great Place of Pharaoh [his tomb] — is in strict good order, its walls are in peace and no damage has occurred therein. Moreover, we are working in the Great Place of Pharaoh in strict good order — doing the will of Pharaoh, our good Lord, having made it a good efficient work of eternal construction.' Something of the personal relationship between the scribe and the Vizier is contained in the last paragraph of this letter, where Kenhirkhopeshef gives news of some private orders Panhesi had placed with the villagers: how five baskets 'for the Lady Heret, your sister' were being woven, how Kenhirkhopeshef would soon deliver to the Vizier a bed that, along with some special tools, he had ordered from the tombmakers. The letter is not humble: it deals with the Vizier, if deferentially, still as one person to another.

In 1205 BC, the seventh year of Merneptah's reign, during the month of May, the statues of the gods that were to stand around the dead King in his tomb were hauled into their places at Panhesi's order. These elegant figures were partly covered in thick gold leaf, and often ritually daubed with shiny-black resins that made their cedar look like polished stone. This marvellous collection had been manufactured in workshops standing beside the royal mortuary temples and its arrival in the Great Place was a signal for celebration amongst the tombmakers. As the sun and the stars moved through the sky, so these gods moved through the landscape of Egypt, and now, as the dead kings moved with the setting sun, so the gods came again to the Great Place; the beginning of the journey of royal resurrection and of the rebirth and fertility of Egypt. Food and drink for feasting was issued to the two gangs and they celebrated with singing and dancing. At one of these little festivals a food magazine in the Great Place was opened and pots of cheese curds were given out. During another, the finest linen cloth, a most courtly luxury, was issued, one length for each member of the two gangs.

The day after the celebration, Vizier Panhesi visited the valley and ordered that the King's outer coffin, which was usually made of wood, should be cut from a block of alabaster as King Seti's had been some ninety years before. This stone coffin, shaped like a mummy and covered in texts, was to hold two inner coffins made of pinewood and inside this triple shell would lie the swathed and embalmed cadaver of the King. This most inventive Vizier had already decided to change the arrangements of the royal sarcophagus: unlike most of the earlier kings who had only one stone box

45

holding their royal coffins, Merneptah's mummy was to be provided with three bulky granite lids which would rest, one on top of the other, in a series of concentric slots cut into the floor of the burial chamber. The innermost of these three trenches would hold the alabaster coffin. Now the eyes of the administration were fixed firmly on the arrangements for the royal funeral and the King's eternal well-being.

The day following the edict, Vizier Panhesi again appeared in the Great Place, this time with a court scribe and a chamberlain. Together they watched as two of the lids that were to cover the royal mummy were taken down through the tomb into the burial chamber. These heavy stones had been brought on barges from the granite quarries at the first cataract of the Nile, to the south of Thebes. Their decorations – for like the tomb, these too were to be covered in texts and gods – had been engraved by granite-masons from Elephantine, the town on the cataract forming the southern border of Egypt. These artists had a very different style of drawing and modelling from that cultivated by the men of the two gangs, and this difference emphasized the alien quality of these darkly shining objects as they were taken into the limestone tomb. Both the tombmakers and the Vizier's commission must have been greatly relieved when the two massive stones, each weighing several tons, were successfully manoeuvred past the gods and goddesses that, along with the sacred texts, decorated the walls of the upper parts of the tomb. The gangs could now happily return to their usual tasks of excavation and decoration.

Surprisingly, some of the work of decorating and inscribing Merneptah's funeral equipment – his coffins, the gods' figures and the like – was done in the Great Place close by his tomb. The scenes that cover the alabaster coffin for example, were carefully engraved there under the supervision of a scribe, Huy, who had been sent especially for the task from the offices of one of the royal temples' treasuries. All the texts and the iconography of the objects destined for the royal burial and the decoration of the tomb itself were controlled and edited by scholarly scribes who had culled the most accurate copies of the ancient compositions – the 'old writings of the tomb' as they were called – documents of leather and papyrus, from the temples' archives. These texts described the fate of the king in the underworld, potent information that was closely guarded.

King Merneptah 'joined with the god who made him' and was 'united with the sun disc' in his early sixties, in the thirteenth year of his rule. Unfortunately, the lower sections of his tomb were still unfinished. Quickly the gangs' carpenters filled the burial chamber with scaffolding made of heavy beams of local wood held together with tensioned ropes and, whilst the King's corpse was being mummified, the room was plastered and the traditional scenes were painted, each in its proper place, in fresh hot colours on its walls and vault. It must have been during this same strange period, when no king ruled and the universe held its breath, that the tomb commissioners discovered a drastic error in their plans. For the massive black granite prism, the final outer cover of the royal coffins, was too large to pass down through the tomb. Hurriedly, all the doorjambs in the upper corridors, each one of which had been carefully sculpted and painted years before, were cut away and their gaudy fragments taken out into the sunlight and dumped at the end of the rocky bay behind the tomb. New plans were then drawn up showing how the King would lie inside his coffins under the three granite lids, and an attempt was made to pass the big black stone into the burial chamber. But in the narrow corridors at the bottom of the tomb there was precious little room for manoeuvre and the block was abandoned half-way down the tomb, shining like a stranded whale.

But now, after seventy days, the King's corpse had been gutted and desiccated on its bed of natron, then basted with resins and gums, wrapped ready for its eternal journey. Light as a blown egg, and hard as a statue, tightly bandaged by his priests, Merneptah lay in the pinewood coffins that had waited five years to hold him. Time pressed on the tombmakers, and the royal funeral, which depended on the movements of the stars and planets, could wait no longer. So, late on a summer day, as the sun dropped through the slot of the horizon and the evening desert glowed, the King was carried over the western hills and down into his underworld. Passing now under the gaze of the gods and goddess of the walls, the procession picked its way down into the tomb through the stacks of royal possessions that had been brought from palaces all over Egypt, then through heaps of amulets and vases, copied in the most part from objects of temple ritual. Then, deep in the tomb, they passed by the great black block, abandoned in the corridor, and down, finally, to the burial chamber. There, under the freshly-painted vault, the men of the gangs lowered the two smaller lids over the encoffined king, each one ringing as it touched bedrock. There, too, they left the procession's paraphernalia: the priests' jewels, the processional statue of Anubis, the jackal-god who had guided them to the cemetery, the King's viscera embalmed in a special casket. Then the priests gathered the gods about the sarcophagus, installed the magic amulets in their places and lit the golden torches that would illuminate the chamber after all of them had gone. Sweeping their footprints away as they went, the priests left the tomb, shutting and sealing its doorways one by one; King Merneptah was set in his underworld, and once again the compact between Egypt and its gods was renewed.

7

FESTIVAL

When Roma, the head of the royal workshops, inspected Merneptah's tomb in the King's eighth year he could not have failed to have been impressed by the skills that were displayed there. Indeed, he could well have wished that such talented artists as the tombmakers worked in his own studios. For the King's tomb was the finest monument of the reign, the sculptures in its upper corridors the equal of any of the time and the architecture and its novelties showed a lively intelligence. (Merneptah's successors judged the stranded lid in the tomb's corridors as a monument to experiment rather than ineptitude.)

The tombmakers' skills had fully matured since the days of Vizier Paser's reorganization and now they were held in due regard by the administration. Supplies and rations for their village were generous in quantity and prompt in delivery; the men of the gangs were rich beyond the wealth of ordinary craftsmen, their houses were well-furnished, their tombs the equal of those of ranking civil servants, and the village temples were richly endowed, the gods' feasts most lavishly provisioned. Indeed, the feast days and festivals had become so large a part of the village calendar that the tombmakers now spent a third of their time in celebration. Their eight-day working week was broken up by two- or three-day weekends, amounting to sixty-odd days in the year. There were a further sixty-five days of festivals dotted throughout the calendar, which they celebrated along with the rest of the population of Thebes, even, it seems, when a royal tomb had to be finished with some urgency.

These extra state festivals included most of the full-moon days as well as others celebrating the beginning of spring, the harvest and the river's flood. The first festival of the Theban year was the Feast of Opet which in Merneptah's day started on the eighteenth day of the second month and lasted for twenty-four days until the twelfth day of the following month – from mid-August until early September. The Opet Feast began when the shrine of the god Amun was carried from the dark sanctuary of his temple at Karnak out into the Theban sunlight to be taken to visit his harem at the temple of Southern Opet – now the temple of Luxor in modern Luxor town. Shaven-headed priests carried the god, enclosed in his gilded house and veiled in linen, right through his vast temple and down to the quay outside, where he was set upon a grand altar at the centre of the cedarwood barge which would convey him to his southern harem. And the entire city of Thebes would come to the river bank to see the god's progress and join the long procession that accompanied the teams pulling the god's ponderous barge upriver with heavy tow ropes. On the immense gold-plated barge, the king and the high priest made offerings of incense and food to the god, in full view of the city, whilst along the river bank paraded all the conglomerated exotica of an empire's capital: from be-feathered African drummers to bands of young Theban girls playing lutes; from naked dancing girls turning rhythmic backward somersaults to blind harpists and the god's priestly singers; from special army units, wrestlers and royal charioteers, to thousands upon thousands of the god's acolytes who had poured out of the temples. Like the modern festivals in Upper Egypt it was a time when people thronged happily and noisily in the streets for hours – but in ancient times how terrific the scale, how exotic the event!

Eight months after the Opet Festival, at the time of the full moon of the tenth month, the second festival of the Theban year, the Feast of the Valley, was celebrated, when Amun crossed the river on his barge to visit the temples of the west. Even the dead came to see the arrival of the sacred bark at the river-landing: prayers on the walls of nobles' tomb chapels ask that their spirits may always be allowed to hear the cries of the boat crews and see the god when the king comes with him to the west. Amun's glittering barge was pulled across the river by a boat of state that held rows of oarsmen. Once more, the king and the high priest were aboard the barge, steering it and making offerings upon the altars set up before the enshrined god. During the next two days Amun would be taken into most of the royal temples where, for a while, he would join the resident gods in their sanctuaries for special rituals and offerings. Small stone sanctuaries were placed along the god's processional routes in which Amun, now mounted in his shrine and set upon a model boat, and his priestly bearers who carried this load on long heavy poles, might rest. At times of festival special loaves were baked in the temple ovens and a strong beer was fermented in the temple's breweries so the priests who carried the god were well fortified for the long ordeal of the procession.

On the first morning of the Feast of the Valley, young priests from the royal temples sat high in the western cliffs at dawn to catch sight of Amun's barge as it was towed from the narrow canal that ran to the temple quay and into the river's stream. As they sat shivering in the pink early morning light, the warm sun touched them as it rose and lit the grey mist in the valley below, some of them scratched their names on the rocks beside them.

Then, as the sunlight touches the tops of the palms and sycamore trees and spreads out through the fields to warm away the river's mist, it lights a flash of gold. The god's barge is on the canal, and down the narrow cliff path the young priests run, down past their temples and along the dykes through the fields to the riverside, there to parade with the Theban god and welcome him to the west. Slowly the long processions of the living and the dead spread through the fields, cemeteries and tomb chapels, through the temples, the settlements of priests and the village of the tombmakers. And as the sun rises higher and the cliffs unfurl like huge white sails, as their shadows shrink away, so the god crosses the white desert land of the dead. With him too come the musicians and the dancers, the army and the singers in a shouting stamping throng of dust, linen, and music. So did the people of ancient Thebes celebrate their gods, and their gods, being like their subjects neither sober nor prudish, blessed the city with their bounty.

Not all the festivals the villagers celebrated were as lavish, or as public, as these two main holidays of the year. At the other end of the spectrum were feasts that were observed only by individuals or single families: the attendance registers of the village scribes often note a man's absence from the work in the Great Place when he was either celebrating 'his festival' or brewing beer for the accompanying feast. There were festivals of the gangs too, which celebrated specific events in the work at the Great Place, like the arrival of the gods' statues which surrounded the dead king in his tomb. And there were festivals for the gods of the village temples, especially King Amenhotep, whose statue, enshrined and veiled like Amun, was carried around the village by the workmen who also served as his priests. Sometimes, King Amenhotep was also carried along the track to the Great Place in festival: 'Twenty-first day of the seventh month, this day of King Amenhotep that goes to the valley, with the workers dancing before him. It was ordered that they go to the store and open four vessels of curd — .'

Other village festivals connected the living with the dead. All the families would go to their tomb chapels, light lamps, tend the small gardens that were sometimes kept in the cemetery and feast in the chapels above the burial vaults filled with their ancestors. Then Kenhirkhopeshef would return to Ramose's chapel to make offerings to his village father on a special stone table that bore the names of the dead scribe and his adopted son. Many of these offering tables have been found at the village, some of them still stained with the charred fat of the cooked meat offerings that they once bore. After the dead had taken their part of this cooked meat, the delicacy could then be shared by the living family sitting above them at their feast in the chapel.

The dead also had separate festivals of their own which they celebrated by an annual pilgrimage to the sacred city of Abydos, where the god of the underworld, Osiris, was buried. On these ancient hallowe'ens the villagers would set up model boats, each one rigged for drifting on the river, pointing north towards the sacred city. The little craft took the spirits on a mystic voyage along the river to the sacred city whre they joined others, in their millions, from all over Egypt, an enormous procession of all the dead that there had ever been. At the front of the spirit multitudes, Osiris's priests carried the god in his shrine out into the white desert to his holy tomb. Then the following day the boats in the village tomb chapels were rigged for sailing upstream and turned southwards so that they might bear the spirits home again. That evening, lamps were lit in the chapels to guide them to their tombs and, once more, the living would make offerings to their dead and to the gods they lived with.

In King Merneptah's eighth year, when Roma had visited the Great Place as part of a royal commission, the Vizier ordered special rations to be given to the tombmakers, so pleased was he with the progress of the work. 'Pharoah let the workmen be rewarded for the tasks which they have executed,' noted the scribe Anupemheb, one of Kenhirkhopeshef's assistants, who then went on to list the full extent of the royal largesse on a particularly large limestone ostracon. In fact, the villagers were already expecting extra rations at this time of the year for the celebration of the Festival of Opet, but in this particular year the tombmakers were especially well provided-for. The food began to arrive a day after the Vizier's order, just before the start of the feast; more than 150 donkey-loads of provisions were delivered to the village, all carefully noted down by Anupemheb. And although some of this food had lain on the altars of the gods the greater part came from the warehouses and the agencies of the royal temples. Fish, for example, of which there were some 9000, was never offered in the temples. Nevertheless it was a staple part of the villagers' diet and now twenty-five donkey-loads of it were sent to the village, along with large quantities of rough salt. There, in the sun, we may imagine, the fish were filleted and salted on the roofs so that they dried quickly in the open air and their stench was not trapped in the houses. None the less the work must have imparted a most distinctive odour to the village for a day or so. Perhaps it was the similarity of this process to the rituals of human mummification that had made fish so unwelcome on the altars of the gods.

A different grade of salt, set in small hard cones, was used at the village, each person presumably grinding a little from his block to season food. Four hundred 400 of these blocks were sent up to the village with the supplies for the feast and, if we estimate that without its servants, each household, held six or seven members, we can imagine that this amount was sufficient to allow each resident his own salt for the feast. And what a feast the tombmakers were handed with their salt! Ten oxen, on the hoof and ready for slaughter, had been sent up to them, enough to provide everyone with several fine meals of a meat that was not everyday fare, for oxen were valuable and consumed large amounts of costly feed. These particular beasts had been fattened in the temples and bore the brand of the gods. When they were killed, by cutting their throats, the blood was carefully collected and used for food. All meats, from oxen to ducks, were spit-roasted whole, but butchery was a fine art, and the villagers would also have cut and boiled their beef in small pieces. Legs were considered to be the finest cuts but we may imagine that none of the rich meat was left at the end of the day, just dry and hollow bones.

To accompany this meat feast other protein-rich foods were also sent up to the village: some four donkey-loads of beans and sweet oils to add savour to the sauces, and enough barley malt (some eight donkeys had sweated up the track to the village carrying sacks of it) to allow every person in the village about four pints of beer. Bread, too, was sent from the temple offering tables in extraordinary amounts, 9000 loaves being loaded on to donkeys for the journey into the desert. Most of this was obviously destined for storage, then re-softening with water before eating, but large quantities would have been consumed at the feast. With each house taking about 150 loaves in an equal division the cellars under the floors of the rear rooms must have been crammed full. The Vizier had sent the village a considerable reward for its labours; thoughtfully, his officers had even supplied eight donkey-loads of natron, the soap of the day, so that the families could wash themselves thoroughly after their feast.

Such tremendous supplies of food and drink ensured that the Opet Festival of Merneptah's eighth year was very well celebrated. Though small feasts may have taken place in the larger rooms of the village houses, these could hardly have held many people, and certainly not have accommodated an ox roast. Still, there was a good deal of open land around the village and we may imagine that the villagers held their public feasting in the open air, perhaps in garlanded pavilions built especially to shade them from the sun. There would have been music and dancing, and certainly red wine to drink, a special luxury. Most guests sat with flowers in their hands. Drummings, rattlings, the bouncing rasp of stringed percussion and the liquid sounds of lutes and flutes accompanied nude dancing girls tattooed with blue patterned dots and small images of the god Bes (an ugly but beneficent dwarf who liked to play the tambourine) who performed in rhythmic acrobatic display.

Serving girls, naked but for a leather thong, stood at the side of each group of banqueters, each seated on their finest chairs, men and women together. It is likely that at the village, unlike the households of the courtiers, the children of the feasters helped to serve the food. Young girls brought the feast to the guests, the ox meat and possibly some desert game, oryx or gazelle, perhaps all basted in sweet-scented honey taken by the village bees from the sacred persea trees of the temple enclosures or the flowers of wild balsam thorns. Most food was held in the hand, meat nibbled carefully off the bone. Lumps of fat were served with cumin and radish oil and bobbing in the juice might be purple juniper berries, imported from more northern countries. There were bowls of brown beans – *ful* – still an Egyptian favourite, bright chick peas and soft lotus seeds, all flavoured with marjoram, coriander and dill. Pungent cilantro leaves and the roots of wild sedges were popular too and, as now, olive oil; the trees being cultivated at Thebes and additional oil imported from Syria and Crete, along with the berries. Large wine jars stood in stands garlanded with flowers and the attendants syphoned it off, blending light and dark together as it ran into the serving jars leaving the heavy must behind at the bottom of amphorae shaped like champagne flutes. Fresh grape juice was drunk too, there were vineyards close to the village, and a festal beer was brewed, flavoured with pommegranates, figs, mint, honey or grape juice – the extra sugars making a heady brew. Along with shining pommegranates, grapes would be eaten at the festival, jujubes, honey cakes, heads of garlic and the delicately-flavoured figs of the sycamore. And after this, perhaps, came more meats, pork, Nile ducks or even fish. Celery, parsley, leeks and lettuce were eaten fresh from the fields.

Traditionally, a male harper sang at these feasts to encourage the revellers to enjoy themselves. One song, already 300 years old, was still popular:

> Follow your desire,
> allow the heart to forget ...
>
> Dress yourself in garments of fine linen ...
>
> Increase your beauty,
> and let not your heart languish.
> Follow your desire and what is good.
> Conduct yourself on earth
> after the dictates of your heart —
>
> Celebrate
> but tire not yourself with it.
> Remember, no man takes his goods with him,
> and none have returned after going!

53

The celebrations lasted for many days and nights, and with exotic foods in such enormous quantities, it must have seemed like a hypnotic ritual endlessly punctuated with bouts of eating, singing, drinking and dancing.

So the villagers sat and swayed with the music and ate and talked, as people will. All the guests wore rich brown wigs and white gossamer linens, bright, loose and elaborately pleated. The women's wigs were especially massive, as wide as their shoulders, and, emphasized in this dark thick frame, their faces were exquisitely made-up: eyebrows shaped to narrow arcs, eyelids carefully painted and coloured. Both men and women wore jewellery: fragile faience bracelets and rings which could shatter almost at a touch, ear-rings and necklaces, and for special feasts large collars made of fresh flowers and aromatic plants strung together with beads and fine linen tassels. Perfumes too, were a major part of this elaborate display. They were a special attribute of the gods and, along with seeding lettuce plants, held to be aphrodisiac. Yellow-scented saffron oil was a favourite perfume, though more exotic varieties were also imported into Egypt, as were some of the cosmetics. Many foreign scent vials have been found in the village and one glass perfume flask, still sealed and as yet unopened, has been found in the Great Place itself. '... I'll pluck garlands for you', says a girl to her lover as she leaves a feast before him, and:

> If you come back drunk
> and lie upon your bed,
> I will rub your feet,
> and the children —
> shall hide behind the gate —

PART TWO
ORBIT

8

FOUR KINGS

The death of King Merneptah brought to an end an era so abundant, so amaranthine, that it seemed it would last for ever. But the climax of the new dynasty had passed. The huge temples that had grown like palm trees in King Ramesses II's reign, with their monumental artifice and frothy decoration, had been the achievements of Merneptah's youth, whilst he was working in the royal administration. As king he had not been able to sustain such national enterprise, and now the mood, the tension, was breaking. Nevertheless, by Merneptah's day, this prosperous age stretched back beyond all living memory, and the Nile's valley, fertile in culture, rich in empire, was sustaining a triumphant state that could contain any calamity that the world might hold.

This was just as well, for the two decades following Merneptah's death saw four kings, from two rival factions, on the throne, while other contenders – a queen and a chancellor – held such sway at the court that they had enough power to order tombs for themselves in the Great Place that rival those of the monarchs they manipulated. The period was one of civil strife. Today its history is blurred and a subject for debate: the identities of the contenders established only by careful studies of the obliterations and restorations of their names in the Great Place, the progress of their feuds charted inadvertently in ambiguous texts or upon the remains of chisel-clawed statues stored in museum basements.

One of the two factions was grouped around the numerous offspring of King Ramesses II, the other around the offspring of his son, King Merneptah. For at Merneptah's death, the throne was taken not by his son but by a step-brother – a son of King Ramesses II. Then, after just four years this King, Amenmesse, was followed to the throne by Kings Seti II and Siptah, each of whom reigned for six years. Of the three, only King Seti II, perhaps a son of Ramesses II, would later be recognized as a legitimate ruler. It was Seti II's principal Queen, Tausert, who became the power behind the throne. In co-operation with the royal Chancellor Bay she supported the young crippled King Siptah through his reign; then, when he died, she extended her influence further into the following reign, that of Setnakht. Today, no one knows where this two-year King sprang from and probably no one would much care were it not for the fact that his son was the third King Ramesses, who in a reign that lasted more than thirty years brought a relatively stable period to the country.

It was the very success of the Egyptian state – its wide power and riches – that helped to upset the national applecart, for as well as courtly intrigues there were great pressures upon Egypt from the north. Biblical stories of the Israelites show much of the attraction and repulsion that foreign peoples – city states, nomadic nations, even itinerant shepherd tribes – felt towards this fat empire in the south of their world. Even in the time of Merneptah, Egypt had to defend itself against the migrations of foreigners attempting to enter the country by force, just as fifty years before Ramesses II had fought similar battles for the security of the Egyptian empire in Syria and the Lebanon. Despite this growing pressure, Egypt had never isolated itself from the world. Foreigners had lived in the Nile valley for hundreds of years, the Egyptian state employing the best that the world had to offer. As befitted an elderly empire, the Egyptian army was now largely staffed by foreign mercenaries, many of whom also lived by the Nile. The court too, held many non-Egyptians within it; even Chancellor Bay, a king-maker in his day, was later described by a scribe as a foreigner – indeed, as a follower of the god Seth, a 'Bringer of Chaos' – and either he or his forefathers may have come to Egypt in one of the tribal migrations that had travelled south to the richest state in the world. Looking back over some forty years to the disjointed decades following the death of King Merneptah, the same scribe recalled:

The land of Egypt was cast adrift, every man being a law unto himself, and they had no leader for many years — empty years when Irsu, a Syrian [Chancellor Bay], was chief having set the entire land in subjection before him; each joined with his neighbour in plundering their goods and they treated the gods like people and no one dedicated offerings in the temples.... But the gods turned themselves to peace so as to put the land in its proper state — they established their son Setnakht ... upon their great throne ... he brought order to the entire land — he slew the rebels — he cleansed the great throne of Egypt — . He established the divine offerings in the temples ... [and then] he went to his rest in his tomb like the gods; there was done for him as was done for Osiris: he was rowed in his royal barge upon the river and rested in his tomb in the west of Thebes.

For the royal tombmakers, the era was one of hard work. In eighteen years they began seven tombs in the Great Place, and before the second decade was out they were working on another. And all the while the authority of the viziers rose and fell with the noble houses that they supported. Remarkably, much of the gangs' work at this time was of an exquisite quality, though it is hardly surprising that some of the tombs they decorated with masterworks around their entrances ended in small hastily-painted, part-finished burial chambers.

It is a great irony that we have far more information about life at the tombmakers' village during these two decades than we have about the petty kings whose tombs they made. These ephemeral masters, each wanting a king's tomb, seem never to have neglected the tombmakers' rations or stopped their work in the Great Place. At the same time, the two decades saw a series of spectacularly scandalous events at the village that occurred in uncanny parallel to the struggles at the royal court. As surely as the kings divided the country, so the village was split into two competing factions engaged in a contest as violent as that of their rulers. That the villagers surmounted all of these confrontations to make such a beautiful progression of royal tombs is quite remarkable.

9

FOREMAN PANEB

It was a most experienced team which, after the burial of King Merneptah, started on the excavation of the tomb for the new King Amenmesse. Scribe Kenhirkhopeshef, now well over seventy, was embarking on the third royal tomb of his career, and Foreman Neferhotep, who was almost as old as the scribe, led one of the two gangs. Foreman Anhirkawi having died in the same year as Merneptah, the other gang was commanded by his son Hay, who had worked in the royal tombs since boyhood, probably as a senior sculptor cutting the wall scenes in the tombs, a 'fashioner of the images of all the gods in the House of Gold'. Hay was aged about thirty-five when he inherited the foremanship and he held the office for forty years through the thick and thin of village life, with remarkably few disputes.

Amenmesse's tomb was planned to be virtually the same design as Merneptah's. The quarrymen, having quickly cut the first corridor, were soon excavating the four-columned hall and the corridors that lay beyond. Within the first year of the reign the engraving sculptors were at work on the outer parts of the tomb, cutting reliefs as fine as any that their fathers had made before them. Then, before the painting of these scenes had even begun, the unfortunate monarch died. A single line of text upon an ostracon describes the return of his mummified corpse from the north of the country for burial in the Great Place. 'Year one [of his successor, King Seti II], day ten of the second month [28 July 1195 BC] the day of the mooring of Pharaoh — at the southern city where he spent days eleven and twelve. He came to the west [i.e. his burial] on day thirteen — alabaster ... gold ...'. Though later kings considered him an usurper, Amenmesse received a proper burial from Seti II, his step-nephew, who, thus legitimized, now ascended the throne.

'Year one, first month of winter, day sixteen, the scribe Paser came with good news, saying: "Seti II has arisen as ruler".' This was the Vizier's message to the gangs in the Great Place, the order to the tombmakers to start planning a tomb for the new King. Just twenty-five days later they were already quarrying high in a side valley that had not been used for royal tombs since the time of the old dynasty. Though the limestone at the valley's head is harder and whiter than the parts of the Great Place where the tombmakers usually worked, within the year the sculptors had made some very fine reliefs around the tomb doorway, working the brittle stone like gem-engravers. Whilst the sculptors were carving these splendid images, the old Foreman Neferhotep became ill and was sometimes unable to go to the Great Place for weeks at a time. A large family now rested around this venerable old man, many of his brothers and their children working in the two gangs. His huge tomb, which dominated the ridge of the western hillside above the valley, had stood empty for a quarter-century. Like Scribe Ramose before him, Neferhotep had no children of his own to succeed him, and so he too adopted a successor in his middle-age: a young stonemason named Paneb who had worked in Neferhotep's gang. This young man came from a village family as old as Neferhotep's: with other workmen, his father Nefersenet had made small stelae to the gods in the settlement huts above the Great Place, and built one of the little shrines high on the mountainside. But it was Nefersenet's young son who caught the foreman's eye, and Paneb exchanged one village family for another.

The household that Paneb entered as heir-presumptive was in the southern part of the village at the end of the high street, a straggling affair with the foreman's clan overflowing into several nearby houses. Neferhotep's household accounts show that he provided well for his family. From a workman in his gang he obtained jars of animal fat, a tasty luxury for a village kitchen that was not feasting. On another occasion he bought a live ox, a considerable expenditure for any village household. The foreman was fond of wine too, and he paid for it twice the price of barley beer, the usual village drink.

Inadvertently the same accounts describe exactly what goods were available to the most prosperous village households of the day and give a good idea of the realistic material aspirations of other village families. We discover, for example, that the foreman and his wife Wabkhet dressed in some style. For the walk to work across the windy cliffs on a cold January morning, Neferhotep might wrap himself in a voluminous woollen cloak with some fourteen yards of fabric in it, and underneath this lavish robe he wore heavy, loose garments of wool and linen, all edged with coloured weavings and embroideries. Whilst he worked inside the tomb, where the temperature hardly varied through the year, he would change into the usual plain kilt of coarse linen and heavy leather sandals that protected his feet from the sharp chippings littering the valley floor. At home in the village Neferhotep and Wabkhet wore fine linens, long loose shirt-like garments exquisitely cut and sewn, and tied at the neck with delicate tassels. Some of the villagers wore red leather slippers similar to those still sold in Eastern bazaars and, in the summer-time, delicate papyrus sandals, beautifully woven from the reeds that grew by the river. Like the linen clothes there were distinct fashions in these sandals, special intricacies of shape and weave. One extravagant pattern, pulled up roundly at the front like the prow of a boat, was called 'Pharaoh's' sandals and was popular for formal occasions during Neferhotep's middle age.

As well as sandals, many of the foreman's household furnishings were made from reeds and rushes: baskets, fans, footstools, storage chests and the springy sleeping mats, that, when placed on the mud-brick benches of the front rooms, served the villagers as beds during the winter months. The fresh plants from which all these things were made grew wild by the river banks and craftsmen bent and trimmed their green stems as soon as they were cut and gathered so that they would shrink and dry into the shapes required of them. Such furniture is still made at Thebes today, and it is interesting to add that one still pays, as Neferhotep did, not for the finished article but for the reed and the labour of the craftsman who works it. In addition to this reed furniture, Neferhotep would have owned expensive wooden chairs, beds and headrests – a cooler if harder alternative to a woollen pillow. Surprisingly, the bed frames, based on designs thousands of years old, had their head end higher than the foot. Plaited strings formed their base, as they did the seats of the wooden chairs, which also had large woollen cushions on them during the winter. Neferhotep's household would certainly have used the fine light linen sheets made in large quantities in the Theban workshops and in winter he would have used blankets too, woven like *flokati* rugs, with a long loose pile to trap the body's heat. All these things were strong and well-made. Indeed, there was little in a rich village household that did not attain some measure of elegance: even the pots and pans were of careful, if traditional, design. And with foreign servants for sale at the ferry-landing, there was little that the foreman's household could have lacked.

Such was the rich household which Paneb would one day inherit. Doubtless Neferhotep made a public declaration before the village elders of his intentions towards his adopted son, then, in the last years of Ramesses II's reign, to strengthen further the ties between the foremen of the two gangs and their successors, Paneb was married to a relative of Foreman Hay's, named Wa'bet. Considering all the stresses that it had to undergo, their liaison proved surprisingly successful: they did not divorce, though it was common enough in the village, and they lived together for a long time and raised several children.

During the second year of Merneptah's reign, when the stonemasons were cutting the new royal tomb, Paneb contracted to have a room in a village house partitioned by a brick wall to separate the domestic area from the workshop. That he bought, along with the room-divider, household goods

– boxes, baskets and, in particular, a woman's bed – suggests that at this time he and Wa'bet moved out of the foreman's household to start one of their own, possibly because they had children to provide for. Though families lived close together in the village, there was no tradition, nor, indeed possibility, of several generations and branches of one family inhabiting a single house.

Paneb's departure from Neferhotep's house must have occasioned great relief, for he had been a wild and unruly youth much given to fighting and drunkenness. Perhaps to fill the silence that his adopted family must have left behind them, Neferhotep adopted another boy, making one of his house-servants, Hesysenebef, a second son. So the same small boy who the village artists drew sitting under the foreman's chair in the sculptures of his tomb chapel, feeding a limestone monkey stony grapes, now moved in Neferhotep's family circle and was appointed to work in his step-father's gang in the royal tombs. Unlike Paneb, Hesysenebef revered his village father, and when he married he named his eldest son and daughter after the foreman and his wife. But despite his new son and doubtless much to the distress of the foreman's numerous family, it was the Heathcliff-like figure of Paneb that Neferhotep still regarded as his successor. A brief inscription scratched into the cliffs behind the village shows that Paneb reciprocated his continued affection and called Neferhotep his 'father' before the gods. Like Hesysenebef, he too named one of his children, a girl, after a member of Neferhotep's family – a confusing, if affectionate, village habit that, as may well be imagined, is the bane of modern genealogists.

Surviving accounts of Paneb's household show the young workman busily acquiring the collection of goods usually to be found in the richer village households: wooden furniture, good sandals, fine linens and copper cooking cauldrons whose metal could be exchanged for grain in times of hardship. To add to the finesse of his daily table, Paneb bought sesame oil which was perhaps served then, as it is today in the Middle East, mixed with spice and water to make a thick savoury paste that is mopped from a bowl with a piece of bread. Even as a young man the foreman-designate looked to his grave as well as his house, as was proper at the village: receipts for his coffins and funeral equipment survive, dating from this period; he also built a tomb, a vaulted burial chamber glittering with yellow and white paintings, now half-destroyed. Above his vault was a chapel with a sharp little pyramid over it and a causeway, a smaller version of Foreman Neferhotep's (which was just above it) ran up to the chapel's entrance. Though lower down in the cemetery than the foreman's tombs the chapel, like Paneb himself, was well enough situated in the village hierarchy.

Though fortunate in his life and skilful at his work, Paneb spent his adult life in the eye of a storm. We cannot tell today whether the long feud that he fought with the foreman's family had been provoked by his harsh treatment of the old man, or whether his relationship with his step-father had been soured by jealous relatives, angry at the outsider who had secured the succession to the foremanship and inherited the Neferhotep's household. Neither can we determine why, one day late in the reign of Amenmesse, an enraged Paneb chased Neferhotep right down the village high street, the elderly foreman only escaping by bolting the wooden door of his house. As he stood outside the barred door of the house he had left some twelve years before, Paneb threatened his village father, 'I will kill him in the night,' he cried angrily, breaking the wooden door-lock. He would have attacked Neferhotep if a guard of men had not been put around him. Later it was reported that 'Paneb beat nine men in that night'. Paneb was a violent man who would sustain high rages for several hours.

On surviving this long and clamorous night, Neferhotep now judged his step-son to be beyond his control and, sidestepping the village assembly who would normally have dealt with such disturbances, he reported his step-son's actions directly to the office of the vizier. Probably this was intended to ensure that Paneb would receive a punishment, either of a heavy beating or, even, a sentence of stone-breaking. Astonishingly, Paneb's electrifying response to his disgrace was that he, a mere stonemason working at the King's tomb, brought a complaint against the office which had ordered his punishment; and shortly after King Amenmesse's death the Vizier to whom Neferhotep had reported Paneb's misdeeds was himself dismissed!

How could this happen? How could a delinquent workman bring down the most powerful official in Egypt? It should be understood that the internal troubles of the court, the age of the petty kings, had begun in earnest: Amenmesse had died after a reign of just two years and was now regarded as a usurper. Political revenge had probably caught up with the Vizier who, after presiding over the funeral of Merneptah and supporting King Amenmesse, was now, quite obviously, very vulnerable. It is likely that the officials of the new King were happy to find any pretext they could to rid themselves of the old Vizier. Secondly, to judge from a later case in which one of Paneb's sons was involved, there was a specific charge that a tomb-maker could make against a vizier or any state official which, if true, was completely damning: that he had knowingly allowed 'irregularities' to occur in the Great Place.

In such a closed community as the tombmakers', the security of the rich royal burials in the Great Place ultimately depended upon every man of the two gangs, the storekeepers, the medjay, the priests and even the Vizier himself, watching his neighbour. Each day more than 100 men passed through the little valley, and it is impossible to imagine that not one of

them would have noticed any 'irregularities' signalling an attempt at robbery: a disturbance in the filling over a closed tomb, or the breaking of a
sealed doorway, or even the pilfering of materials and tools from the work
gangs, of objects from the royal burials at the time of funeral. The men of
the two gangs were placed under a specific oath to report untoward happenings in the royal valley and in one inquiry into such 'irregularities' it
was held that a man who had held his tongue when he saw a tomb being
entered and robbed was as guilty as the robbers he had seen at their work.

So, just as his son would do again (perhaps in imitation of his father),
Paneb may simply have reported to the officers of the court that the Vizier
had failed to control 'irregularities' occurring in the Great Place. If this is
true, it required a cool nerve, for Paneb must have had to swear to his
statements, and the penalties for perjury ranged from mutilation to death.
But the courtiers wanted to be rid of the Vizier so they used Paneb's
complaint as the mechanism by which they engineered the great man's
downfall. For whatever the precise details were, the effect of the recalcitrant
stonemason's rhetoric upon the usurper's Vizier is clear enough: he lost his
post shortly after the new King came to the throne.

Paneb's action, opportune and decisive, must have greatly impressed his
fellow-villagers, if, indeed, he still needed such advertisement. Vindicated in
this extraordinary manner, he now set himself firmly against Foreman Neferhotep and his large family. It was precisely at this moment, during the
first year of Seti II's reign that Foreman Neferhotep fell ill and was unable
to work at the royal tomb. Paneb must have thought that he would soon
be claiming his inheritance, but the old man recovered sufficiently to work
in King Seti II's tomb for four more years. Then, suddenly, the foremanship
passed to Paneb, the old man being killed, a papyrus tells us, 'by the
enemy'. Who this 'enemy' was, exactly, it is difficult to say. Perhaps Neferhotep was murdered in the political disturbances that ran through Thebes
at this time. Perhaps, though this is less likely, for even his bitterest critics
do not accuse him of it, he was killed by Paneb himself. What is certain,
however, is that Seti II's new Vizier, the man whom Paneb had inadvertently
aided to office by his denunciation of a few years before, now appointed
Paneb to the foremanship.

In an account of these events, written years later, Neferhotep's younger
brother accused Paneb of bribing the Vizier for his foremanship with a gift
of five servants from Neferhotep's household. The claim is suspect: it is
improbable that a vizier with all the resources of the state at his command
would be swayed by a gift of five servants; perhaps Paneb was simply
ridding his new household of some white elephants. In either case the
statement reveals that even before his appointment to the foremanship,
Paneb was enjoying the right of disposal over Neferhotep's household;

he had never been dispossessed of his inheritance, and had succeeded directly on the death of his step-father. At all events, the result of Paneb's promotion was to split the village into two factions: those who supported Neferhotep's venerable family, and wanted the foremanship to remain within it, and the friends of Paneb – a quick-tempered man attracted by power and prestige but also an excellent foreman who insisted on the highest standards of craftsmanship in the work at the royal tomb. Raucous and violent as he may have been – and Paneb's antics grew far worse during the years of his foremanship – a personality like his was no stranger to the villagers. Scribe Kenhirkhopeshef even possessed a text in his library describing just such a man. Today, despite the fact that the papyrus is in poor condition, we can still marvel at this remarkable document, the first dispassionate study of a specific human character that has come down to us, the best description of an ancient man as a living personality that we may ever obtain. A man that Kenhirkhopeshef's papyrus calls a 'follower of Seth'. Now Seth, the brother and murderer of Osiris, was a god who embodied disorder and foreignness, storms, invasions and confusion; all the dark alternatives to the good order of the Egyptian state. It was Seth who engaged in combat with his nephew Horus, out to avenge his father's death and claim his proper birthright. While this young man was the Egyptian embodiment of familial love and the rights of the just, Seth represented the rule of might over justice. Clearly it was a parallel not lost upon the members of Foreman Neferhotep's family whose grumblings and denunciations echoed the cosmic drama of Horus and his uncle.

'Followers of Seth', says Kenhirkhopeshef's papyrus, were readily identifiable in society by their appearance and behaviour. Commonly they had red faces and red hair, and they were violent and often lonely people who drank to excess. Drunkenness, indeed, brought even those who followed Horus temporarily under the influence of his uncle Seth. Quite early in his career Paneb had gained notoriety in the village for his drunken rages, which may well have caused much of his violent behaviour. Though common enough at feasts and sometimes considered even as a holy state during particular religious ceremonies, drunkenness was usually considered a bad thing. Along with the other students at the scribes' school, Kenhirkhopeshef had had many moralizing maxims about the demon drink dinned into him with copy-texts that were as much an aid to sober citizenship as they were to good grammar and literary form: 'Do not indulge in drinking beer for fear of uttering evil speech — If you fall — no-one will hold out a hand to you — Your companions will say "Out with the drunk" — You will lie on the ground like a little child.'

Exhibiting extraordinary self-awareness, Paneb acknowledged his affinity with Seth, for when his eldest son was born during the middle years of

King Merneptah's reign, he named him Aaphate, which means 'great of strength', Seth's most common epithet. Just as Paneb contained an awkward mixture of violence and creativeness - an unwitting forerunner of some of the bohemian artists of the last two centuries - so it would be wrong too to see Seth as simply a destructive god. His mythic conflict with Horus reduced all the struggles and tensions of ancient society to the metaphor of a simple combat and provided a yardstick for human behaviour. And in other sagas of the gods we even find Seth defending the order of the universe against invasion, for the devil was seen as an integral part of the universal order, a fallen angel, the god of the dark side of Egyptian society; a necessary part of its full form.

It would be wrong, therefore, to imagine that Kenhirkhopeshef's careful description of the 'Followers of Seth' was merely an ancient identikit for prejudice: what it gives us is a clear picture of a person who is still with us, someone in whom grandeur and folly are inextricably mixed:

The Marks of the Followers of Seth

The god in him is Seth ... he is a man of the people — He dies by a death of ... the fallings ... sinews ... He is one dissolute of heart on the day of judgement ... discontent in his heart. If he drinks beer he drinks it to engender strife and turmoil. The redness of the white of his eye is this god. He is one who drinks what he detests. He is beloved of women through the greatness — the greatness of his loving them. Though he is a royal kinsman he has the personality of a man of the people ... He will not descend unto the west, but is placed on the desert as a prey to rapacious birds ... He drinks beer so as to engender turmoil and disputes ... He will take up weapons of warfare — He will not distinguish the married woman from ... As to any man who opposes him he pushes ... Massacre arises in him and he is placed in the Netherworld. . . .

10

DREAMS

We know from the sculptures that he supervised that Paneb had a fine eye
for the values of his art: that he flew into rages we may read in the village
texts; but that he was afflicted by insecurity or ambition is much more
difficult to discover. Indeed we may doubt that, even if the foreman had
these feelings, we could recognize their operation in such a remote world.
Most of the ancient kings, after all, are only bland stone faces and a name,
and most of their subjects lack even this fragile identity. Yet, uniquely, at
the tombmakers' village we can find proof that a wide range of subtle
feelings were experienced.

Among a jumble of writing on a papyrus in Scribe Kenhirkhopeshef's
library is a book of dreams. Even in Kenhirkhopeshef's time the text was
ancient – like Chaucer in a modern edition – but it clearly still possessed
relevance for the scribe or he would have washed it off the papyrus and
replaced it with different writings, as he did with other texts. In fact, the
dreams in this book inhabited an environment similar to that of the scribe's
village and they are filled with the claustrophobic pressures characteristic
of small communities. Certainly then, Kenhirkhopeshef's Dream Book describes some of the thoughts and passions that ran through the villagers
minds while they slept.

The scribe's papyrus preserves around 108 ancient dreams describing an
exhausting range of some seventy-eight activities and emotions: from sailing, weaving and brewing to pounding, pickling and copulation; from plastering, sightseeing and stealing to carving, waving and stirring. The largest
category, some 17 per cent of the total, is that of 'seeing', next comes
'eating' and 'drinking' with some 15 per cent each; 'receiving' and 'copulat-
ing' follow with about 5 per cent each. The text is laid out in columns,
enabling the reader to locate his dream and then quickly its interpretation.
Running vertically down the height of each page is a column of characters
containing the phrase 'If a man sees himself in a dream'. Horizontal lines
of text running off this title in rows each give brief descriptions of a separate
dream, and then, after a short space in the same line, its equally brief
interpretation.

A typical set of dreams and their interpretations runs:

If a man sees him-self in a dream	dead	good: it means a long life in front of him.
	eating crocodile flesh	good: it means acting as an official amongst his people [i.e. becoming a tax-collector]
	with his face in a mirror	bad: it means a new life.
	uncovering his own backside	bad: he will be an orphan later.

First, it should be remarked that there are some purely linguistic con-cordances in the dreams and their interpretations that are not apparent in the translation: for instance in the ancient language the terms 'backside' and 'orphan later' form a pun which, in ancient eyes, powerfully reinforces the validity of the interpretation. Punning, a simple device that shows a magic unity in disparates, is given significance in many ancient writings, whilst another even simpler method of interpretation merely reverses the dreams' contents: thus a happy dream will often be interpreted as signifying sadness, a dream of plenty will signify scarceness, a dream of loss, of gain, and so on. It is a common device of dream books up to today. While many of the ancient dreams and their interpretations have splendidly Freudian overtones, even, indeed, in the principles of inversion and punning, there is a basic difference between the professor's attitudes and those of Kenhirk-hopeshef some 3000 years earlier: Freud viewed Viennese dreams as being motivated ultimately by the dreamer's wish to express his own desires; the Theban dreams are seen as divine signals predicting the future. In their most important aspect, however, the two systems, ancient and modern, correspond: for they both provide the same therapeutic service of helping the dreamer to understand the significance of his dream.

Unlike the Socratic investigations of Freud, it is the very lack of precision in the ancient text which allows the interpreter a wide degree of personal choice. Both the descriptions of the dreams, which are never more than a single phrase, and the fact that similar dreams often receive differing inter-pretations permit a wide variety of choice in determining their significance to the dreamer. And to further fortify the dreamer's personal predilections, the papyrus is clearly divided into two parts, the two categories 'good' and 'bad'; the word 'bad' always being written in red ink. So the papyrus clearly leads the dreamer towards his conclusions by offering a variety of suggestive alternatives, a system similar, in some degree, to the Freudian method of inviting the dreamer to discover, through his own interpretations, the significance of his dream. In a broad sense, both ancient and modern systems serve as an aid to greater self-awareness, and ultimately attempt to influence the dreamers' behaviour. Both systems, then, have an eye clearly fixed upon the future. Unlike psychotherapy however, Kenhirkhopeshef's Dream Book simply makes straightforward predictions of a dreamer's fate; though often these are no less interesting than the dreams themselves, and tell us a good deal about ancient village society and its pleasures and hazards.

More than 35 per cent of the Dream Book predictions concern the dreamer's direct gain or loss, either by such happenings as receiving a house, an inheritance or a new wife, or, in the case of loss, by calamities such as robbery, taxation or becoming an orphan; 25 per cent of the dreams predict purely physical events, good or bad, which will happen to the dreamer's person, these being as diverse as eating too much food or being starved, being in pain or having an illness made better; 15 per cent simply predict feelings: from the pleasures of 'sitting with the villagers' and having 'gossip about one cease', to the experience of bitterness, anger or deceit. Another 15 per cent of the interpretations predict that the dreamer will be placed in a situation where ethical judgements will be made about him by the gods, and his sins will be forgiven or retribution will occur; 10 per cent concern changes in the dreamer's authority and prestige in the village, from prophecies telling of an appointment to an important office or 'acting as chief', to others that simply describe how the villagers will become aware of the importance of the dreamer and what he has to say. Occasionally the assessment of a dream as 'good' or 'bad' hints at the significance with which dreams were invested and the power that such interpretations wielded in village society. The 'bad' prediction that the dead wanted something (this after a dream of 'putting one's face to the ground') probably signalled that the dreamer should expend fresh efforts on the graves and shrines in the village cemetery, while the 'good' prediction that the dreamer would have people assembled for him 'by his god', after a dream of 'bringing in cattle' seems to hint at an evangelizing spirit in the community.

Taken together, the dreams and their interpretations not only allow us a glimpse of how sections of an ancient village dealt with anxieties about the future but they also give subtle glimpses of the individual in the village community. If, for example, a man dreamt that he was writing, this might be seen as 'bad' predicting the reckoning-up of his misdeeds by his god; clearly feelings of guilt were abroad. If he dreamt of making love to his wife in the daylight this too was 'bad' for it meant that his god would 'discover his misdeeds'. In fact the interpretation of sexual activity in dreams is particularly unusual and demands a closer look. To start with, the range of sexual behaviour experienced by the villagers in their dreams seems extraordinary in both its detail and its interpretation. Whereas dreams of bestiality with desert rats, kites and pigs were considered 'bad omens', copulation with mothers and sisters was 'good'. However, dreams of copulation 'with a woman' were labelled 'bad', while even to catch a glimpse of a female's private parts in a dream signified 'the last extremity of misery'. Happily this evil omen might be quickly allayed by a dream of plunging into the cold waters of the river, which signified the 'absolution of all ills'. Perhaps such interpretations were ultimately concerned with the socially disruptive effects of promiscuity in the little village, although to assert this may be to impute a false moral tone to the Dream Book. Certainly there is little evidence at the village that eccentric sexual practises were more common there than in any modern community. Despite such eccentricities we can see from the Dream Book that Paneb, Kenhirkhopeshef and the rest of the village shared the same feelings of guilt and fears of loss of prestige, the same enjoyment of life and family that people experience today. A striking similarity with modern religious thinking is revealed by the constant references to a clear ethical code, and by the belief that the gods were reckoning up and judging human behaviour, and could even see into people's hearts.

The sharpest difference between ancient and modern experience revealed by this book is the extent to which the dream interpretations – the predictions of the future – are concerned with food shortages or violent death and mutilation. However lurid their imaginings, in reality few of Freud's patients faced such fundamentals. Further, a quarter of all the ancient dreams, and these equally in both the 'good' and 'bad' categories, are concerned with aspects of manual labour. Basic differences also arise where economic circumstances are concerned: the ancient text underlines, for example, the village's ultimate dependence upon the royal palace, from whose doorways both good and bad things could issue. Further, a fifth of the dream interpretations are concerned with the giving and receiving of gifts, which, in their widespread use, were a vital part of the village economy and a major element in the system of obligations, relationships and alliances running through the little community.

But what was Kenhirkhopeshef to do when he awoke agitatedly in his bed, alarmed by his dreams and frightened by his memories of their interpretations? Happily, his Dream Book also included a special spell to be recited upon waking which would dispel all demons and their evil omens. The papyrus specifies a recitation, which was to be accompanied by the eating of fresh bread and green herbs moistened with beer. So if, in the middle of a warm night, you saw the startled old scribe trotting through his house anxiously chanting spells – 'Come to me, come to me, my mother Isis; behold I am seeing what is far from my city', – he was off to visit his cellar where he had stored some food and drink against such an emergency.

11

KENHIRKHOPESHEF II

In the era of the four kings, as pharaohs and viziers came and went every few years and the two gangs worked furiously to make tombs for them, the usual close supervision of the royal burying ground was relaxed and slowly the men of the gangs were able to erect some of their own monuments in the sacred valley. On the flood debris above the old huts in the centre of the valley, Foreman Hay and several of the workmen set up small prayerful stelae which showed them worshipping the gods. Scribe Kenhirkhopeshef went one better and had a shrine cut for himself in the cliff face at the head of the valley: a niche in the rock, painted with fine figures of Osiris, Hathor and Isis and faced on either side with stone lintels bearing his name and titles. Two doors probably closed the interior of the shrine off from the valley; now it is completely ruined, indeed, it may well have been anciently defaced for its presumption. In its day, however, it was a unique monument, demonstrating the freedom and authority that the tombmakers briefly enjoyed in the royal burial ground during the period of four reigns.

There are other glimpses of the old scribe, full of years and wisdom and not without a certain guile - necessary perhaps in an age of transient kings and violent young foremen. On a broken ostracon we find him furiously denounced by an unknown plaintiff for aiding the cause of a certain Rahotep who was in trouble with the village tribunal and needed an ally in the upper ranks of the community. While Rahotep 'shaved the head of the scribe', his denouncer reports, he suggested to his client that, in exchange for large amounts of fabric and yarn, Kenhirkhopeshef might help him to 'conceal his misdeeds', a request to which the scribe had promptly agreed. Such 'gifts for a purpose' were an accepted feature of village society, part of the daily intercourse of civility and obligation and, as a man of his time, we should not judge the scribe too harshly. Similarly, Kenhirkhopeshef also indulged himself in another way, one which would properly scandalize most civilized people today, for, just a few years before the uproar of Amenmesse's usurpation and the murder of Neferhotep, Kenhirkhopeshef found himself a wife. Close to his seventieth birthday he married a village girl, Naunakht, who was little more than twelve years old. It was not the disaster that it might at first appear. Certainly, Naunakht memories of the old man were fond enough, for when she married again she named her first child – for she had no children with the scribe – Kenhirkhopeshef, and he was always her favourite child.

Marriage at the village was a contractual partnership between two people, the man usually supplying two thirds of its joint property, the woman the remainder. Though there was no religious ceremonial connected with it, matrimony was regarded as both normal and desirable in the village, where both wives and husbands were considered as independent citizens who, though each with clearly defined roles in the village, held equal civil responsibility. Divorce, especially among the families of the workmen, was not uncommon, and many people married several times over, usually after amicable property settlements had been arranged between the parting family by members of the village tribunal. As a young bride, Naunakht would have found herself rich and privileged by village standards and in her later years, an elderly and forthright matriarch at the head of a large family, she bequeathed the property of her first marriage with the scribe to the children of her second.

Kenhirkhopeshef's marriage to Naunakht seems to have been the action of an elderly bachelor providing for his dotage and making arrangements for the disposal of his property after his death. Kenhirkhopeshef was childless and that Naunakht later left some of his property to the children of her second marriage shows that he made special arrangements for her to receive property apart from the one-third share of the marriage's wealth which automatically fell to the wives either at divorce or on the death of their husbands. It is possible that as well as marrying the young girl Kenhirkhopeshef also legally adopted Naunakht so that she would become his legitimate heir, for other women were adopted by their husbands in similar circumstances. Such complex and careful arrangements, though typical of a society which held most humane attitudes to the family, are hardly what the modern world would associate with the predicament of a 'child-bride'; nor is there any evidence of a cruel use of children at the village.

A similar gulf between ancient and modern is found in differing approaches to old age and retirement. Just as life at the village was too rich, too ritualized, too filled with wonders to sustain the monotonous regularity of modern industry, just as there was no annual timetable for the work in the king's tomb, so neither was there a set age for retirement. In Kenhirkhopeshef's last days at the royal valley, a period interspersed with long absences due to illness, the old scribe must have sat shaded and warmly-wrapped and watched the work at the royal tomb, an honoured figure at the end of a long career, whilst his long-time assistants, the scribes Anupemheb and Paser, saw to the running of his office.

By the period of the brief reigns of the four Kings, Scribe Kenhirk-hopeshef was old indeed. Even as early as the reign of King Merneptah we can detect changes in his handwriting, from a large vigorous script to a cursive, less legible style whose uneven shapes suggest that at seventy, Kenhirkhopeshef could no longer see as well as he once had. Now the ageing scribe could well have fought the encroachment of old age, for there are several papyri of the time containing recipes purporting to prevent greying hair (natural dyes and balsams), baldness (animal fats and prayer), and even impotence (ointments and more prayers). And on the back of an old letter from the Vizier's office, he wrote a chant against the evil influence of foreign demons that 'fed on excrement — and lived on dung': 'Get back Shehakek, who came out of heaven and earth ... Nedrakhsemem is the name of your mother, Djubeset the name of your father. If he comes against the Scribe Kenhirkhopeshef, son of Sentnefer, I shall call to....' Knowing and naming your enemy has always been half the battle. The scribe folded his papyrus into a small square wad, tied it with a flax string and hung it around his neck. Other villagers wrote the same spell on potsherds and small fragments of stone, then drilled a hole in them so they might suspend

them from a cord around their necks. It was to be repeated 'four times over a stem of flax, the stalk of which is made into an arrow. ...' Disease was seen as an attack by evil forces, its remedies, if such charms were effective, designed to combat the imbalance in the individual that had allowed the demon its foothold inside him. So concerned was Kenhirkhopeshef with the efficiency of his charm that he named his real mother on it, rather than Wia, Ramose's wife, his village mother.

Doubtless, on the days that he worked, the old scribe carried a stick with him on the walk from the village to the valley which would have been inscribed with a text similar to that on the staff of another villager: 'Come, my stick, so that I might lean on you and follow the beautiful west, that my heart may wander in the Place of Truth.' There must have come a time though, when even the walk over the hills to the royal valley was too much for the old man and he moved only around the village where his young wife kept house for him. Certainly, now, he could have sat with the other old men in the open area by the village gate, in the blue shadow of a wall, with the dust hanging golden-grained in the evening light, whilst they talked together. Men who had worked together for more than half a century, who had grown old with each other and who still deferred to the old scribe, their senior, even in their retirement. It was at this time, perhaps, that Kenhirkhopeshef wandered along the base of the cliffs running past the shrines of the village and scratched his name and titles on the rocks there, remembering his real father of long ago, before Scribe Ramose adopted him in the village: 'Scribe in the Place of Truth, Kenhirkhopeshef, his father Panakhte'.

The old scribe must have been well over eighty when Paneb was appointed to the foremanship, and he must surely have viewed the young man's progress with some amusement. Better than most at the village he knew of the 'Followers of Seth' and he, too, had little time for the finer conventions of village life. As a village elder, of course, Kenhirkhopeshef would also have been caught up in the constant denunciations and recriminations of Neferhotep's family when Paneb became foreman, and he seems to have taken Paneb's side in the dispute; Neferhotep's family claiming that, like the erring Vizier, he had taken a bribe from the new foreman to help 'conceal his misdeeds'. So we may imagine him discussing the affair with the other village elders – for the dispute seems to have caught up even the old men of the village. Sitting in the sun with his cronies, his tomb built, his affairs settled and the two gangs working away in the Great Place on a multiplicity of tombs with workmen the equal of any he had seen in his youth, Kenhirkhopeshef could look forward to receiving, as the old prayer asked, 'a goodly burial after an old age'.

Kenhirkhopeshef made very few monuments for the village or its shrines. Even his own tomb chapel was undecorated and, being cut in poor rock at the end of the village terrace of tombs, is now ruined. In its day, though, the tomb had a spacious chapel with an impressive stairway running up to it, along which the scribe's sarcophagus was dragged. A single statue of the scribe and Naunakht was found by the tomb and this alone allows its attribution to Kenhirkhopeshef; the scribe's substantial insurance against oblivion did not serve him well. Surprisingly, it is the scribe's fragile library and the stony notes of his work in the Great Place that have ensured that Kenhirkhopeshef's name will 'live for ever' as he would have wished. One of his manuscripts records that it later became the property of Naunakht's children; some of them also appear to have formed a part of the library of another family of village scribes.

It was not only the disposal of his property and his household after his death that Kenhirkhopeshef had to concern himself with. Just as the kings performed the funeral rites for their predecessors to assure their full legitimacy to the throne, so village children had also to bury their parents to qualify for their inheritance. Indeed common law decreed that whoever buried a person inherited a large amount of that person's property. Childless Kenhirkhopeshef must, then, have made special arrangements for his own funeral. In fact we do not know how, or even where, the old man finally died, aged about eighty-six. One old man is recorded as dying in the house of a friend; but it must seem more likely that our scribe, with his prosperous household and a young wife to care for him, expired in his own home. At all events, specialists from the gangs would certainly have been at hand to mummify him and, quite probably, a special day would have been put aside for his funeral rites. Then, like Ramose before him, his body, clad in cedar coffins, would have been dragged up the long causeway of his tomb. 'In peace, in peace to the west, the Place of Truth, the place of rest amongst those that did right' cried the funeral procession as Naunakht and the women of the scribe's household wailed before his coffin, set upright outside the tomb chapel. Then Kenhirkhopeshef's spirit was magically reunited with his body and, with Naunakht momentarily clutching the foot of the coffin in a ritual attempt to prevent her husband's inevitable descent into the grave, the burial party carried the scribe out of the sunlight of his chapel down into the burial vault, where he was set to lie amidst a motley collection of tomb furniture collected over a long lifetime.

Later that year, Naunakht would have made offerings to the dead scribe in the courtyard of his chapel during the village festivals. Then, before long, she married again, and brought to this new marriage part of Kenhirkhopeshef's property; some of these belongings had certainly come from the household of Scribe Ramose. Naunakht and her second husband, Khaemnum, were together for more than thirty years and in that time the couple had eight children. She always retained the title of a 'Lady of the House' – the full mistress of a village household – to the end of her days despite the fact that her second husband was a comparatively lowly workman in one of the gangs of the royal tomb. Like his mother, the second Kenhirkhopeshef, her eldest son, regarded the memory of the old scribe with inherited affection, for when he inscribed his name with that of his children on a cliff in the Great Place he wrote his genealogy over the earlier text of Scribe Kenhirkhopeshef's in which the scribe had commemorated his descent from Panakhte. By his superscription the young Kenhirkhopeshef gave the dead scribe descendants who would continue the family tradition at the Great Place.

Some fifty years after Scribe Kenhirkhopeshef's death, Naunakht made a written will describing in detail her wishes for the disposal of her large estate and this document gives a sharp taste of the strong-minded old lady.

In a declaration before the village court she first describes her legal status in the community: 'I am a free woman'. Then she scrutinizes her family with the testiness of old age: 'I brought up these eight servants of yours [a pious reference, before the village court, to her children] and gave them everything that is proper to their station. But I have grown old and they do not look after me in their turn, Whoever has aided me, to them I will give of my property; he who has not aided me, I will not give of my property.' Naunakht excluded four of her children from inheriting either her property or the property of Scribe Kenhirkhopeshef 'my husband', but to her son Kenhirkhopeshef, always the apple of her eye, she gave a valuable legacy: 'as a special reward, a washing bowl of bronze, over and above his fellows'.

12

PANEB II

With the village split by the feud between Paneb and Neferhotep's family, with king following king to the throne every year or so, Kenhirkhopeshef could have wished for quieter times in his old age. Indeed, on occasion there was fighting of such violence at Thebes that it would later be remembered as a 'war'. Foreman Neferhotep had been killed at just such a time. Sometimes the tombmakers felt so insecure in their isolated desert village that they fled, presumably for the safety of the eastern city or the fortified compound on the west bank. Such crises would become common enough during the next 100 years, times when the rule of law broke down, often while there were bands of marauders in the area: mercenaries or bedouin who had discovered that Thebes was virtually defenceless. The tombs and temples were especially vulnerable, not only to these plundering invaders but also to bands of Thebans who took advantage of the temporary state of anarchy to reach out and take the treasures that surrounded them. In more settled times the sacred sites were guarded both by the medjay and by the eye of every citizen. Obviously no one in the tombmakers' village could suddenly attain wealth or fine possessions without their neighbours' knowledge. The villagers lived in such close proximity that even an everyday visit to a shrine or temple or another village house would be observed by a neighbour. Similarly the storing of plundered goods in one of the houses would hardly have passed unnoticed; and that would have placed the entire community at risk.

Yet, in the sixth year of King Seti II, a village woman, Heria, on trial before the elders, was found with stolen temple property in her house. Heria was originally charged with stealing a copper chisel from a workman who said that he had buried it in the floor of his house, presumably before the tombmakers' families had temporarily left the village for the safety of Thebes, and Heria had taken it in his absence. In her defence Heria swore an oath before the villagers that she had not taken the tool, but when the elders had her house searched after a village housewife's denunciation – 'I saw Heria when she took your tool' – they not only found the chisel, but what was a good deal worse, some ritual equipment from the village

79

temples, also abandoned when the workmen fled. With everyone gone, Heria, probably as a member of a robber's gang, had seized her chance and stolen both the chisel and the gods' treasures. Heria's thefts and perjury horrified the village tribunal, who declared her 'worthy of death'. After her trial she disappears completely from the surviving records and in all probability the unfortunate woman was sent over the river to the court of the High Priests of Amun who, along with the King and the Vizier, had the power to pass sentence on such a serious crime.

That these little wars of Heria's day were factional struggles around the throne and not a united Thebes fighting to repel marauding foreigners receives oblique confirmation in an account of another hearing held before the village tribunal in the year previous to Heria's trial, when Foreman Hay himself was accused of 'speaking against the King'. Hay's accusers were four workmen of the gangs and it would seem that the political factionalism shaking Thebes found reflection in the village. Foreman Hay was himself an elder and entitled to sit in judgement at the village court so his own trial, which must have been quite an event, was witnessed and judged by all the men of the gangs. Facing his four denouncers, the foreman coolly denied all knowledge of their accusations and said that at the time they claimed to have heard him utter his seditions, 'as for me, I was sleeping'. Then the four men were themselves brought before the court, whereupon, despite Foreman Paneb's encouragement, they suddenly retracted their former statements. 'Tell us what you heard', he demanded, but now they would only tell the court 'we did not hear anything'. Understandably, the tribunal then became very angry, and its spokesman gave Foreman Hay's timorous accusers a severe dressing-down: 'As truly as Amun lives and as truly as the Pharoah lives, there exists nothing in the story about speaking against the King. — and if you hide today only to speak of it tomorrow, then may your noses and ears be cut off. '

The four men were threatened with the type of mutilation sometimes carried out on perjurers if they continued their gossip but refused again to substantiate their claims before the court. As well as this threat, each of the four men was sentenced to suffer 'ten solid blows with a stick'. Such a sentence for merely gossiping may seem harsh, but it can be imagined how sly rumours would fuel the civil unrest running through Thebes. Evidently there was also some antagonism between the two foremen; Paneb and Hay were as opposed to each other as the warring kings: 'I will come up to you on the high desert and kill you,' Paneb once threatened the hapless Hay. And the desert, regarded as a malevolent and untrustworthy environment by most Egyptians, was where one felt threatened at the best of times. It was also the cliff-top path between the village and the Great Place.

But after a short while in office Paneb made peace with Hay, and soon they were busy supervising together the speedy completion of the work in the tomb of King Seti II: 'In the sixth year of King Seti II, on the tenth month's sixteenth day [mid-March 1189 BC], the Chief Medjay Nakhtmin visited the gangs at the King's tomb saying "The falcon, namely King Seti II, has flown to heaven and another has arisen in his place".' Three months later the gangs were already working on the tomb of the new King and the relationship between the two foremen had become so amicable that one of Hay's most skilful painters was taking time away from the work in the royal tomb to aid in the preparation of Paneb's own funeral equipment.

Throughout all this hard work and reconciliation, the family of Foreman Neferhotep still smarted under the injustice of Paneb's appointment. After the death of Seti II they seized the chance to denounce him for the theft of some of the King's burial equipment, stolen, they claimed, whilst the gangs were placing it in the royal tomb during the King's funeral. In that uncertain era it was highly probable that Seti II's burial had been hasty and perhaps that his tomb furniture had been disturbed or plundered. The detailed list of objects that Neferhotep's family provided indicates that the plunder of the tomb were common knowledge, for if it were not, no villager would readily admit to such detailed information of the crime without exposing himself, by implication, to a charge of complicity. Their list is an impressive one: parts of the tomb's doors, a chariot's coverings, incense, wine and statues with the King's name on them. All it seems were taken by Paneb, Neferhotep's family even providing a finishing touch to their denunciation in a passage implying that Paneb had sat drunkenly on top of the royal sarcophagus after the King had been placed inside it! Foreman Neferhotep's brother, Amennakht, who compiled this list of crimes, also mentions in his rambling account an earlier robbery where a scribe had a hand cut off for a similar offence – for a moment, it seems possible that old Kenhirkhopeshef himself will be involved along with the erring foreman.

In his rebuttal, Paneb simply repeated the oath he had taken not to 'upset a stone in the neighbourhood of the place of Pharaoh'. At his trial two years before Foreman Hay had used a similar formula to clear his name, and so powerful were these oaths, so severe the penalties for perjury, that the charges before both of them simply crumbled. The foreman's words were trusted, but the vindictiveness of Neferhotep's family seems, not surprisingly, to have angered Paneb, whose attitude towards them now became hostile. Later Amennakht recounted that Paneb even stopped him from going to the foreman's tomb chapel to make offerings to his spirit. Not only did Paneb send a member of his gang to see that this harsh command was obeyed, but he even shouted to the villagers himself 'don't let any member of the family of Neferhotep be seen going to make offering to Amun, their god'. But failure to offer to the ancestors or the gods was a serious lapse and, despite Paneb's orders, some of the villagers ventured to continue the family's duties – doubtless keeping an eye out for Paneb as they did so. But Paneb caught them at it, and according to Amennakht, threw stones at them; one may imagine how, faced with the enraged foreman, the pious desire to aid Neferhotep's spirit somewhat abated.

With this feud raging in the village it was probably a good thing that the gangs suddenly found their work at the Great Place had been increased. For the new King, young Siptah, wanted three tombs: one for himself and two for his protectors, Queen Tausert and Chancellor Bay. At this frantic time the gangs' work shows no evidence of the pressures mounting in their private lives. Rather we see the same pattern in the tombs as before: elegant beginnings then hasty conclusions; fine wall scenes around the tombs' entrances, and unfinished burial chambers below. Be that as it may, the work involved in merely quarrying three tombs together was terrific; their three doorways being grouped together close by the tomb of Seti II: the King's and the Queen's were of the usual design, with the Queen's smaller but just as carefully made; the Chancellor's smaller still. His tomb, though, was unique in the Great Place, for rather than the usual texts covering both sides of the first corridor of the Kings' tombs, the Chancellor's had a series of scenes cut right along the walls that showed him worshipping the gods; today the rest of his tomb remains a mystery, for it has long been flooded and filled with sand and rock.

The gangs' progress in these tombs is documented in a series of records of inspections that took place early in Siptah's reign: from the first year, on the second month's twelfth day, when the Vizier came to see the beginning of the work, to the second year when the inspectors saw that it was continuing deeper into the rock. A yet more vivid indication of the gangs' frantic pace are the notes scribbled by an accounting scribe recording the rate that chisels were issued from the stores. These chisels were heavy long-pointed spikes that, with the massive cedar mallets still favoured by sculptors today, the quarrymen used to rough-quarry the corridors. Flakes of limestone still bearing the glistening marks of these copper chisels are common enough in the Great Place. The records show that Hay's and Paneb's gangs had each taken thirty-seven chisels from the valley stores and that only one remained in stock, along with two spikes that were blunted and two that were 'old' – that is, whose heads had mushroomed after continued use making them too short to be effective. According to the same records the copper of another broken spike had already been re-smelted to make sixteen small chisels which, shaped like modern steel-engraving tools and fitting comfortably in the artists' hands, were used to cut the reliefs on the tombs' walls.

Clearly the men were working very hard, most of them employed in quarrying: three men working side by side at the rock face, about twice that number smoothing the rough-quarried surfaces of the walls, and the rest carrying the rock and chippings out of the tomb. Typically at any one time one or two men of each gang would be ill, and a further two or three would be set to plastermaking – baking and sieving the gesso that occurs naturally in small pockets in the desert about the Great Place. This plaster was used to fill the holes and cracks that appeared in the tombs' walls and ceilings during the course of the work and, later, painted on the walls to give a fresh even surface for the draughtsman's guidelines. Until the first corridors were smoothed and whitened in this way there was no work for the skilled painters and engraving sculptors in the tomb, a fact that both Hay and Paneb readily turned to their advantage for, during the early stages of the work, several of these specialists were employed in the village cemetery working on the foremen's own tombs. Paneb was building a new monument for himself and his wife to replace the earlier tomb made years before when he had been a stonemason and Hay had some of the skilled men of the gangs working to improve his burial vault.

All this the recording scribes faithfully wrote in their work-registers: in the first year of King Siptah, on the fourth month's twenty-third day, for example, we find that two men were absent from Paneb's gang, one nursing a scorpion-bite, the other, the painter Neferhotep, working with the fore-man himself. From the next day's records we find once again that 'the chief', Paneb, is with the painter and that the two of them are working on Paneb's coffin; a project that would continue sporadically over the next year. Such coffins were works of art, brilliantly coloured and beautifully made, and Neferhotep was one of the best painters, having made coffins for several men in the gangs, and even one for a medjay who, the receipt carefully notes, was obliged to provide his coffin's expensive wood himself. Nor was Neferhotep merely a craftsman, for he was also skilled in the ritual of vivifying his works of art, of making them live as aspects of the people they would hold. In a receipt for another of his coffins, he says that 'I opened the eyes of the coffin of Ramesses the doorkeeper'. That he became rich by such labours is apparent from other agreements that have survived. In one of them he agrees to a price for buying a live ox, and such animals could only be afforded by the richest village households.

Though this use of the craftsmen's labour by the foreman and scribes was regarded as perfectly proper, as we have already seen, there was one especial aspect of Paneb's tomb-building that was not and that, as you might expect, soon attracted the beady eyes of Foreman Neferhotep's family who did not hesitate to denounce him. Paneb, Amennakht claimed, took stones from the work at the Great Place and used them to build four columns in his village tomb chapel. At first sight the accusation seems strange: why, in a landscape of limestone should anyone bother to carry stones for miles over mountain-tracks from the Great Place to the village cemetery, simply to stand them in a tomb cut into the same formation of limestone as the Great Place itself? The reason is not hard to find. Paneb had carried off cut blocks, stones that were carefully shaped, every surface expertly smoothed to be close-fitting to its neighbour. In an age when masons had only soft copper chisels, each block represented considerable time and effort, for several smiths and chisel-sharpeners had to work behind the finishing sculptor. At the tomb of Seti II the two walls that ran up to the doorway, and the doorjambs of the entrance itself, had been made out of these blocks; today they are half-denuded. We can guesss that after the King's funeral, when the entrance to the tomb had been covered with chippings, the tops of these walls still protruded and were taken down by Paneb's gang who, as Neferhotep's brother carefully reported: 'took them away to his tomb every day, and he erected four columns in his tomb with these stones — and he plundered the Place of Pharaoh — and the people who passed nearby saw the stonecutters when they were standing on top of the work of Pharaoh and they heard voices'. With so many people watching and waiting for him to make a slip, Paneb could never have got away with it. When we find him swearing an oath that 'should the Vizier hear my name again I shall be dismissed from my office and become a stonemason once more!' We can guess that he was being brought to book.

Paneb was not alone in his disgrace, for at the same time - 'Year one of Siptah, the fifteenth day of the tenth month' - one of his many children, his eldest son, Aaphate, was sentenced by the vizier's office to be beaten, perhaps because of involvement in some of his father's activities. For the most part, however, Aaphate had profited from his father's promotion; now deputy of his father's gang, the usual post for a foreman-designate, he could look forward to a good life in the work of the Great Place.

Although Paneb may have named his eldest son Aaphate, 'great of strength' in the image of the god he followed, for most of the time the boy was not only at odds with many of the villagers but also with his father. Once again, Amennakht gleefully supplies us with all the details as he observes the friction inside his adversary's family. One day at the village, he tells us, Aaphate ran away from his father's house and went to the doorkeeper's and there took an oath saying: 'I cannot bear with him; my father made love to the Lady Tuy when she was the workman Kenna's wife, he made love to the Lady Hunro when she was with Pendua and when she was with Hesysenebef! And after that he debauched her daughter too.'

84

12 The face of an unknown villager, from a votive statue that was probably set up in the presence of a god in the darkness of one of the village shrines.

13 Workman Penbuy's portrait, from a statue that he dedicated at one of the village shrines.

14 An unknown village woman from her votive statue.

15 Ramose, the 'honest scribe', prays to the rising sun; detail of a relief carved upon a capstone of a small steep-sided pyramid that topped one of his tomb chapels in the village cemetery.

16 The murdered Foreman Neferhotep, Paneb's 'step-father'; a fine detail of a wooden door-frame from his tomb.

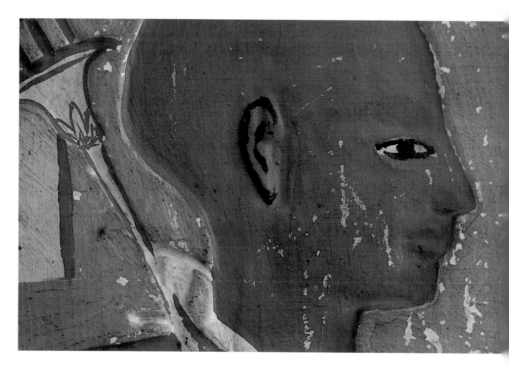

ove 17 Unfinished section of the
ceiling in the tomb of Seti II; the basic
grid system and the first stages of
painting are still visible. Flying
vultures are a common motif on royal
tomb ceilings; for a finished version
of this subject see Plate 26.

ight 18 The sun rising at dawn,
carrying with it two aspects of the
dead king: the ram-headed god who is
his flesh, and the scarab beetle which
holds the magical potential of the
royal resurrection.

Below 19 The 'chariot battle'
ostracon from the tomb of Ramesses
It shows an Egyptian queen (left)
fighting an archery duel with Pharaoh
(right).

21 The oracle that 'looks into men's hearts': the face of Amenhotep I carved some 400 years after the king's death, at the height of his oracular powers.

Opposite 20 The village temple of Amun of Ramesses II, its paving worn smooth by the ancient people.

22 The heraldic cartouches of a Ramesside Pharaoh, cut lightly into the schist cliffs of the quarries of the Wadi Hammamat.

The last woman of this list, Amennakht adds sourly, was seduced by Aaphate as well! If we believe story, Paneb was indeed an ancient Benvenuto Cellini, not only seducing many of the village wives and building large monuments for himself, but at the same time, with Foreman Hay he was supervising no less than three fine tombs in the Great Place.

And this soon became four, as poor young King Siptah, crippled by polio and king only by the assent of Queen Tausert and Chancellor Bay, ruled just six years until, aged about twenty, he died. When the King had been laid in his elegant grave, one completed even down to its huge burial chamber, the royal commissioners came again to the Great Place to search for 'a place of piercing' for the tomb of the new King, Setnakht. The commission had been frequent visitors to the Great Place in the past few years, for they had overseen the three tombs of Siptah, his Queen and the Chancellor. Now they chose quite a different site for the new tomb, one right at the valley's centre, close to some of the earlier tombs of the dynasty, and there Paneb and Hay set their gangs to quarrying. Within a year engraving sculptors were at work in the first corridor and as soon as the craftsmen had cut their carvings and painted them the quarrymen were at work again, cutting at the rock face at the far end of the finely decorated corridor. Then suddenly all work stopped as, only a short distance into the rock, their excavation collapsed, the steps of limestone falling, booming down into an echoing cavern. When they had cut a hole big enough to climb through, some of the workmen were lowered down into the darkness, where, in the flickering light of their lamps, they saw first a flat floor, then a doorway and a rough but regularly cut chamber. Along with the two foremen, the more experienced workmen must have realized what had happened; after they had passed through the doorway into another rough chamber, and reached a large hall with four square pillars through a second door, their fears were confirmed. This room at least was readily recognizable as a room in a royal tomb. On the walls those that could read hieroglyphs found the names of King Amenmesse, the usurper, buried just thirteen years before: the quarrymen stood in the chariot hall of his tomb. The collision of these two tombs indicates how much pressure the gangs were working under. The entrance to Amenmesse's tomb, a white scar on the valley's golden landscape, must have been clear enough, but in their haste the quarrymen misjudged the distance between their excavation and the sealed tomb beside it, and blundered down through the roof of a small chamber running at right-angles to the central corridor of this tomb.

As the men of the gangs passed through the hole in their excavation and down through the ceiling into the dark tomb, they entered a rare underworld where some of the gangs' older painters and sculptors had executed some of their finest work. How sad then they must have been when, at the orders of the Vizier or, perhaps, of a high priest, they were sent down again with mallets and chisels to cut the gods from the walls of Amenmesse's tomb. They were probably led by a temple priest, an expert on the decorations and iconography of the royal tombs. Certainly a senior scribe of the village was present – perhaps Paser, who had announced Amenmesse's death to the gang years before. There too would have been the foremen, Paneb and Hay, watching their workmen as the chippings hammered from the walls flew in wide arcs across the corridors and rattled on to the tomb floor. The tomb is now part-filled with flood debris so we cannot tell if the King's burial or those of his mother and royal wife, buried with him, were plundered at this time: presumably the splendid statues of the gods that stood around every royal sarcophagus would have been taken from the tomb when the gods of the walls were destroyed. No surer example of the new King Setnakht's attitude to his usurping predecessor may be found than this malefic attack upon the tomb. And in no other place may the gulf between the aims of ancient and modern artists be so clearly seen as in this tomb where some of Egypt's finest sculptors mutilated their own masterworks. Henceforth the usurper would not lie in a royal underworld; for the workmen had not destroyed mere works of art, but had taken away the King's gods.

Following the destruction of Amenmesse's tomb, the unfinished corridor above was abandoned. Now, in great haste to provide a proper burial for King Setnakht, who was ailing, the gangs went back into the fresh-sealed tomb of Queen Tausert, where they enlarged the doorways and extended the corridors further on into the cliff and cut a second suite of rooms for Setnakht's burial behind those of the Queen; a tomb within a tomb. Here and there in the Queen's tomb they quickly altered some of the wall scenes, changed a few of the names and tampered with the figures. Then, having reigned for just two years, Setnakht died. The granite-masons of Elephantine having already cut his sarcophagus, the founder of the new dynasty was placed peacefully in his freshly-painted tomb.

Setnakht's son took the throne, naming himself King Ramesses, the third of that line, and like his illustrious namesake he brought a comparative stability to Thebes and the tombmakers' village. Paneb and Hay continued to supervise their gangs during the King's first few years. All through the previous decade, while Paneb endured a hail of gossip and criticism and kings came and went, the two foremen had overseen the excavation and decoration of five huge and splendid tombs; a period in the village's history of furious and quite unprecedented activity. Hay continued his foremanship for decades to come, eventually passing it on to his son in the twenty-second year of Ramesses III's rule. Neither Paneb nor his son Aaphate enjoyed so tranquil a fate: after just six years of the new reign both of them completely disappeared from the village records. Like King Amenmesse before them, they had fallen foul of the state.

13

THE FOREMAN'S BROTHER

Much of our information about Paneb comes from the writings of his antagonists – and most of these are implacably hostile. Even the scribes who compiled the attendance registers of the Great Place give us unusually detailed, and always unfriendly accounts of the foreman and his actions. No other foreman in the registers, for example, is described as having sent a man from the work in the royal tomb to feed his own ox. It comes as no surprise to discover that the ox-feeder in question was, in fact, a member of the family of the dead Foreman Neferhotep.

The largest source of information about Paneb comes from the dead foreman's own brother, Amennakht. It is a single papyrus, written to Amennakht's dictation during his old age, when he was an old man looking back over the injustices of a lifetime: Amennakht might well have expected to have taken the foremanship of his childless brother, instead of which the interloping Paneb replaced him, not only in the family inheritance but also, one suspects, in Neferhotep's affection. Amennakht is therefore completely hostile to his adoptive nephew, indeed, the sole purpose of the document is to denounce him to the authorities. Yet it is wise to balance such an ingenuous record of a life of crime against other facts. Paneb, after all, spent some fifteen difficult years in the foremanship and throughout that period maintained a skilled and loyal workforce at a time when quantity of tombs rather than quality of workmanship was the main consideration. He also supported a large family and, even upon the admission of his worst enemies, was not only popular with the men of his gang, but much beloved by the village women as well.

Amennakht introduces both himself and his cause with great directness at the beginning of his memoir: 'I am the son of the foreman Nebnefer. My father died and the foreman Neferhotep, my brother, was put in his place.' Then he describes Paneb's promotion to the foremanship 'though it was not his place', before continuing over some sixty-seven lines of rambling memoir. Occasionally the text is incoherent and in the three millenia since its competition, it has become frayed and damaged. Its last lines suggest that it was written while Paneb was still alive, for after describing his iniquities, Amennakht concludes that 'such conduct is indeed unworthy of his office. But, still, he is keeping well though he is like a madman, and yet it was him who killed these men.' Although the text promises yet more revelations, it is broken off at this point. This lament about Paneb's continuing good health suggests that Amennakht made his statement to serve as evidence at an inquiry into the foreman's activities by Ramesses III's first Vizier, Hori. Just such an enquiry is described, at a later date, in a document reporting a speech by Paneb's younger sons.

In its essence Amennakht's papyrus is a simple catalogue of crimes: accusations that tumble out indignantly, one after another. It writhes with dislike for Paneb and revels in the mean-minded emotions of a village feud. Paneb is accused of every offence from petulance to royal tomb-robbing, from claims that he manipulated high offices of state to the observation that he forced an adoptive brother to feed his ox without payment, and this 'for two whole months'. Amennakht's statement, a verbal declaration, is in great contrast to the suave hand of the scribe who wrote it down in four columns in round rolling letters across three gummed sheets. If we are to glean any facts from it we must attempt to penetrate the emotions filling Amennakht's mind as he spoke and match them against what we can assume to be the truth. For here history is tempered by a desire for revenge.

In all, Amennakht accuses Paneb of sixteen separate offences of which just four are crimes that, however imperfect our knowledge of the ancient legal codes, we may classify as state crimes. Three of these, Paneb's contriving the dismissal of a vizier, bribing another vizier for his foremanship and robbing a royal burial, were old allegations and, as we have already seen, had not merited any action on the part of the authorities for well over a decade. Only the fourth of these serious charges, that of robbing a Queen's tomb, appears to be new, and this, as we shall see, represented a real pitfall for Paneb.

Out of the remaining twelve offences with which his adoptive uncle accused him, six concern family quarrels, such as the non-payment for feed for the wretched ox-minder or the alleged seduction of a relative, and six are village affairs of a similar nature. How, then can one discern the truth under the shrill coating of ancient malice with which Amennakht decorates his case? First, we should probably acknowledge that, like all the best gossip, the central facts of Amennakht's stories were based on reality; after all, the public events the text describes were well known to both the villagers and the officials of the administration, and there would have been very little point in inventing them. We may assume that if Amennakht says that a vizier was summarily dismissed then this, in fact, did happen; however, we should probably be sceptical about the implied extent of Paneb's contribution to this incident. Similarly, the accusations that Paneb stopped villagers from making offerings at Foreman Neferhotep's tomb chapel, threw stones at them, and got very drunk at their parties all refer to public happenings and were therefore probably rooted in fact. Paneb's own declarations under court oath – that, for example, he had not robbed a king's tomb – would also be public knowledge, as would his son Aaphate's revelations of life with father.

However, Amennakht's reference to other, more secret, crimes – to Paneb taking tools from the Great Place and bribing Scribe Kenhirkhopeshef (long dead at the time of Vizier Hori's investigation) – concerned discreet activities which surely require further confirmation: certainly, the claim that Paneb stripped the Lady Yemyemwah of all her clothes 'and threw her on top of a wall and seduced her' is an equally difficult charge to prove. Yemyemwah was Amennakht's and Neferhotep's sister and had probably grown up alongside Paneb in the foreman's household. Though the wording of the text is ambiguous, it seems hardly likely that Paneb actually raped his adoptive aunt, for there is no mention of punishment for what would surely have been considered a crime. One can imagine that all of Paneb's sexual activities with an adoptive relative, willing or unwilling, would have been viewed with a somewhat jaundiced eye by a brother already jealous of the newcomer's influence over his family. Similar objections may also be raised about the list of village wives which Aaphate accused his father of seducing. Several other denunciations from the same period in history contain such lists, and, usually, as in this case, three women are named. As it is most unlikely that seduction was considered a crime, we should probably consider this list's inclusion in the denunciation as an attempt to show Paneb as a sower of social discord, a 'Follower of Seth' intent on upsetting the social order. Amennakht's particular choice of women in the statement does, however, demonstrate a certain skill in trouble-making, for one was the wife of a close companion of Paneb's and another was the wife of a prominent villager, an unusually literate tomb-painter. This lady, Hunro – 'little Hathor' – later divorced her artist husband and married again; Amennakht tells us that throughout both of her marriages she remained Paneb's lover. Interestingly, Hunro's second husband, Hesysenebef, was the child adopted by Foreman Neferhotep after Paneb had left his household (the same little boy who feeds the monkey stony grapes on the foreman's statue). Hunro had two children whilst she was married to Hesysenebef and they were named after Foreman Neferhotep and his wife Wabkhet – Amennakht claims that Hunro's daughter, too, was Paneb's lover and also the lover of his son Aaphate.

Perhaps we should dismiss these claims as mere scurrilities since Hunro and Hesysenebef were married for just three years, and at the time of Paneb's trial, Wabkhet, Hunro's daughter, was only a small child. Interestingly, the exact date of Hunro's marriage to Hesysenebef is recorded for us on another document, her divorce settlement, written on a large limestone flake: 'Year two, the twenty-third day of the twelfth month of King Setnakht. The day when Hesysenebef dismissed Hunro. "I gave her during three years, in every single month twenty-eight pounds of wheat, making nine sacks".' Hunro in return contributed a bolt of cloth to the marriage's wealth: she was a weaver, probably in the workshops of the Temple of Ramesses II, where her marriage settlement was found. There had been an argument about this cloth, both about its quality (of which a merchant had said 'it is bad'!) and its value. Finally though, everything was settled and the couple parted. During their brief marriage Hunro and Hesysenebef, by this time a prosperous member of the village working in Foreman Hay's gang, set up a fine stela by the temple of Ramesses II showing members of their two families worshipping the spirit of Foreman Neferhotep. The sculptor drew him dressed in finest pleated linen and standing on the deck of a celestial boat loaded with offerings – far removed from village feuds and the broken tombs of usurping kings.

One of the parties to Hunro's and Hesysenebef's divorce settlement was a villager named Hay, called the son of Siwadj to distinguish him from the foreman of the same name in whose gang he worked. Another of Sidwadj's sons figures in a further accusation in Amennakht's papyrus: of all the incidents recorded in the document perhaps the best single example of how an innocent action can look like a heinous crime when viewed through an evil eye. At two points in his denunciation, Amennakht accuses Paneb of entering and robbing village tombs. In all probability, the charges are baseless. If such serious offences could have been proved, Paneb would have been convicted of them years earlier, for Amennakht alleges that Scribe Kenhirkhopeshef was bribed in connection with these robberies and this dates to the first two years of Paneb's foremanship, before the scribe's death. Amennakht claims that Paneb went into 'tombs though they were not his and he stretched his legs. He was with workman Kenna.' (The same Kenna whom, according to the papyrus, Paneb had cuckolded!) 'Leg-stretching' refers to the villagers' method of climbing down the vertical tomb shafts, fitting their feet right and left in slots in the opposite walls. Once in the burial chamber, Paneb was alleged to have stolen the very bier on which the coffin lay, and to have 'carried off all the objects that one gives to a dead man and stolen them'. We can tentatively locate the tomb Paneb was supposed to have robbed for, although Kenna was a common enough name in the village, only one, the son of Siwadj, had a family tomb in a part of the village cemetery close to the tomb Paneb built for himself.

By Paneb's day the village cemetery was very crowded and many of the old tombs had collapsed; groups of villagers went to inspect these cave-ins, usually with the pious aim of putting the exposed burials back in good order. It is possible, then, that what caught Amennakht's jaded eye was merely Paneb assisting his friend in this work or even searching out a place in the crowded cemetery for his new tomb. From the graffiti of inspectors at the Kenna, son of Siwadj, family tomb we know that it was opened several times in village history for just such refurbishings, and we may be sure that, if Paneb and Kenna had really been tomb-robbing in broad daylight only a stone's throw from the village walls, they would have incurred more than a few confused lines in a text written twelve years after the event.

Nevertheless, as we attempt to separate malice from fact in this extraordinary text, we can assert with confidence that the fiery foreman was no Ramose: that he *did* drink heavily and fly into theatrical rages, that he *did* seduce village wives and was indeed a 'Follower of Seth'. Through Amennakt's envious accusations we can see a real man: angry, passionate and, in all probability, one of the best foremen that ever oversaw the gangs, a pious worker in the Place of Truth. No man is merely black or white, but rather a mass of contradictions, and Paneb more so than most.

What finally brought the foreman before Vizier Hori's tribunal on trial for his life? The very form of the papyrus's text provides the clue. For there *is* some shape to this wandering, apparently incoherent declaration. In its own way it tells a story. Not in the rounded form of a literary document with a beginning, a middle and an end, but as an illiterate man used only to random conversations would express himself. Neferhotep's brother had many bitter memories and they spilled out of his mind like a jumble of footnotes to a catalogue of major crimes. Amennakht starts his denunciation by describing two weighty offences, follows this with some village gossip and then recounts some family injustices, before returning to his central theme. Almost at the end of his recital he describes the crime for which Paneb was caught and, finally, as a bitter afterthought, spins off again into more grumbling details of the family feud. But if Neferhotep's brother shows us his own oratorical shortcomings, he none the less tells us Paneb's ultimate crime: 'Charge concerning his [Paneb's] going to the burial of Queen Henutmire and taking away a goose. And he took an oath by the Lord concerning it, saying "it is not in my possession", but they found it in his house.' This, then, was the crime Paneb committed and for which the penalty was removal from the village and, almost certainly, death: the theft of a gilded goose, the sacred animal of the god Amun, from the tomb of a wife of Ramesses II, a daughter of Seti I.

It is the very brevity of Amennakht's account that convinces. It tells no more, one might imagine, than any Theban of the day would wish to know of a crime so damning for the villagers that it would be especially unwise for an innocent party to have intimate knowledge of its circumstances. Certainly for a foreman of the Great Place to have been caught at such a crime – a leader of a community that daily passed the doors of tens of royal tombs, whose whole existence was founded upon trust or, at least, mutual observation – must have made the village very nervous. Almost certainly other villagers were involved, probably Aaphate, Paneb's son, who disappears from the records with his father. The papyrus goes out of its way to name Paneb's friends in the gang, distinguishing them carefully from those it describes as suffering from the foreman's exploitation. It may well be that Amennakht was not simply denouncing Paneb but, as the brother of a respected former foreman, also attempting to dissociate the elder villagers from the crime. Maybe we should excuse Amennakht from the charge of merely blackening his enemy's name and allow that he was also trying to show Vizier Hori how, unlike the fiery Paneb, most of the villagers were good men of Horus, not 'Followers of Seth'.

One thing is certain, however, the golden goose found the foreman out. By robbing the tomb and committing perjury, Paneb was guilty of two heinous crimes: in 1175 BC, as winter visited the land after the Nile's flood, a single line upon an ostracon refers to his end: 'Year six, the fifth month, "the killing of the chief".'

14

FRAGMENTS

Today, the personalities of people like Paneb and Kenhirkhopeshef are preserved chiefly in the records of their relationships with the other villagers: receipts, letters, wills, even denunciations. Most of their contemporaries survive only in scraps, fragmentary literary caricatures. Scribe Nekhenmut, for example, exists only as a name in a few rough graffiti that he scratched on the Theban cliffs, in a scrappy memorandum of the work in the Great Place, and as the recipient of a single, now anonymous, letter.

Nekhenmut's graffiti tell us that he was a priest at one of the village temples; the records of the royal tomb that once, when rations were delivered to the gangs, he quarrelled with some of the men. But Nekhenmut only comes to life as the recipient of a letter sent to him by an angry workman:

> To Scribe Nekhenmut. Why are you falling into bad behaviour? Nobody's words penetrate your ears except your excessive conceit. You are not a human being. You do not make your wife pregnant like other men. You are very, very rich but you do not give anything to anybody. He who has no child adopts someone's orphan to bring him up. It is he who will later bring water for his hands [i.e. act as a son].

While we may pity poor Nekhenmut, perhaps lonely, probably selfish, we can admire such directness of expression between one villager and another and also appreciate how a letter like this would act as a medium for dealing with stress, for letting off steam inside the community. Everybody lived close together at the village, so claustrophobically close that individual solitude must have been rare and, in all probability, was considered a disagreeable condition; as it still is in many non-western cultures today. Broad tolerance governed the villagers' behaviour and accommodated virtually all individual foibles. Just as the pleasures of a gay party or a full table were never the sum of village aspirations, so most village villainies and quarrels were not as divisive as the conflict between Paneb and Neferhotep's family.

When national events impinged upon the villagers' daily lives – when three royal tombs had to be made in six years, and when the villagers were forced to flee for safety to a nearby settlement – we begin to see clear evidence of stress and even, on occasion, disillusionment. Often these feelings are revealed in ironic drawings: emphasizing the sad gulf between the sacred office of divine Pharaoh and the mortals competing for possession of it, or making more general observations, no less perceptive, about the world in which they lived. One of the village artists made a sharp comment upon the court rivalries that had brought such danger to the village and caused the tombmakers so much hard work. In a halting red line on a limestone ostracon, the artist drew two chariots facing one another (see Plate 19). One of the chariots holds a charioteer who steadies the horses and stands next to the damaged figure of a king. Both are in poses similar to those in the battle scenes on the walls of Theban temples. The other chariot holds a queen dressed in long transparent clothes, and she is loading a bow in a very business-like manner. Her opponent seems to be doing the same thing. Between the two chariots arrows fly in mid-air, loosed from the bows of both parties. This is certainly not a scene copied from a temple wall, for there we would never see, as on this stone, two regal Egyptians fighting each other. Obviously the most likely candidate for the identity of the battling Egyptian queen is Tausert, the most powerful presence behind the throne for two reigns, and a lady with her own tomb in the royal valley. The king she fights doubtless represents one of the monarchs who followed Merneptah briefly to the throne. But so charming is the drawing, so lively are the horses, so carefully judged the gesture of loading the bow, that its acidic comment is almost obscured. For here one of the royal tombmakers has taken elements from traditional triumphal scenes and turned these bland sentiments into a comment on contemporary history; a time when Egyptians fought not uncivilized foreigners, but each other. It is difficult to say to what extent we can define this drawing as satire. Like artists of all periods the ancient draughtsmen worked inside conventions, using particular poses and attitudes almost instinctively. Egyptian art supplied the ancient people with a discreet vision of themselves, one remarkably different from any modern concept of man; a public vision of a stressless, solid society, as unruffled as a Victorian prime minister. But with his small sketch the village draughtsman has given us the equivalent of Queen Victoria and Bertie sparring together with boxing gloves and safety helmets.

The huge public image of a strong, calm state that offered all the security of a pious feudalism reflected conditions that had not existed at Thebes for a long time. Slowly, during the first century of life at the tombmaker's village, the mood had changed. Individuals started to appear, people who worried, prayed to personal gods, recorded personal experience rather than bland sentiment, and who were, perhaps, more superstitious (for they had sensed the unknown). These people would go to their graves not merely as happy servants of the state machine assured of their place in the next world by the status of the man they served on earth, but as individuals who had provided themselves with their own magic passports and amulets for their journey and who, once they had arrived with the gods, would stand singly before them for judgement. The innocent little drawing of the fighting king and queen is only a tiny part of this gradual change of attitude.

Just as the artists had a wide repertoire of standard poses on which they based even their most original compositions, so the villagers based their perceptions of their roles in society on a series of grand images, most clearly spelt out in such stories of the gods as the battle between Horus and his uncle Seth. This understanding of their role was the oil of their daily society; the relationships, rules and ruses of the gods in the sagas were echoed in the tombmakers' social behaviour. Kenhirkhopeshef's study of the 'Followers of Seth' shows careful analysis of character and indicates how sensitive this world was. Similarly the composite attributes of female gods as terrifying lionesses, mothers, destroyers of mankind and bringers of song and beauty, show the same subtle complexity.

As if emphasizing this subtle understanding of the individual and the social order, there are many deliberate inversions of the conventions in the drawings that the villagers made for their amusement. We find a mouse in his chariot sternly directing an army, but facing the wrong way, and similar scenes tell us that the mouse's chariot is carrying him off to fight a war with cats, who usually lose, like Tom of Tom & Jerry's cartoon films. In the village scenes, similar havoc is created by the reversal of roles, with anthropomorphic coronations and party scenes showing mice dressed in clothes and attended by cats. Here cats fan the mice and serve them food, they even, on occasion, carry the mice babies in warm shawls from which tiny faces poke, surprised apparently at such obliging felines. Other animals join in their parties: foxes and donkeys play double pipes, smiling crocodiles strum lutes contentedly, while outside in the garden more cats herd geese to market, blackbirds with baskets climb ladders to pick figs, and hippopotami, high in the trees, flit from bough to bough.

It is all part of a rustic fairyland that has existed since people kept farms and invested their animals with human roles. But in Egypt, where the gods themselves were often animals – Horus a hawk, Seth a strange hound – cats that were conquered by mice might also have a deeper significance. For Seth was sometimes manifested as a hippopotamus and a donkey, blackbirds were common signs of ill omen, and crocodiles, after all, ate people. These scenes of Punch and Judy simplicity are nightmare fairytales. All the bad things of the world, the overturning of the normal, are contained as a cat and mouse war; Mickey Mouse performs the same vicarious service in our own century. Of great interest is the elusive longevity of these simple tales, for the Egyptian animal battles went straight to Rome where they decorated taverns and were as popular in their day as hunting prints in public houses are today. The foxy piper emerges in a dozen roles in European folk tales; not the least, perhaps, disguised as the Pied Piper of Hamelin. The three papyri and dozens of related ostraca with animal scenes that still exist are evidence of a rich tradition of folklore that has survived, fragmented, to our own times. In the great mass of Egyptian art, however, they are very rare, and most examples that have survived come from the tombmakers' village; part of a vanished pictorial tradition that stood quite apart from the public art of the temple and the tombs.

Perhaps the most famous Egyptian animal drawing, showing a fabulous feline battle raging whilst donkeys dressed as priests offer to the gods and a horrible group of donkey harpists, leonine lutists and simian flute-players produce cacophonous serenades, also comes from the tombmakers' village. On the reverse of the papyrus are a series of high-flown titles suggestive of the beginning of a scribe's letter to a vizier. Like the charm that Kenhirkhopeshef manufactured from a similar letter, it would seem that a document of the royal administration had been washed and reused for the scribe's own purposes.

The rest of the sheet is filled with scenes of a very different character and these tell not of an individual's relationship with the state, but of his relationship with sex and sexuality. For while the animal gremlins fill a third of

the long sheet with their topsy-turvy world – the ancient unconscious tightly held inside the scribal registers – the pictures of sexual games covering the rest of the sheet are very different and quite serene. Although some of these scenes are adapted from the decorations in the royal tombs, this was probably not done for satirical effect but is merely the result of the artists' adaptation of the poses they drew most frequently in public art. With no less than twelve positions of sexual intercourse on this single sheet, we may suppose that the scribe was flexing his imagination to the full towards the end of his work. All twelve of vignettes show these similar participants: a priestess of Hathor and balding, knobbly-faced men, a type one recognizes from other drawings on ostraca found in the village. Most of the scenes also have a third party in them, a huge phallus which swings pendulously between the couple, even, on occasion, being supported by some helping handmaidens. Sex between the priestess and the man is diagrammatically insistent, pornographic. Yet it is drawn with such vivacity that the dullness that usually afflicts such scenes is quite absent. The comments scribbled quickly in the margins express enjoyment and delight: 'Come behind me with your love', 'Oh! sun, you have found out my heart, it is agreeable work'.

It is the priestess who speaks so clearly, and both words and pictures show she is a happy participant in the revels. As the man pats her backside, gently cradles her head, even seems to gasp at her prowess, so she pulls him carefully to her, holds his head like a baby's in her hand and continues to care for the old reprobate even when he has fallen, dead drunk, out of their bed! The inscriptions that accompany all the village erotica concern pleasure; none refer to violent or perverse activities, all show this same, perfect, stressless world. Yet we should not forget the horrid animal chorus, the jumbled unconscious, the ancient fear, that fills a third of the erotic papyrus. It is almost as if this were an acknowledgement that in the mind of the individual, as distinct from the bland sentiments of so much of ancient

Egyptian art, such strata of unreason did exist, as they have done in every society: half-perceived fears and dark superstitions subtly colouring the relationship between people and people and their gods. The generation that followed Paneb's would witness an increase in this dark interaction, both at the village and in the city and temples of Thebes itself.

15

ORACLE

The battle between Neferhotep's family and Paneb is unique in village history. Usually, if people could not accommodate each other they resorted to litigation before the village's own tribunal. Most such hearings were concerned with the simple disputes of village life, and here more than anywhere else one discovers that, along with a love of the process of litigation itself, there was an overriding and almost modern sense of fair play in the little community.

On three separate occasions, for example, the chief medjay, Mentmose, was brought before the elders by the workman Menna, who claimed that he had received no payment for a large jar of fat which he had given the policeman in trade. Menna should have known better: medjay were notorious for not paying their debts and fat was, after all, at more than two and a half *deben* of copper for each pound, an expensive commodity, a whole jar being equivalent to the price of a small sheep. The case dragged on for eighteen years. Eventually Mentmose settled for a complicated exchange of goods that included a young bull which would have been of sufficient size, if Menna so chose, to be spit-roasted and so provide a new jar of fat in exchange for the one that he had given to the policeman all those years before. Nothing daunted, apparently, by his long wait for payment, Menna had entered into other agreements with Mentmose during the time of his legal battle with him and was also suing another workman before the tribunal in a different court action. Menna's dealings show that such complicated exchanges were not undertaken in a spirit of true trade or even with the intention of making a fortune, but simply as part of a bargaining process between people in a secure community.

If the recalcitrant medjay had not eventually paid up and the village tribunal had decided against him, bailiffs would have been sent first to collect the debtor and bring him before the court, then to the debtor's home to extract either the goods or their just equivalent. The court's bailiffs were the doorkeepers of the royal tomb. Usually allotted to each of the gangs, the two of them kept the storerooms in the Great Place and were under the control of the senior scribes. Along with the medjay, doorkeepers were also used by the state scribes to collect the wheat taxes levied upon farmers throughout Egypt: they were in fact the pointed end of the law. As the wheat-collecting was frequently accompanied by beatings and searches to find hidden stores inside peasant houses, they were not greatly beloved by the community at large. One such doorkeeper, a senior, who worked at the Great Place and regularly acted as a bailiff of the village court during Mentmose's and Menna's time was Khaemwase. The village scribes record him collecting an ass for payment, and taking a woman debtor down to answer to a court in session in the compound of Ramesses II's temple. One debtor, though, was not impressed with the gravity of the law or the person of Khaemwase, its erstwhile representative. 'The magistrate sent the door-keeper Khaemwase, saying "Go to his [the debtor's] house and bring whatever you will find there".' So Khaemwase duly set off and finding the debtor's house empty he entered it and took the clothes that were the subject of the dispute. Then the debtor returned and with scant respect for this representative of law and order, he 'beat Khaemwase, seized the clothes which he had brought from his house and took them away'. 'I am still unpaid today,' the plaintiff complained mournfully.

Penalties for non-payment of a debt or an agreement could be severe and sometimes a debtor was required to pay two or three times the value of the goods that he owed. The kindly Foreman Hay, however, was contented in his own lawsuit with retrieving the value of the donkey he had loaned to a workman and which had died under his care. Such disputes were common, as the relatively rich tombmakers frequently loaned their beasts to both the medjay and the servants who brought water and provisions up to the village.

But there were also quicker ways of obtaining justice than the lengthy processes of litigation. A certain Nekhenmut, for example, one of Paneb's successors as foreman of a gang, had recourse to a god to have some stolen belongings restored to him. During the festival of King Amenhotep, whilst Foreman Nekhenmut was at his house in the village, he claimed that thieves broke into a storeroom he owned by the river bank and stole bread, cakes and beer. It seems that the thieves, too, wanted to join the god's feast. In his denunciation of the crime, the old man grumbled on about further robberies to his household and then, finally, addressed the god, King Amenhotep, directly: 'act, my Lord, so as to restore my loss'. As the village patron, King Amenhotep had the highest shrine in the complex of small temples grouped together at the northern end of the village, across the head of the valley. Though small and old, this shrine was one of the most revered and it was filled with statues of the villagers, all standing together in the god's presence. Fine stelae offered to the god were set into the shrine's walls.

At the time of his festivals, the god's statue was taken out of his temple and carried around the village and even occasionally taken to the Great Place. There storerooms would be opened and wine, beer and cheese curds given to the gangs, who would spend the day dancing and feasting with the god. Unlike the shrines of Amun at Karnak which were closed to view, King Amenhotep appeared to the gaze of his worshippers as he was carried in a sort of sedan chair by six ritually-purified workmen accompanied by workmen-priests with large ostrich-feather fans who carefully and rhythmically enveloped the sacred image in clouds of incense, a form of processional that is still favoured by the Holy See some 3000 years later. As Amenhotep I went about his peregrinations he often arbitrated in village disputes, as did other statues of the King kept in various shrines throughout Western Thebes. As he was carried through the village questions were asked of him and the statue would answer by 'nodding its head' or moving backward and forwards. It is quite wrong to put these movements down to simple connivance on the part of those carrying the god. Still, in Luxor today, during funerals, where corpses are similarly carried upon wooden coffin boards, bearers often feel the dead person's spirit pressing down upon them or hurrying the procession to the graveyard. Occasionally the spirit will slow the bearers down, rarely it will fix to a spot outside the graveyard and then a special tomb must be built to accommodate the demanding corpse. Just as it would be callous to suggest that these modern mourners deliberately play games, so it would be pointless to attribute modern tricks to the movements of King Amenhotep's statue. The god simply moved or nodded, and his bearers felt the pressure.

The villagers' appeals were delivered directly to the god, who acted as a higher court over the tribunal of elders at the village. The villagers also asked King Amenhotep simple questions, often personal anxieties transmuted into formal oracular requests:

> 'Is it he who has stolen my mat?'
> 'Shall the god appoint Seti as priest?'

> 'Will they mention me to the Vizier?'
> 'Are these dreams which one sees good?'
> 'Shall one [the King] give us the rations?'

The village scribes would write all these questions on to little stones, each one inked separately so as to change a simple request into a tangible object.

The system was a miniature version of the oracle of Amun of Karnak that, in the days of the old dynasty, had risen with all the mystic force of a state god to appoint the Kings of Egypt themselves. 'The procession made the circuit of the temple hall — searching for his majesty on every place. On recognizing me, lo, he halted. I threw myself upon the pavement — he set me before his majesty — he was astonished at me. The secrets in the hearts of the gods were revealed before the people.' So recounted a scribe of the old dynasty who witnessed a prince's successful fight to succeed to the throne which, in fact, he gained only after the oracle of Amun had recognized him as the rightful king.

The oracles also had powers to 'see into people's hearts', demanding higher loyalties than the traditional more easy-going deities. They also brought with them a crippling fear of deity and its fateful capriciousness. Just as all believers who appeal to such supernatural powers to settle their future lives return to them again and again, so in the last decades of the Theban Kingdom, when the kings had retreated to the north of Egypt, far away from the High Priests of Amun and their fearful statues, all the major state decisions were sanctioned by the oracular gods.

In Foreman Nekhenmut's day, however, people were still self-confident enough to talk straight back to an erring oracle and even barter with the god as one might with a travelling merchant. At one Opet Feast procession a workman appealed to a statue of Amun to help recover some stolen property 'and the god nodded very greatly'. Then he read out all the names of his townspeople and at one point the god nodded, meaning 'it is him who has stolen them', at which the alleged culprit piped up and said, 'It is false, it is not I who have stolen them.' The god, it is reported, was then exceedingly wroth but, nothing daunted, the accused man then went off to another oracle who, he thought, would be a better judge of his actions. This god, too, accused him of the theft. Indignantly the poor man then went to a third oracle and cried before it, 'Help me, Oh beloved Lord! It is not I who took the clothes.' His hopes were finally dashed when this god too, declared his guilt to the assembled crowd. Then a beating by the god's priests produced an effect that the combined offices of the gods had not achieved, and the man agreed to return the clothes to the workman and was even made to swear an oath that 'If I go back on what I have said I will be thrown to a crocodile.' It seems, then, as if the unfortunate appellant had regarded the 'stolen' clothes as his rightful property.

Slowly, however, the gods gained ground over such independent Thebans. Neferabu, for example, a painter at the royal tomb, was blinded by them:

I am a man who swore falsely by Ptah, Lord of Truth,
and he made me see darkness by day.
I will declare his might to the disbeliever and the believer,
to the small and the great:
Beware of Ptah, Lord of Truth! —
He caused me to be as the dogs of the street,
I being in his hand:
he made men and gods to mark me.
I being as a man who had sinned against his Lord
Righteous was Ptah, Lord of Truth, towards me
When he taught a lesson to me!
Be merciful to me, look upon me with mercy!

The blinded painter had his poem written carefully upon a special stela on which was also carved a scene showing him praying to the vengeful god. So concerned was he about the complete recording of his composition that it covered both sides of the stone.

In the dusty and crowded environment of the village and the royal tomb infectious eye diseases must have been common, and indeed, more than a dozen serious disorders of the eyes were recognized and treated by the Theban doctors. The root of these afflictions was believed to be in people's behaviour: either they, like Neferabu, had annoyed a god who had visited blindness upon them, or their blindness had been prompted by malice or perhaps envy, the ancient evil eye. 'Be merciful, for you have caused me to see darkness by day because of those women's talk,' the blinded wife of another village painter begged Thoth, the moon-god, believing that gossip had prompted her illness.

The names of celebrated eye-doctors have survived from the period a thousand years or more before the tombmakers' village was founded and one imagines that, whatever the modern opinions of their theories, such fame must have attended success. But the formulae they have left us to reproduce for their medications, which contain such ingredients as tortoise brains and caustic soda, to be applied directly to the eyes, smack more of desperation than of reasoned treatment. It is difficult to believe that the same physicians who had so carefully observed and described a wide variety of eye conditions would not have used their sharp diagnostic eye to recognize that these written remedies were hardly efficacious. We must imagine, then, that it was the practical application of simple nursing methods – irrigating damaged eyes with water, carefully removing foreign bodies from them and sheltering them from bright lights and further infections – that these doctors used as their really effective cures. But, as the villagers believed that illness was visited upon them by the gods, so ancient medicine treated the whole person, not merely the injured body, and it was by these criteria that the ancient doctors were held to be efficient. Neferabu's blindness was probably treated with simple medications of honey and kohl, the traditional cosmetic and a mild antiseptic, applied to his eyes. At the same time, prayers, spells and sympathetic support were treatments afforded to the frightened artist. Eventually Neferabu managed to treat his condition himself by recognizing its root causes: blasphemy and perjury.

> I was an ignorant man and foolish,
> who knew neither good nor evil —
> I called upon my mistress,
> I found that she came to me with sweet breezes.
> She was merciful to me,
> having made me see her hand.
> She turned to me again in mercy,
> she made me forget my sickness,
> for the Peak of the West is merciful
> if one calls upon her.

Perhaps Neferabu was lucky: we can imagine that he might have been temporarily stricken by a blood clot which spontaneously dissolved, or some such similar happening. Or perhaps we might term his blindness hysterical, caused by a pious terror of his own actions, and when he repented, his punishment, blindness, simply vanished with the sin. But such explanations were quite irrelevant to Neferabu, for both he and his friends had recognized the cause of his illness and the cure had completely vindicated their diagnosis. Neferabu, a village elder with a large family, set up several stelae that publicly recorded those awesome events. And as the prayers of a blinded painter have a particular pathos, one is thankful that his gods cured him.

16

SCRIBE AMENNAKHT

There was something of a power vacuum in the village following Paneb's execution. Whilst Foreman Hay continued to oversee one of the gangs, a rapid succession of four elderly workmen filled the foremanship of the other in the space of just ten years. The second of these short-lived foremen, named Amenemopet but called by the diminutive Ipy, was the brother of Neferabu, the painter blinded by the gods for his impiety. Their family was an old one, artists at the royal tomb and painters of coffins at the village since the days of Scribe Ramose.

Ipy was an old man when he took the foremanship and it is likely that he died after a few years in office. His eldest son Amennakht, a painter like his father, should have taken the post in his father's place but he was only a young man of some twenty-five years, and another elder workman, Nekhenmut, a friend of Paneb's and a member of his gang, was appointed in his place. Although Nekhenmut also died after only a few years in office, on this occasion the foremanship was secured by his family, where it remained for many generations. One consequence of this was that Amennakht's family tended to side with the villagers who were still at odds with Foreman Paneb's family and friends. All this would hardly be of interest were it not for the fact that this Amennakht, the son of Ipy, quickly found his own, quite novel, route to promotion inside the village heirarchy. For just five years after his father's death we find him proudly recording his appointment as a scribe of the royal tomb in an inscription in the Place of Beauty, close to the appointment notice that Scribe Ramose wrote 100 years before. The damaged text may be restored to its original length with the aid of another version that Amennakht wrote on the cliffs of the Great Place: 'Year sixteen, the third month, the Overseer of the City, Vizier To, came to appoint Scribe Amennakht, son of Ipy, as scribe of the tomb.'

By this time, the mid-point of his reign, King Ramesses III had stopped the dynastic squabbles and civil warfare that had plagued the country for generations and had also fought two major campaigns to secure Egypt from imminent threats of heavy foreign settlement. Large-scale building projects had been under way at Thebes on both banks of the river since the first years of his rule and outstanding amongst them was the temple complex that had been built, within sight of the tombmakers' village, at the southern end of the line of mortuary temples on the west bank. This had originally been planned as a somewhat sophisticated imitation of Ramesses II's temple, which stood less than a mile away to the north. But certain telling changes had been introduced into its architecture since the early years of the reign. Now the royal temple was surrounded not only by plain white walls but, in a second phase of building, by a fortress with an extra girdling wall built high and strong with battlements and ramparts. So although Amennakht's notice of appointment may seem every bit as proud and self-assured as Scribe Ramose's had been before him, the village world was changing. Immense old Thebes, fat and pious, rich and wicked in its imperial old age, was no longer the centre of Egypt that it had been in the days of Ramose's youth. Slowly it was becoming a sacred city, an embodiment of the national culture far removed from the day-to-day affairs of government. Following a fashion started 100 years before, Ramesses III now lived in cities in the Nile delta. The move brought Egypt into closer contact with the other powers in the region and enabled her to confront the nomadic tribes who were pressing ever closer to the Nile valley. It also released the King from the constraints and pressures of the vested interests in the old capital city.

This change of atmosphere at Thebes is clearly reflected in the differing monuments that the two scribes, Ramose and Amennakht, have left us. Ramose, the honest scribe of Ramesses II's day, built whole temples next to the village and stocked both them and the other monuments there with statues, stelae and stone doorways, all inscribed with his name, and that of his Vizier and King. Amennakht, though he became equally as eminent as his ancient counterpart, has left just five stelae as his memorials for eternity and three of these are dedicated to Ptah, who as the god of writing and the arts was his professional patron. By Amennakht's time, the village shrines were jammed with stelae and statues of the gods and dead villagers. Even the houses were burdened with such pieties, for along with the traditional little shrines of the household gods, small busts of the families' ancestors were now installed in the main living rooms. Stillborn babies were sometimes buried under the floors. Amennakht's stelae dedicated to the god Ptah reflect the central occupation of both the scribe and the numerous members of his family. For not only would the family he headed hold the centre of the village during its most dangerous crisis but it also supplied the royal tombs with some of their most talented artists. Amennakht, the son of Ipy, founded six generations of scribes who flourished for more than 100 years; a family of intelligent and independent Thebans. Indeed, it was

Scribe Amennakht himself who composed the poem praising Thebes quoted in the opening chapter of this book:

> What do they say —
> those who are far from Thebes?
> They spend their day blinking at its name,
> if only we had it, they say —

Like Scribe Ramose before him, Amennakht owed his promotion to the position of scribe of the royal tomb to the direct intervention of a vizier, and this official, named To, not only became the benevolent overseer of Amennakht and his family, but of the entire village. In gratitude, Amennakht named one of his sons after the Vizier and, towards the end of Ramesses III's reign, he noted happily in a single line in his accounting book that, after organizing the ceremonies of the royal jubilee, To had been promoted to the dual vizierate of both Upper and Lower Egypt.

Amennakht had established his village household with his wife, the daughter of the Foreman Hay, even before he was appointed as a scribe. The generous rations of wheat allotted to the two foremen and the scribes enabled their households to barter for luxuries with the surplus left over from their kitchens, and Amennakht's house was provided with the most expensive furnishings, the heaviest of copper ewers and cauldrons, and fine furniture. Like the leading villagers, the scribe had a large wardrobe of fine linens, kilts, cloaks, tunics and sandals. Even after his promotion to scribe, Amennakht still continued the craft of painting that his father had taught him, contracting to decorate some of the villagers' coffins. The felicitous mixture of art and scribal accountancy seems to have affected the rest of his household, for several of his sons claim to be scribes in their inscriptions whilst they were also some of the best painters in the gangs. The scribe's large family - and Amennakht had at least nine sons - seems to have inhabited a group of houses at the south end of the village high street. Certainly, the little house upon whose wall Amennakht wrote his name could never have accommodated all his offspring, let alone his household servants, and as a nearby house bears a similar inscription of his eldest son Harshire, we should probably take this whole area, dominating the length of the high street, to be the family domain.

It must have been here then, that King Amenhotep's statue stopped one day during its procession. Minutes before, a sculptor of the tombs named Kaha had appealed to the oracle: 'My Lord, come to my help today. My two garments have been stolen.' Amenmose, a junior scribe, a priest of the village shrines and a soothsayer, was sent for. His grandfather, a friend of Scribe Ramose's, had been a leading figure in the village, a magician, doctor and scorpion-charmer, and had evidently passed his esoteric gifts on to his family. Amenmose joined the procession to read out the names of the village houses as the god was carried down the main street. Then, as the oracle was carried around the corner by Amennakht's house, it indicated that Kaha's clothes were there, 'in the household of his daughter'. Appalled by the accusation, Scribe Amennakht addressed the god directly. 'These clothes of which you talk; is it the child of Amennakht that has taken them?' The god told him that it was. Possibly the ownership of these clothes had been disputed. Equally, it is possible that the unfortunate scribe knew nothing of his daughter's doings. It seems unlikely that the scribe himself, with his chests full of fine linens, would have stolen a workman's wardrobe; indeed this was not the oracle's charge. Certainly, we can imagine how after the god's decisive intervention the two garments were quickly discovered and returned to sculptor Kaha and that afterwards the embarrassed scribe had many things to say to his household.

This statue of King Amenhotep not only judged the living in the village but also the dead, and in the graveyard to the west of the village they were crowded in upon each other with little room for more. The supervision of the graveyard had become a serious problem for both the village tribunal and the district officers, who were responsible for order among the monuments of the west bank. For now the hillside above the village was covered with tomb chapels, and the rock beneath, a loose khaki-coloured shale, was honeycombed with innumerable vaults. Almost half the hillside had been quarried away. The best position for tomb chapels and vaults – high on the hillside in the strong limestone cliffs – had long been occupied by the chapels of leading villagers, whilst the families of lesser workmen had taken the lower sites on the hill in the poor rock down by the village. Even Scribe Kenhirkhopeshef had been forced to make his chapel in a site at the southern tip of the graveyard which, though high on the hill, was set in the heavily fractured stone that subsequently collapsed. Long since, most of the villagers had made do by cutting their burial vaults down from tunnels off the burial vaults of their ancestors. The old chapels above ground had become family shrines whilst underneath lay the family, generation after generation, in vaulted chambers cut one after another ever deeper into the rock, each connected by short stairways. In compensation, perhaps, for the lack of space above ground, the workmen had started to decorate some of these dark burial vaults with bright paintings, commonly using just whitewash and natural red and yellow ochres for their palette. The shale in which most of these vaults were excavated was so friable that the tombmakers could only fashion rude caverns. Inside these oval caves the workmen built small rectangular barrel-vaulted rooms of mud brick, like pitched tents, and it was these little rooms that they decorated with such verve, with scenes of gods and the life in the other world, in a manner that was exactly what you

would expect from skilful craftsmen who, released from the constraining
iconography of the royal tombs, were painting for themselves and their
friends.

By Scribe Amennakht's day, subsidence and collapses in the cemetery
were common, as were collisions between new excavations and old previously sealed vaults that might contain burials laid down centuries before.
Then a committee of village elders and district officers would sally forth
into the cemetery and inspect the newly-discovered tomb with an archaeological precision. One such event happened on a rest day from the work in
the royal tomb in the twenty-first year of Ramesses III's reign, when one of
the villagers, Kha'nun, was working in his tomb chapel. Cutting away in
the hillside low down in the cemetery, he broke through into an old burial
chamber. Together with one of the district officers, who he had most sensibly informed of his discovery, Kha'nun climbed into the chamber and
briefly inspected the burial, then reported his find to the village elders. The
following day a committee, consisting of three village elders, Amennakht,
a recording scribe and the district officer, all went up to the cemetery to
inspect the tomb. At first they were puzzled by the burial, for neither the
coffin nor the scanty grave goods by it had a name upon them. Neither
could they detect the entrance to the old vault. This was important, for the
vault was connected to the surface by a shaft whose mouth would be close
to a family tomb chapel, and that would help to determine whose ancestor
had been brought to light. It was the experienced eye of a foreman, Khonsu,
old Nekhenmut's son, that rescued them from their dilemma, for, as the
official report frostily observes 'he made a discovery as he sat drinking'.
Khonsu detected that the entrance to the ancient tomb was in the wall of
a nearby chapel where another villager, Amenemopet, stood working with
two of his friends. Standing in the tomb Scribe Amennakht shouted up its
shaft to Amenemopet: 'Open up north of the pillar in your chapel, where
I can see the mouth of the shaft.' Thus Amenemopet and his friends uncovered the top of the hidden shaft. Scribe Amennakht, leaving Khonsu
sitting in Kha'nun's tomb, went into Amenemopet's chapel next door and
climbed down the freshly-opened mouth of the dark shaft to arrive back by
the side of the inebriated foreman again. 'Come and see the place which
opens into the tomb of Kha'nun', the energetic scribe shouted back up the
shaft to Amenemopet, and thus inadvertently left us the first record of a
common delight in modern Thebes – squeezing along the dark and dusty
tunnels that connect so many of the ancient tombs and wondering what
you will find at the end.

Poor Amenemopet must have been dismayed at this turn of events for
although he disclaimed all knowledge of the new-found shaft, it was clearly
a part of the tomb in which he and his friends had been working, which, he

claimed, had been granted to an ancestor of his by a mayor of Thebes as long ago as the days of the old dynasty. But his ignorance of this shaft and the unknown burial in the chamber at its bottom cast considerable doubt upon the validity of this inheritance, and such was the pressure to obtain sites in the western graveyard that other people soon began to claim his tomb as their own. So, the next month, the whole problem was put before the oracle of King Amenhotep. Amenemopet says that he stood obediently before the statue and its bearers, and the King said to him 'walk to a tomb amongst the ancestors' and he 'gave me the tomb ... by a writing'. Probably the oracle made a choice between a number of alternatives that had been written out and placed before him. Finally, after a good deal of oath-swearing, 'to have my nose and ears cut off' if perjury was committed, Amenemopet was recognized as the true owner of the tomb and started work in it once again. Presumably he and his friends now planned further burials for themselves in the chamber below. But this was not the end of the matter. Three years later the village court heard a complaint from Amenemopet that another villager had thrown one of his family's burials out of the tomb chamber. The case dragged on and the graveyard, undermined by all its funeral vaults in the rotten rock, received more and more mummies, rich and poor alike, whilst the village elders tried to keep some order in the place.

The following year another burial was exposed in a ruined tomb close to Amennakht's own funerary monument. Once again the commission was convened and once again Foreman Khonsu and the district officers (the reporting scribe, on this occasion Amennakht himself, does not report whether the foreman was drunk or sober) sallied out to the cemetery, where the two scribes hastily made an inventory of the grave goods before resealing the tomb. Along with two mummies in their coffins, they found two luxurious cosmetic boxes, one for a woman, the other for a man. The man's held razors, cloths and the like; the woman's tweezers, cosmetics, perfumes and a small blue-glazed charm: the contents of many a modern handbag. There were also furniture and clothes in the tomb, presumably from the couple's household, but no name was found in the chamber. It had been a rich burial but placed in an unstable vault in the rock of the tottering hillside.

At the same time as recording these early archaeological excavations in the village cemetery, Amennakht was also supervising 'every task in the Place of Pharaoh', where his activities left their mark on the surviving work-records. He also officiated at the village tribunal, indeed it was Amennakht who recorded the final settlement in the eighteen-year litigation concerning Medjay Mentmose and the jar of fat, and he also oversaw many other contracts and bargains that were struck in the small community. On a small weight one finds an inscription stating that it had been 'checked by the Scribe Amennakht'; on an ostracon he noted that when he arrived at the Great Place one day with a gang of thirty-two men, they found, to their surprise, 'a donkey which had passed inside, as well as an old man'. It sounds as if the guards had been sleeping late again.

As a man of his time, Amennakht was as affected as the other villagers by the growing fear of the gods' capriciousness, of the power of fate, and he owned a calendar which told him the days that were lucky and the days that were not. Such calendars were of ancient origin but were coming into common use again in Amennakht's time. Each day of this calendar was divided into thirds and each division was separately described as auguring well or ill. In the entire ancient year of 365 days, a fraction over half the days were considered 'good' in all their thirds, a tenth held mixed fortunes, and the remainder were days of complete ill-omen. Some of these almanacs also forecast the fate of those born on specific days:

> Whoever is born on this day will die of old age.
> Whoever is born on this day will die of plague.

It is probable that on the days these calendars identified as inauspicious, no work was done at the Great Place. Some days, indeed, were considered so dangerous that the almanac advised its readers to stay indoors altogether!

But such dates in the calendar were only a small percentage of the many breaks in the work at the royal tomb: there were also state festivals, personal and family festivals, regular rest days and other village events. Like most non-industrial societies, Pharaonic Egypt usually underemployed its labour force: late in the reign of Ramesses III it is probable that the tomb-makers worked only one day in four at the royal tombs. And in the early years of the reign the Feasts of the Valley and of Opet were made six days longer than in Ramose's day and some eleven days longer than they had been during the old dynasty.

Quite unusually, it was decided that Ramesses III's tomb would be excavated as a continuation of the first tomb of his father Setnakht – the one that had collapsed into Amenmesse's. Perhaps it was felt that, like the villagers' own cemetery, the royal burying ground was running out of suitable sites for tombs. However, by turning at right-angles near the end of the tomb's original corridor, and then back again after a short distance, the tomb was continued on a parallel course to its original axis and further collisions were avoided. Throughout the long reign the gangs quarried ever deeper into the cliff and finally cut a huge and quite complete tomb. It was the first one they had finished since the reign of King Merneptah.

As a senior scribe Amennakht officiated during a visit to the Great Place of specialist stonemasons brought for a specific task in the King's tomb:

The King's butler Amenkhew brought the four chief alabaster-cutters — together with two men [labourers?]. They were escorted down the sloping passage [of the King's tomb] and the Scribe Amennakht shut them in the tomb. They spent the night working the outside and inside of the alabaster shrine until dawn. They finished it and it was painted with figures.

This alabaster shrine was probably designed to hold four pots containing the King's viscera, which would be removed from his corpse during the process of mummification. Unless this special task had to be performed in concert with the movements of the heavens or the like it is difficult to imagine the need for a night-shift; but then so little of the ritual that surrounded the work of making royal burials is known to us. Despite such fits of hard work, the long reign allowed the gangs a respite from the furious activities of the previous two decades. Nevertheless, though Ramesses III's tomb was finished years before he died, pigments were again issued to the draughtsmen in his twenty-ninth year, and the gangs returned to the tomb, where they cut right through Setnakht's wall texts to make a series of eight small chambers, four on each side of the corridor. These little rooms were miniature warehouses, their walls exotically painted as if filled with the paraphernalia of a royal palace. One scribe, perhaps Amennakht himself, wrote brief labels over each of their doorways: 'The Treasury', 'The Hall', 'House of Food' and so on. These little rooms are unique and it is easy to imagine that individual inspiration, probably the King's, prompted their appearance in the royal tomb.

The gangs also made tombs for several of the Crown Princes: one in the Great Place itself and others in the Place of Beauty, where the earlier kings had made tombs mainly for their wives and mothers. The fragmentary ostraca of the village scribes give us brief glimpses of the progress of the work: 'The tomb of the King's son — work in it finished in year twenty-four'; 'Working in the tomb of the charioteer of Ramesses III'. This last was probably the tomb of the Crown Prince in charge of the royal stables, the 'first king's son of his Majesty, Prahirwenemef'. Old Nekhenmut, Ipy's successor as foreman to Paneb's old gang, built himself a shelter in the Place of Beauty during the excavation and decoration of these princes' tombs, as, doubtless did others in the gangs. Here too, Nekhenmut's son, Khonsu, had a stela carved upon the cliff face with a scene showing himself, a group of workmen and Vizier To all praying to Meretseger, the goddess of the peak rising above them.

Nekhenmut and Khonsu supervised at least five tombs in the Place of Beauty. All were for Ramesses' Crown Princes, all were as regular and neat as a close in a housing estate, brightly coloured and of equal size. Their wall scenes show Ramesses III leading each of his sons into the presence of the gods. The atmosphere in them is almost festive: gay and light with careless mannered drawing. But why, one might wonder, was such a uniform group of tombs required for five crown princes at the same time? It is possible of course that they had died in an epidemic, perhaps the victims of an ancient virus. Alternatively it has been suggested that the five princes were killed by their father at a single stroke. From the first days of his reign Ramesses III had been determined to avoid the dynastic vendettas that had bedevilled his predecessors: even the scenes in his temple showing the processions of princes left their names blank, their order indeterminate. This explanation is more faithful to the spirit of the age, for such things were real possibilities. Even the King himself had been the subject of a lurid harem plot hatched in his Theban palace involving magic, poison and judicial corruption. Several of the conspirators, queens, courtiers, judges and army men, were tried and either executed or invited to commit suicide. The conspiracy may well have been an attempt by a group of Theban nobles, many of whom bore their city's name as part of their own, to dispose of an absentee king. When Ramesses III stayed at Thebes security was strict.

During the later part of the King's reign Thebes finally ceased to be a political centre in the nation. The massive royal temple compound on the west bank with its fortified wall was the major royal presence at the Southern City. Two Syrian-style military gateways gave access to the teeming fourteen-acre city inside. The houses of the temple's administrators and priests, traditionally situated in rambling enclosures outside the temple walls, had been brought inside the fortress, where the staff were accommodated in regular rows of rectangular houses built between the temple magazines and the fortifications. By the side of the royal temple a palace contained the King's bedroom and harem whilst loggias and other royal apartments were set high in the fortified gateways. The King had withdrawn from Thebes and this massive fortress had become the centre of royal power in the old sacred capital. Still, with the great royal building projects mostly completed, with harvests as rich as ever and the wealth of the city and its temples growing and growing, what did it matter if Thebes was becoming a political backwater and the King and his court were far away, or if the quality of the workmanship in the royal tombs was generally poor, slapdash even, when compared with the work of Paneb's and Neferhotep's gangs? Certainly the villagers' art was decidedly inferior to the magnificent scenes that far less privileged workmen had carved on to the walls of Ramesses III's mortuary temple. Indeed, with its curious colours and idiosyncratic styles, the work of the village painters and sculptors was now quite different from the art of the rest of Thebes. And this, symbolically, exemplifies the village's growing plight. For the King had left Thebes, and the villagers were the King's men, working on the royal tomb, provisioned from the royal temples. Their exclusive community had existed for centuries with little direct contact with the usual processes of daily life and food production. The men that made the royal underworlds, holders of esoteric skills and mysteries beyond the imagination of most of their countrymen, lived like orchids in the desert. But Egypt was changing and the survival, not of the state, but of the individual inside the state machine, was becoming the villagers' first priority.

17

STRIKE

In about the twenty-fifth year of King Ramesses III's reign, one of Amen-nakht's junior scribes, a certain Neferhotep, wrote a letter to the office of the Vizier To telling of the gangs' progress in the Place of Beauty: 'I am working on the princes' tombs which my Lord [the King] has commissioned to be made. I am working very well; do not let my Lord worry about them for the work is excellent. I do not become negligent at all.' So far so good, it seems; but then the letter continues:

> We are impoverished. All the supplies for us that are from the treasury, the granary, and the storehouse have been allowed to be exhausted. The stone [of the Place of Beauty] is not light. One and a half hundredweight of grain has been taken away from us ... [i.e. is missing from the ration] ... make for us a means of keeping alive ... we are dying, we do not live at all. '

Why had the villagers suddenly become so desperate? The Nile flood was still as regular and as rich as ever and supplies of fish and other foods were delivered regularly to the village by its own servants. It hardly seems possible that in an age of such plenty the royal tombmakers would actually be starving, and one imagines that the office of the vizier would not seriously believe it possible either. After all, the village grain rations were always at least half a month in arrears; the scribes kept careful account of that. And even if, by some administrative quirk, the village really was hungry, the tombmakers were wealthy men and could easily have bought wheat in the Theban markets. Further, some of the villagers had special food stores away from their village: Foreman Nekhenmut, as we have seen, was robbed of bread and other foods from his storeroom by the river bank. So there never had been a real fear of hunger at the village, and the disruption of their supplies described in the letter would hardly have caused the physical suffering that Scribe Neferhotep suggests.

None the less, it appears that a large part of the monthly wheat ration was not arriving at the village and, with the limited storage facilities available in the little houses, there would indeed have been a wheat shortage within a few weeks. With some 500 people dependent upon the regular

23 The splendid ruin of the Ramesseum, a centre of west bank administration in the time of the tombmakers.

Overleaf 24 Foreman Anhirkawi with his wife, children and grandchildren, painted in the family vault by a village outline draughtsman.

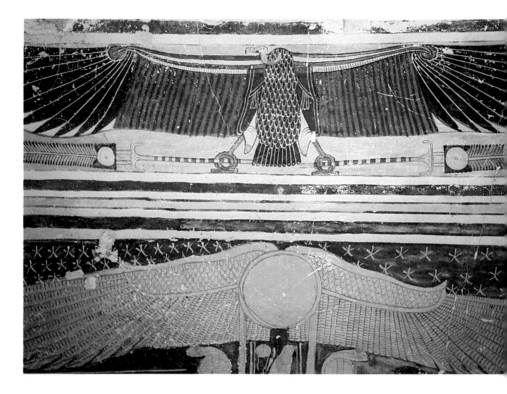

Village artists at work: *Previous pages* 25 A double image of sunset. The goddess Nut swallows the sun and the dead king who will pass through her to be reborn from her womb at sunrise. *Above* 26 Ceiling leading to the burial chamber of Ramesses VI's tomb. Here, the sun's vultures give way to the winged sun-disc that travels through the night underworld. *Below* 27 Anubis revitalizes the mummy of tombmaker Nakhtamun. The colour scheme of this burial vault is reminiscent of the ceilings of many royal tombs.

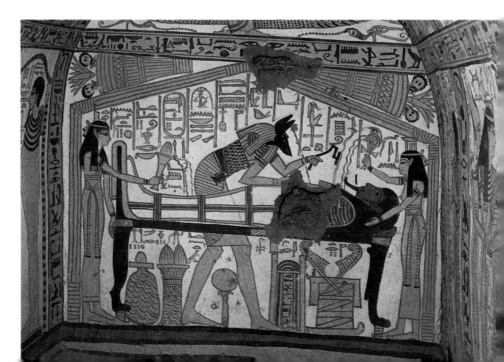

Village artists at work: 28 Detail of an astronomical ceiling. Such star charts were used by temple priests to measure the hours of the night: the stages of the dead king's journey to his dawn resurrection.

29 A typical wall in Ramesses IX's tomb, lit by sunlight. This work, of outlining, graving and colouring, attained an especial brilliance in the last tombs that the villagers made.

30 The supreme example of the outline draughtsmen's skills: Prince Montuhirkhopeshef offering to his gods, a detail from his tomb in the Valley of the Kings.

deliveries of such rations to the desert village – the sixty or so tombworkers as well as their families and servants – the village had become a large consumer of the state resources at Thebes. And wheat had a remarkably stable market value, one sack of about a hundredweight – one *khar* – being worth about two-fifths of a pound – two *deben* – of copper. A workman's monthly ration, four *khar*, would feed about sixteen people on the village diet. Foremen and scribes' rations were more than a third larger than that – a total of eleven pounds of bread per family every day in a diet that also included a variety of other foods as well. So with families and dependants numbering, on average, eight or ten people, it was a very generous ration, one unequalled in other ancient societies and, indeed, in many countries today. Through the reduction of their grain ration the tombmakers were actually being deprived of a regular income, being caught in a *financial* squeeze. What at first sight appears to be a pathetic appeal for sustenance is nothing less than a heart-felt complaint by a member of a professional middle class couched in the hyperbole of the day.

Late in the second month of Ramesses III's twenty-ninth year – in July 1152 BC – Scribe Amennakht was also caught up in these disputes about the wheat ration. 'This day,' he announced to the gangs, 'twenty days have elapsed in the month and rations have not been given to us.' In the pounding summer heat he walked down from the valley of the village and across the sand to the temple of King Horemheb which stood next to the looming temple-fortress of Ramesses III. There, royal officials 'brought forty-six *khar* of wheat' which were delivered to the villagers just 'two days later'. It is on the same ostracon that he used to record his protest that Amennakht also noted that 'The office of the King promoted the Vizier To to be the Vizier of the Land of Upper and Lower Egypt'; an indication perhaps that the administration had not performed well, and that the amalgamation of these two offices was an attempt to increase its efficiency. Amennakht went to a royal temple to protest at the lack of rations because it was from the temple granaries that the village wheat came. Presumably this was also where the officials that controlled the grain supplies worked. At a most conservative estimate the grain magazines of the temple of King Horemheb could hold – and this in an enclosure that has not yet been fully excavated – sufficient stocks to last the village for ten years. And the 120 magazines of Horemheb's temple were of comparatively modest size; the twenty largest buildings in the vast complex of granaries built by the temple of Ramesses II – long barrel-vaulted chambers of mud brick – each held more than two years' supplies for the village! The reserves of grain at Thebes – taken from all over Egypt – were colossal. Why then, this sudden squeeze?

For one thing, it is likely that the extravagant enterprise of Ramesses III's building programme at Thebes had temporarily depleted the Theban grain reserves during the last ten years of the reign. Although the temple granaries could easily cushion the effects of a succession of bad harvests – a reputation that these 'granaries of Pharaoh' hold in the Bible – after many years of feeding large workforces of masons and labourers stocks may have been unusually low. As an outlying flank of the royal economy, the tombmakers had become highly vulnerable to fluctuations in the royal fortunes and, in times of stress, would be the first to feel ill effects. There was also a growing corruption at this time: one small temple alone lost more than 90 per cent of its northern grain revenues to corrupt officials; this amount, though a mere drop in Egypt's ocean of grain, would have sustained the village ration for a third of a year. And this embezzlement went undetected for ten years.

Vizier To's appointment to the dual vizierates seems to have brightened the tombmakers' immediate prospects and mollified the fears of the village elders. First, it seems, they began to investigate and overhaul the gangs of men acting as servants and food-suppliers to the village – a tactful move if the tombmakers were suffering a loss of prestige and feeling that, like Thebes herself, they were set apart from the main enterprises of the age. In the month following Amennakht's complaints in Horemheb's temple, he and his fellow-scribe took stock of the village servants. There were some twenty-three of them in all: six water-carriers; three gardeners, each with an assistant, who grew produce in fields specially allotted to the village; four fishermen who supplied fish to the village in quantities set by the scribes; three woodcutters who brought the fuel for the village bread-ovens; a potter and a washerman. And as well as these, there was also a storekeeper whose son made plaster; destined, presumably, for the improvement of the village houses. The assignment and augmentation of these village servants was overseen by doorkeeper Khaemwase who acted in his legal capacity as assistant to the scribes: 'Statement of the doorkeeper Khaemwase before the scribe of the tomb and the two foremen — I will allot twelve water-carriers to the right hand, and twelve to the left, total twenty-four.' And along with these water-carriers, there were fourteen woodcutters, twelve gardeners and eight potters and, intended, perhaps, as a sweetener for the unhappy community, a cake-maker was allotted to each of the gangs. Previously their pastries and sweet cakes had been sent to the village from the temples.

Although the Vizier may have calmed the fears of the village elders, the men of the two gangs were far from happy, for the food deliveries to the village still arrived late and in paltry quantities. Their confidence in the administration was badly shaken. Slowly, the wealth of the tombmakers was being eroded, and they felt neglected and ill-cared for.

Tempers finally broke on 14 November 1152 BC, in the twenty-ninth year of the King, when the two gangs stopped their work and marched together out of the Great Place. The senior men, the two foremen, their deputies and the Scribe Amennakht had no idea where they had gone. They walked down from the village in search of them to the huge complex of Ramesses III, now set behind its massive fortifications, and walked right through it, but still could not find the gangs. Leaving Ramesses' compound, they went along the line of royal temples and eventually found the men sitting together behind the temple of Tuthmosis III, one of the old dynasty's legendary kings, whose temple's magazines had often supplied the villagers in the past. Gathered together on this patch of high ground right in the centre of the necropolis, their presence alone advertised their discontent. The elders called out to them but were met, Scribe Amennakht recorded, with 'great oaths'. 'We are hungry,' the crews claimed; 'eighteen days have passed this month', and they had still not received their proper rations. So the elders went back to the village, a short walk across the little white desert, and in the evening, as the light shone across the silver sand and lit it like the surface of the moon, the gangs too, returned home.

The next morning the men set off across the mountain to the Great Place, but still they were not in a mood for work; again they left the royal valley. This time they headed for the temple of Ramesses II, whose altar-offerings had so often supplied the village with copious deliveries of bread. The men entered the temple compound through a small gate in the south wall of the enclosure which gave them access to a corridor running along the side of the temple and into the courtyards of the vast grain magazines. By entering the temple compound the gangs had taken a serious step. One of Amennakht's colleagues, the scribe Patwere, two doorkeepers and some of the guards of the Great Place now kept an official eye on the angry gangs. But the chief medjay Mentmose, he of the litigated fat jar, sympathized with the men's cause. Telling them that he would bring the Mayor of Thebes to see them, he went down to the river, crossed over to the east side, met the Mayor and told him that the tombmakers had entered the temple's compound. Unfortunately the Mayor's remedy for the situation, if such there was, has been lost to us in a break in Amennakht's papyrus but certainly he did not produce a solution, for the strike continued. Things were not too bad, however. Whilst Mentmose was seeking out the Mayor, Scribe Patwere had seized the opportunity of being away from the royal tomb on a work-day and bought himself fifty-five little cakes, of a special variety that was not baked in the village. Possibly they had been made in the ovens of a nearby temple compound which had often baked sweetmeats for the village. At all events, the receipt of this purchase written amongst the account of the strike again emphasizes that the villagers were striking more because of low morale and diminished income than the hunger that their speeches proclaim.

No one came to see the men as they sat by the grain magazines, and at the day's end they decided not to return to their village but to spend the night by the temple's gate. There they must have sat in the evening on the warm sand and talked, eating their bread and onions and drinking their beer, the yellow light glancing low across the fields and the farmers leading their animals past them as they walked home in the golden light. Then as the sun died, the huge seated statues of King Amenhotep, still standing in the ruins of his temple, faded black in the starry sky. The next day, a rose-misty autumn dawn, the temple priests took statements of the men's grievances. Once again the workmen appealed for the King to remember them: 'It was because of hunger and thirst that we came here. There is no clothing, no fat, no fish, no vegetables. Send to Pharaoh our good Lord about it, and send to the Vizier our superior that we may be provided for.'

After the men's statement had been recorded, the rations of the previous month, now some six weeks late, were finally handed over to them and the men left for their homes. The following morning, they returned to work in the Great Place. Medjay Mentmose still remained incensed at the neglect of the men and, as the gangs were at the police post by their settlement above the royal valley, he addressed them in a fiery speech: 'Look, I will tell you my opinion. Go and gather your tools, seal your doors, bring your wives and your children and I will lead you to the temple of Seti I, and I will let you settle there.' But the gangs had had enough and they returned to work. After all, the novelty of their actions must have produced considerable strains within their ranks. They stayed angry enough, however, to walk out of the Great Place again the following month; this time a nasty quarrel broke out between a workman and two foremen and the scribes who went to collect them. 'By Amun and by the ruler whose power is greater than death, if they take me up from here today, I will lie down in my tomb!' swore workman Mose, who refused to budge. But by taking the names of the gods in such an angry way, Mose had committed blasphemy; neatly sidestepping the whole issue of the strike, the village elders beat him for his swearing, there and then.

Once more the gangs were encouraged to return to work, but this did not prevent them from walking out again a short while later, to the shouts of the scribes and foremen, who, in their turn, had become exasperated. This time the men were cleverer and colder in their negotiations and when the district officers and Scribe Amennakht went to see them to get them back to work they were given a new and more serious statement of the gangs' grievances by two of the senior workmen, who stood in front of the others and represented them. 'Tell your superiors we will not return!' they said. 'It was not because we hungered that we left the royal valley. We have an important statement to make: Evil is done in this place of Pharaoh.' The men of the gangs, like the foremen and the scribes, were bound under oath to report any irregularities that occurred in the Great Place and they knew that even Paneb, whilst he was still a stonemason, had denounced a vizier and caused his dismissal. Now the angry workmen were pointing the same dangerous finger of accusation, but this time, without naming names, they made a veiled threat to those members of the administration whom they held responsible for their diminished rations. As before, we should doubt their claim of having been reduced to poverty. Just three months before the strike one of the two men now airing these menacing grievances had spent the equivalent of four months' full wheat rations on a coffin and other pieces of funeral equipment, and there could be no clearer indication that it was the village's living standards that were under threat. We may detect in the men's actions all the indignation of those who felt entrusted with deep secrets and grave responsibilities, yet despite this had been forgotten by their masters. Don't forget us, they seem to be saying, for we are part of your wider fortunes in the royal administration; loyal servants we may be, but we demand your proper attention. The lack of focus in their complaints shows the diffuse air of demoralization which had spread throughout the village.

However vague these charges of tampering with the royal tombs may have been, they were serious enough to prompt Scribe Amennakht to wash down the old papyrus on which, amongst other things, he had already recorded the main events of the gangs' strikes, and compile a full record of the new disputes. It is this document in all its sharp detail that has survived: a report written by a scribe who felt himself vulnerable to the gangs' accusations, making careful note of all their claims and listing those, such as Medjay Mentmose, who had supported the workers' actions. Scribe Amennakht knew that the gangs' denunciation was a two-edged sword and could easily rebound upon them if the claim, rather than being accepted, was held to be malicious and without foundation. With the gangs and the village elders at odds, mud had started to fly once again.

Vizier To heard of the village strikes later that same year, when he was sailing downstream from Thebes collecting together the gods of Upper Egypt from their temples to join the ceremonies of the King's thirty-year jubilee, which was to be held in the north of Egypt. (A further indication of the lessening political importance of Thebes.) He left a message for the villagers with the chief of the Theban medjay: 'It was not because I had nothing to bring you that I did not come,' he said. 'As for you saying "do not give away our ration", do I, the Vizier, give in order to take away? If it had happened that there was nothing, even in the granaries, I would have given you that which I found.' It was a cleverly paternal speech that pushed the villagers' grievances aside whilst at the same time telling them that he knew of their hardships and cared about them all. This was followed by an announcement by a village scribe that half a month's grain ration would be distributed on the spot – but as this was only half the amount already owed them the gesture was hardly the example of regal largesse that the Vizier had intended! It also revealed a lack of proper communication between the Vizier and his villagers.

Four days later, when only a fraction of the proper amounts had been supplied for the monthly ration, Foreman Khonsu himself took a hand in the workmen's dispute. He was convinced that it was the lower administration which was stopping the village's full rations and that the Vizier still did not know the sad story of the past three months. Members of the Vizier's staff were staying on a river boat moored at Thebes, perhaps the same vessel that had earlier collected the half-month's grain rations from the temple magazines of Upper Egypt, and the foreman believed that a direct confrontation was the best course. As scribe Amennakht parcelled out the grain ration Foreman Khonsu addressed the men: ' take the ration and go down to the harbour.' Then the Vizier's staff would see the truth of the matter with their own eyes. The foreman's words swayed the men and when the scribe finished dispensing the ration they started off out of the royal valley once again. But the sight of a village elder deserting the ranks of the administration and siding with the men of the gangs proved too much for Scribe Amennakht. As the gangs passed the first checkpoint on their way up out of the Great Place, he angrily threatened them: 'I have given you a hundredweight of wheat in this hour, do not go to the harbour; if you do I will put you in the wrong in any court you go to!' The scribe's own record of the affair relates that he finally won the day and, ignoring the pleas of Foreman Khonsu, the men returned again to their work. (Incidentally, on the same day that Amennakht wrote all this into his records he also recorded that Scribe Patwere, the man who bought sweet cakes at Ramesses II's temple in the early days of the strikes, had died. He must have been a close friend of Amennakht's, for the scribe had named his third son after him.)

Two months later the villagers were protesting in the temples yet again. This time the Mayor of Thebes intervened and supplied the village with some twenty-four sacks of grain which, he specified, were to serve only until the royal administration had managed to organize regular supplies once more. Some of the villagers believed the Mayor was one of the officials holding back rations from the village. People felt that they were being cheated and feelings continued to run high. The villagers knew the route by which their grain usually reached the village and now they were trying to discover where it had gone. 'I will go to Thebes and to the High Priest of Amun and there accuse the Mayor of Thebes of not giving us the bread of the divine offerings from the temple of Ramesses II. He has committed a great crime!'

There was more to be said, too, about the 'evil done in this place of Pharaoh', for under the stress and agitation of the strikes the old village feud re-emerged. One of Paneb's youngest sons, Pa'anuket, was now working in a gang at the royal tomb, and he seized upon the mood of dissatisfaction in the village to make his own, very specific denunciations. In a statement to Scribe Amennakht and Foreman Khonsu whom he calls 'my superiors — the controllers of the tomb' he claimed that two prominent workmen - one a son of Scribe Amennakht, the other a long-standing friend of his family - had been stripping stones from a royal tomb in the Great Place. This, as Pa'anuket pointed out, was exactly the same crime that his father had been accused of many years before. Even one of the men who had earlier spoken up to denounce 'evil done in this place of Pharaoh' was himself now denounced by Pa'anuket; and not only for stealing stones from King Ramesses II's tomb but also from a tomb holding some of the royal children. For good measure Pa'anuket accused yet another man, a close associate of Amennakht's, of taking a branded ox from the temple of Ramesses II and now 'it is standing in his stall'. This same man was also accused of seducing the obligatory three women and, like Paneb's alleged amours, these were the wives of prominent villagers, one being the wife of one of Scribe Amennakht's sons. 'Now,' said Pa'anuket, 'let me see what you will do to them or I will make a complaint to the Pharaoh my Lord and also to the Vizier.' It was a statement worthy of Paneb's own accusers.

Quite suddenly the proper quotas of rations began to reach the village again and now, for the first time, a number of workmen - including Scribe Amennakht's eldest son Harshire, then training for his father's post - were put to checking and distributing the rations as they arrived at the village, doubtless to ensure a fair distribution. The anger in the gangs subsided, and throughout the two remaining years of Ramesses III's reign the village's food was delivered regularly and its accounts properly maintained.

18

VIZIER AND HIGH PRIEST

The strikes created a new situation at the village, for never before in its history had the scribes and foremen – the 'chiefs', as they were known – sided so completely with the authorities and against the workmen as Scribe Amennakht and Foreman Anhirkawi had done. They had told their men that they were asking for more than they could hope to get. Scribe Amennakht, indeed, had even threatened to take the workmen to a court, and thus throughout most of the strikes the men of the two gangs had acted alone. Only at the very beginning of the trouble had the chiefs supported them, as was their traditional role as the spokesmen and protectors of the men. The immediate effect of this split in the village ranks had been to promote new spokesmen for the two gangs: at different times they had been led by some of the senior workmen, a chief medjay, and even the most junior of the two foremen, Khonsu, impulsively acting against his colleagues. Nevertheless, real authority still resided in the handful of families from which the chiefs came. It was on their recommendation to the office of the vizier that all new appointments to the gangs were made from amongst the workmen's numerous children, who had mostly to leave the small community when they were grown. Even promotion inside the gangs, from the posts of workmen and quarrymen to those of painters and sculptors, was decided by the chiefs alone. Along with a small group of senior workmen whom they had promoted, these same men also sat on the bench of the village tribunal. Thus they controlled not only the work at the King's tomb, but also the life of the village.

Such arrangements were, of course, traditional, and generally worked harmoniously and effectively; indeed it is largely the activities of these chiefs that the scribes have so richly documented. Now for the first time a class-division had opened up inside the small community. This split was emphasized by the differing degrees of wealth inside the village: for even those at the periphery of the chief's power-base, like the doorkeepers who, as the civic representatives of the state, also acted as bailiffs and tax-collectors, were, by village standards, relatively wealthy men. The doorkeeper Khaemwase, for example, who before the strikes began had reorganized the village servant-allocation, owned oxen worth the equivalent of several years' grain rations for a man of the gangs, whilst his direct superior, Scribe Hori, not only owned several of these mountainous beasts, which required a continuous heavy expense in feed, but could afford to barter two of them in part-exchange for some of his funeral equipment. If at the time of the strikes the men of the gangs felt their wealth and status were being slowly eroded by the diminishing ration, these village elders seem to have remained as rich as ever. There were now two separate groups living at the village, and their aims and fortunes were not bound as closely as they had once been: the traditional pattern of village society had changed.

This division at the village followed realignments, and even conflicts, inside the state administration. There had been no material reason for the villagers' rations to begin to dry up. Egypt was as grain-rich as ever. As we have seen, even at the height of their protests the Mayor of Thebes had a sufficient surplus in his granaries to give a large quantity of grain to the tombmakers when they appealed to him in person. But at the same time the King's own representative and the village's immediate superior, Vizier To, had been embarrassed by the meagre supplies that his officers commanded in the Southern City. Certainly, this was a consequence of the King and his court moving from Thebes to the north of Egypt. As early as the reign of Merneptah, Scribe Kenhirkhopeshef had complained to his vizier of a breakdown in the supply of materials for the work on the King's tomb, caused, he noted, by the absence of the court from Thebes. How much worse, then, the situation had become now the court had left the Southern City for good and the Vizier was a remote politician governing, for most of the time, from a palace some 500 miles away. Neglected by their traditional benefactors, the villagers found themselves caught between different sections of the government and supplied by neither. In this situation they appealed, as we have seen, not to Vizier To in the distant delta, but to the local power at Thebes, the High Priest of Amun: 'I will go to Thebes, to the High Priest of Amun, and there accuse the Mayor of Thebes ...' an angry villager cried after months of protest.

The royal cure for these administrative bottlenecks had been to appoint Vizier To as the dual Vizier of Upper and Lower Egypt, thus uniting disparate offices of government. Then, at a later date, an intermediate supervising body between the tombmakers and the Vizier was appointed: the Theban High Priests of Amun, the overlords of the colossal temples of Karnak. Within a few years of the strikes the High Priests were in direct control of the work in the Great Place: transmitting correspondence between the scribes of the King's tomb and the Vizier, delivering the village rations to the tombmakers, and taking charge of the resmelting and supply of copper chisels and some of the other building materials.

The temples of Karnak were the most powerful institutions at Thebes, the religious heart of Egypt, and through the ages various kings had deliberately appointed non-Thebans, tried and favoured bureaucrats, to the office of the high priesthood – doubtless so that they might keep close control of the god's enormous domains. But such was the gravity and splendour of this immense office that, like Thomas à Becket in his time, the kings' appointees usually surrendered their temporal allegiance to the great god Amun and maintained a hegemony quite separate from the royal administration and the civil authorities of Thebes. Nevertheless, inside this framework the High Priests were always loyal to the kingship, indeed in the performance of their duties as Amun's priests they acted as ritual substitutes for the king while many of the major events of the religious calendar were still conducted by the king himself who sailed south especially to lead the ceremonials.

Following the example of his predecessors, Ramesses III had appointed two non-Thebans in succession, both sons of his chief taxing-master, to the office of high priest. This tax official, a certain Priest Merybast, came from Hermopolis 100 miles north of Thebes, and had taken up his position as the highest economic functionary of the administration in the fortified compound of Ramesses's temple on the Theban west bank. Not only did Ramesses appoint his sons to the high priesthood but, after Merybast's death, he gave the post of taxing-master to the High Priest's children. Thus this one family held considerable sway over the affairs of Amun and Pharaoh for a long time, and played a major role in the rebalancing of power in the Southern City. Indeed, it may well have been during the early phases of this change, whilst the Vizier's officers and the High Priest were setting up their new lines of authority at Thebes, that the supply of villagers' rations had dried up. Three years later, however, the administration was working in reasonable harmony again, and the villagers enjoyed regular supplies for the next forty years.

Following the new connection between the High Priests of Amun and the tombmakers it is no great surprise to find that late in the reign of Ramesses III the villagers were working on reliefs in a temple at Karnak, that of Amun's son Khonsu, which, unlike Ramesses III's splendid temple across the river, was being cobbled together by the Amun priesthood from the stones of older buildings. Here the villagers made their characteristic reliefs inside the innermost chambers of the temple, miserably poor work for the most part in sandstone, a medium that they were not used to handling. Off and on they would continue to work in this ugly little building for several generations. It may well have been the direct influence of this work with the High Priest and his colossal temples that prompted the increase in the size and dignity of the royal tombs of the Great Place. For from this time onwards, the corridors of the royal tombs stand as firm as the inside of the Theban temples. The bright reliefs on the doorways proclaimed the power and piety of the high priesthood in financing such enterprises on the west bank of Thebes and, their ultimate allegiance to their ephemeral ruler, the absent king.

Ramesses III was probably the last king in whose reign Thebes maintained the delicate balance of a true feudal state. In the early decades of his rule the country regained some of its old confidence, and though future kings would still hold the trappings of Pharaoh and be honoured in the Theban temples, the unity of the pious state would split into the joint components of public politicization and individual piety. The news of Ramesses III's death, in the thirty-second year of his rule, travelled swiftly to the men of the Great Place: 'Third month of summer, day sixteen [18 April 1149 BC] Chief Medjay Mentmose came to say to the people of the tomb: "The Falcon King Usermaatre-miamun, Son of Re— [Ramesses III] has flown up to Heaven, and the King Usermaatre Setepenamun [Ramesses IV], son of Re Ramesses-miamun sits on the throne of Re in his place".' That same day the scribe's work-journal noted simply that 'The Falcon has flown up to Heaven.' Though the kings lived and died in the north of Egypt, they would always return to Thebes for their burial in the Great Place. On 6 June that same year, the royal funeral equipment was carried to the tomb, the heavier pieces of statuary and furniture being dragged up the long valley leading from the plain, in temperatures of well over 100 degrees Fahrenheit. Twenty days later the royal funeral procession brought the King himself to his tomb, where he was laid in his fine pink sarcophagus; as the Greek traveller Herodotus would report some 600 years later, the time between death and burial in royal Egypt was precisely seventy days.

Four days after the burial, a senior member of the new King's staff came to the Great Place and confirmed some promotions in the two gangs. Before setting off for the north again he also rewarded the gangs for their efforts under the summer's sun. As well as receiving silver vases 'from Askelon' (probably sent originally to the vizier's office from Palestine), Foreman Anhirkawi received gifts of fine linens, oils, honey and cream and some extra supplies of basic foods. So delighted was he at this most unusual display of vizierial benevolence that he had its details written upon two stelae which were set up in his tomb chapel and the village Hathor chapel; a permanent record of his high favour at the royal court.

Unfortunately, the official response to Pa'anuket's complaints about the 'evil done in this place of Pharaoh' is lost to us but as the people whom he denounced seem to have suffered not the least discomfort, we may safely assume that the dog it was that died and that Pa'anuket was condemned for perjury. Certainly his name disappears from the village records after this time, and it is especially interesting, therefore, that an inscription of a certain Pa'anuket is to be found on the rocks of a desert quarry some seventy miles from Thebes, deep in the Wadi Hammamat. Miscreants were often sentenced to stone-breaking as a punishment and it is likely that Paneb's son ended his days in this desolate corridor of bruise-black rocks, quarrying its hard stone.

There was a kind of a mania for blocks of such stone in the reign of Ramesses IV. In the first year of his rule there were two major expeditions to the quarries of the Hammamat, in the second, another, and in the third a colossal expedition of more than 8000 men and a group of court officials was led to the quarries by no less a person than the High Priest of Amun, Ramessesnakht. All these expeditions were recorded in inscriptions both official and unofficial, in grandiose hieroglyphs cut on to the hard rock of the windy valley by skilled sculptors and by the graffiti of workmen and junior scribes who tapped away on the cliffs to leave a lightly cut but permanent record of their adventure in this place, with its cruel climate and dangerous quarries. Concerning the gigantic expedition in the King's third year, the official record carefully lists all the participants of this daunting trip and numbers them in their professions, all that is except 'the dead; who are excluded from the list; 900 in number'. Huge blocks of stone were dragged slowly to the river from the Hammamat, some recorded at sizes that must have weighed forty tons or more and would have required hundreds of men to haul them on rollers of wood and balls of stone to the temples of Upper Egypt where they were destined to be used either as building-blocks or for statues. When the massive stones came to western Thebes, after being rafted across the Nile, they were pulled to the temple stoneyards by gangs that sometimes included not only the servants of the village and, even, units of the Theban medjay, but also the royal tomb-makers themselves.

Two vast temples had been planned on the Theban west bank, one of them to be half as large again as the fortified temple of Ramesses III, whilst a series of statues and other constructions were to be added to the temple of Karnak on the east bank. The priesthoods of other temples of Upper Egypt in the cities of Coptos and Armant led separate expeditions to the Wadi Hammamat for building-stone. Further colossal temples were planned at Abydos and Memphis; if his projects had come to fruition, King Ramesses IV would have been the greatest builder in Egypt since the pyramid age some 1500 years before.

In his fourth year, in an inscription cut upon a huge granite stela erected

at Abydos, Ramesses IV addressed an ominous prayer to Osiris, the god of
the dead:

> And you shall be pleased with the land of Egypt, your land, in my time; and for
> me you shall double in its long duration the prolonged reign of Ramesses II, the
> Great God; for I have done more mighty deeds and benefactions for your house
> — daily during these four years than those things which Ramesses II, the Great
> God, did for you in his sixty-seven years — Give to me the rewards of these great
> deeds which I have done for you, even life, prosperity and health, a long existence
> and a prolonged reign; make strong my limbs and preserve me; be with me as my
> God and excellent protector.

The text is unique, its prayers individual, even personal. Was the energetic
monarch ill, did he know somehow that time was running out for him? In
contrast with the beginning of his reign there are indications that the King
had urgent intimations of mortality and now wished to provide for his
future life. In the first year of his reign the King had taken less interest in
his tomb in the royal valley than any other monarch of his dynasty; each
of whom had overseen the most frantic bursts of tombmaking in the first
months of their rule. It was not until Ramesses' second year that a royal
commission arrived from the north to search for 'a place of piercing' for
the royal tomb; but once the work was underway, the gangs were quickly
enlarged from about 40 men to 120, an extraordinary event that might also
reflect some of the mounting anxiety being felt by the King and his court.
It is interesting that there is no evidence whatever that these extra gang
members were accommodated at the tombmakers' village, which certainly
would have been filled to overflowing by them. Nor can the rather dubious
benefits of these extra workmen be seen at the royal tomb itself - quite the
reverse, in fact, for the royal tomb is exceptionally small. It is probable
therefore that this increase reflects the temporary admission of the village
servants into the ranks of the tombmakers, perhaps to help with the hauling
of the hard stone from the quarries. There is strong evidence that some of
the villagers, perhaps even these fresh recruits to the gangs, were involved
in the quarrying expeditions to the Wadi Hammamat. For it was not only
the village trouble-makers who were sent to break stones: other villagers
seemed to have joined the quarrying expeditions as foremen, sculptors and
scribes. Some distance from Pa'anuket's graffito on the black schist cliffs of
the lower parts of the wadi are also the inscriptions of a 'Foreman Khonsu'
and a 'Scribe Neferhotep', both names of village personalities at the time
of the strikes; as the King's own men, accustomed to the management of
labour forces, they would have been useful additions to his quarrying projects.

So involved were the villagers with these royal expeditions that a papyrus map of the quarries, the 'Mountains of Bekhen' (now the oldest surviving map in the world), was made by a village scribe. It shows quite accurately the long track through the desert – now a tarmac road that leads to the Red Sea – the ancient wells that tap subterranean rainwater trapped against the impervious rock and a small temple built for the desert gods. Like modern geological maps of the same area, the scribe's plan clearly shows that two types of stone were to be found in the Wadi Hammamat: the even-grained schist, perfect for small statuary but far too brittle for spanning building blocks; and a fine-grained light-pink granite that was not only used for the king's sarcophagus but also for the vast temples that had been planned to stand in western Thebes. The marks of the ancient quarrymen's wedges can still be seen on cliffs of both these rocks in the wadi. With a careful eye, the ancient cartographer has indicated on his map where these two types of rock are to be found: detailing how the track through the wadi of black schist is littered with pink fragments of alluvial granite washed down from the quarries higher up. Here, amidst the pink granite, quarrymen of the old dynasty had also mined seams of gold, the 'gold of Coptos', a wickedly tough enterprise in which the cliffs were pounded into dust and then carried to wells nearby where the fine gold could be washed from the pulverized rock. On his map the village scribe has coloured two of the mountains in the midst of the granite cliffs a different colour and these he has called 'the mountains of gold'. But this terrible mining had stopped by Ramesses IV's reign. His men were not there for gold but for the stone that had held the lode seam; his quarrymen probably used the gold-miners' cuttings to hasten their work.

One especially large block was taken from these 'Mountains of Bekhen', destined for a sculptor's workshop at the side of the temple of Ramesses II. Here masons worked upon it before it was dragged up the long winding road to the tomb to become the royal sarcophagus. It was the largest ever to be hauled into the Great Place, a vast hollowed slab of pink granite some ten and a half feet long and seven and a half feet high. As the royal tombs were becoming increasingly more like temples, open and impressive, with their entrances closed only with wooden doors, such massive sarcophagi sealed with their equally massive lids offered the only real physical protection for the king's mummy. Today, they stand at the heart of these vast tombs as monuments to royal insecurity.

The ill-starred Ramesses IV died in the summer of his sixth year of rule. Of the temple that he had planned to stand beside that of Seti I at Abydos only the ground where it was to have stood had been cleared and some of the foundation trenches cut. At Thebes, on the west bank, the two massive temples lay in the first stages of construction; a small sandstone temple had been hastily erected during the last years of his reign to accommodate the

King's mortuary cult. At the Great Place, the ambitious King was laid inside his huge sarcophagus, taken out of the desert at such a terrible cost.

That the huge gang of 120 men was not employed in the King's own tomb is apparent from its size: after five years of work the tomb still had not progressed beyond its first corridors and the little chamber at its end. Like the kings of the period before Vizier Paser's reorganization of the work in the Great Place, Ramesses IV was buried in a makeshift tomb, the quarrymen's unfinished cuts being quickly plastered over and made to serve as miniature versions of the chambers that should properly have laid all around the sarcophagus hall. A simple low niche, not a room, held the King's gods, a low passage the royal servant figures. The grotesque sarcophagus, over seven feet high, seemed to fill the little burial chamber.

At the time of the funeral there had been great haste amongst the plasterers and painters who worked hard to ready the dwarf tomb for the royal burial. And as each makeshift room was finished, the scribes noted the progress of the work. Each room should have been 'drawn in outline, engraved with chisels, filled with colours and completed', though by the later stages of the work the first two of these processes were passed over: the rough-quarried walls being quickly covered with plaster and painted with abbreviated versions of the correct scenes. At the tomb's centre, the scribes noted, the King lay in his sarcophagus enclosed by four gold shrines and a linen pall; and when the funeral rites were concluded the tomb doors were 'bolted and fastened', as one by one those officiating progressed up the corridor to the daylight. Later, all this information was gathered together and drawn on to a papyrus in a single plan, probably by Scribe Amennakht, and it remained in his family's archives until the end of the village's history. But in taking their notes at the tomb the scribes had been careless: when Amennakht came to draw this final plan he found that he lacked some of the basic measurements of the tomb, now shut tight with the King inside it. You will find, therefore, that some of the tomb's architectural details, quite obvious when you stand inside the tomb, do not appear upon the ancient plan that Amennakht drew with the aid of his memory and incomplete work-notes. The plan is a strange mixture of precision and inaccuracy: the ill-shaped excavation beyond the burial chamber, for example, is obviously asymmetric to the eye, yet our scribe, so precise in many of his measurements, drew these parts of the tomb quite wrongly. Similarly, he overestimated the work that the decorators were able to finish before the tomb's closure – rooms listed as 'drawn in outline' and 'engraved with chisels' were, in reality, often simply plastered over and quickly painted.

Without exaggeration, one can estimate today that there were nearer twelve men working to finish the tomb than the 120 that the King's officials had appointed to the gangs just four years before. Like so many of the reign's memorials the reality of the royal tomb did not match the King's ambition, indeed the great gang of 120 men was halved within a few years of Ramesses IV's death, when the villagers were told that the Vizier himself would come south to Thebes to supervise the cut-back of the workforce to its previous size. The workmen and their chiefs convened a large public meeting to decide who would stay in the two gangs and who would be demoted to become, as the Vizier's office had decreed that they should, the 'Personnel that shall carry supplies for you'; presumably the process actually consisted of the newer gang members returning to their former occupations as village servants.

When the representatives of the Vizier and the tombmakers first met, things did not go well, a serious dispute breaking out between the Vizier's scribe and one of the village draughtsmen, the artist Nebnefer. But the chiefs were determined not to lose the Vizier's confidence at this most critical moment and when, a few days after the village meeting, the Vizier judged in favour of his scribe the chiefs made their sympathies plain and the village tribunal swiftly sentenced Nebnefer to 'a hundred blows with a stick and ten brand marks; and let him cut stones in the Place of Truth until the Vizier pardons him'. It was an acid demonstration of where the ultimate loyalty of the village hierarchy lay, for in passing such a severe sentence upon one of their own villagers, the chiefs now tacitly affirmed their continuing fidelity to the Vizier despite their growing association with the High Priests of Amun. Shortly after this adjudication the Vizier also confirmed the chief's recommendations for the reductions in the gang sizes and, as if to emphasize the King's continued role as the village's ultimate master and provider, his representative held the next meeting with the tombmakers by the side of a royal granary where rations were given out to some of the men of the gangs and a number of village women. Then he was gone, and the village must have sighed with relief.

Some three months later, at the height of the summer's heat in late August, when the Vizier's party was planning to leave Thebes for the cool of the delta, the village chiefs sent one of their doorkeepers over to the Vizier's boat. 'This day', wrote the recording scribe, 'the chief workmen, the scribe of the tomb and the entire gang gave two chisels of silver to the Vizier — and the Vizier went north on that day.' It was a most grateful present to the Vizier from the tombmakers who had survived the cut-backs; and a present that, with the value of silver some sixty times that of copper, represented more than a lifetime's rations for the family of a man of the gang.

It they had ever needed such a reminder, the Vizier's trip must certainly have impressed upon the villagers who it was that still controlled Thebes. None the less, although the civil administration of the south stayed in the hands of the King's own men, slowly, and almost by default, the High Priests of Amun were becoming the true masters of Upper Egypt, a vast unarmed temporal presence in the soft heartland of the state. The great old city, venerable and vulnerable, rich in age, gold and indiscretions, had been abandoned to the priests. Henceforth it would be visited only occasionally by the highest officials of state: royal commissions and Viziers temporarily filled with all the erratic generosity and fierce ambition of absent parents. This, then was why the Vizier and his staff had made their summer journey: a tour into the fiefdom of the High Priests of Amun to reassert the royal presence in the hot Southern City.

A few years later, Scribe Amennakht died. Though still in his early sixties, he had probably been ailing for some time, for his son Harshire had been appointed as a full scribe some time before. Though indirect, our information of the event is simple enough: amongst the official records of the Great Place a scribe set to copying out Amennakht's accounts noted that they had come 'from the hand of the scribe Amennakht, who is dead'. He was probably buried in the village cemetery, in a family vault under a tomb chapel close by the tomb of Scribe Kenhirkhopeshef. Today the ruin of the heavily fissured cliffs of the area has destroyed all traces of it, but references to Amennakht's tomb are in numerous texts, one of which describes Amennakht himself inspecting his family tomb as a member of a village tribunal. Amennakht's will was written on a space in the same papyrus that holds the plan of King Ramesses IV's tomb. His executor was the scribe Hori (in all probability, Amennakht's son Harshire – literally, 'little Hori' – had been so named to distinguish him from this 'big' Hori, the family friend), and he was so conscientious in his division of his colleague's household that even the worn reed matting of its floors and benches was accounted for.

In fact this division would have been little more than a redistribution of the family belongings into the households surrounding Amennakht's: Harshire and his wife, for example, lived just around the corner in the high street, though in a house so small that he may well have moved back into his father's, where, amongst the other memories of his childhood, he would have recalled the dreadful drama of his sister, the oracle and the workman's clothes. The small house that Harshire left behind him was to serve as a library, an archive that would hold the family's papers: both records of the work in the Great Place and the family's personal documents. Three thousand years later the same archive, much enlarged by Amennakht's successors, would become an archaeological treasure trove. It is an especial irony that whilst the fragile records describing the life and work of the tombmakers of this period have survived in abundance, several of the monarchs of the same period would exist only as the most flickering of presences in scholarly debate were it not for the tombs that the two gangs made for them. Indeed, without tombs to fortify their claims to eternity, scholars might well have relgated some of these flimsy kings to the status of spelling errors on the part of a hurrying scribe.

A pious hope remained in Egypt that the generous age of the great Ramesses would continue with his successors: evidenced by the fact that the seven kings who followed him to the throne all took the name of their near-mythical predecessor. But not one of this procession of Ramessides had even the pretensions of the fourth of their number; neither were they long-lived. Five of them succeeded to the throne within the quarter-century following Ramesses IV's death. Yet even as the kings seemed to fade away from Thebes, diffused by these short reigns; even as a variety of convulsions shook the tombmakers' village, the gangs held fast in this dimming era and made the most vivid monuments of their entire history. It was the final flower of the Theban Empire, a series of incredibly skilful, rather foppish, large-gestured tombs, decorated, on occasion, as finely as miniatures on a papyrus sheet; tombs that settled lightly on the royal valley like butterflies clustering in an overripe orchard.

19

PAINTERS

Four fine tombs remain in the Great Place from this forty-year phase of tombmaking, and all of them follow the familiar pattern of bright beautifully-sculptured entrances leading to unfinished burial chambers: often mere caverns filled with eccentric decoration. It is the four tombs' paintings that are the villagers' final masterworks: brightly-pigmented, rich-textured, alive; sequences of irridescent patterns that seem like eastern carpets hanging from the walls and ceilings. It is an effect that was hard-won by using a great number of skills. First, on the bare white walls and ceilings prepared by the quarrymen and plasterers outline draughtsmen sketched out the ritual scenes. This network of lines – drawn by snapping a paint-dipped string hard against the plaster – served as guides for the enormous compositions, the vast mixtures of figures and texts, that would cover the entire tomb, each with its exact location. After careful checking, these outlines were then worked by sculptors into fine relief, the craftsmen often finishing-off the details with tiny wooden-handled chisels held in the palms of their hands. Only then did the artists start to paint the great white walls: first colouring the sculptors' work, then redrawing the edge of each image, figure and hieroglyph alike.

On the papyrus plan of the tomb of Ramesses iv, the scribe described these basic processes as 'drawing with outline, engraving with the chisel, filling with colours and finishing'. Thus there was a clear distinction between the two types of painter: the outline draughtsman and the colouring artist. In the haste prompted by a premature royal death, this long process was often abbreviated: the colour painters following straight on the heels of the plasterers, daubing their scenes directly upon the rough white surface without the benefit of the outline draughtsmen's drawings. It is in these hasty, brightly-coloured paintings especially that we can see the hands of individual painters and as our eye follows their brushes across the surface we can feel the excitement of watching an ancient artist at his work. But much of the work in these tombs was sculptured in relief before such painters began. Even when there was a decline in the skills of the outline draughtsmen the sculptors that followed them were sufficiently expert to provide the sharp

edges, almost like enamellers' *cloisons*, for each separate figure and hieroglyph, on which the colour artists could lay their pigments as thick and
crusty as a gothic illumination. After this careful decoration each sign and
figure would be outlined in red ochre using a heavily-charged brush, with
the hesitant strokes of a conscientious copyist. By the time of the Ramesside
kings painting these hieroglyphs and figures had become work like a jew-
eller's: the paints being used in dense colour combinations, one upon another, to produce a studded texture similar to the decorations on the village
coffins. In work like this the pigments are transmuted into precious objects
in themselves, each hieroglyph, each figure, a separate gem. It is these same
pigments that, in the reign of Ramesses IV, we find Harshire and Amenhotep, the young sons of Scribe Amennakht, drawing supplies of from the
storehouse for their work in the royal tombs.

During the gangs' history there were limited numbers of painters working
at any one time – usually aided by apprentices and assistants – and this
seems to hold true of these four Ramesside tombs. It would be wrong,
however, to imagine that the murals they made were an opportunity for the
individual expression cherished by Western artists. These paintings are the
creation of an entire community, and in their subject-matter and style
follow a tradition which the village artists had inherited from more than
two millennia of royal culture. None the less, we may yet detect individual
hands working inside the grid of these tomb-paintings and, sometimes, by
comparison with the little stelae that the same artists have decorated and
'signed', even put names to them. In such visual, detective work Scribe
Amennakht's children often figure prominently: village texts tell us that the
scribe himself was a tomb-painter before his promotion; that Harshire, his
eldest son, carried on this tradition before he succeeded to his father's job;
that his second son, Amenhotep, was a supervisor and a fine painter of
royal tombs for almost fifty years and, after the foremen, the most senior
member of the two gangs; and that even a third son, Pentaweret, was an
artist of the royal tombs. A study of their handiwork reveals that these
brothers were colour artists. Whole passages of painting in some of the
Ramesside tombs may be attributed to them, especially less elaborate sections, often ceilings, where they were working directly on to a gridded white
surface without painting over previously sculptured relief. Just as the drawing of the hieroglyphs and the handling of the paint are reminiscent of the
coffin-paintings of the time, so they remind us that, as his father Scribe
Amennakht had done before him, draughtsman Amenhotep too did his
share of coffin-painting.

As well as working in the kings' tombs and on the villagers' own funeral
articles the village painters also decorated the private tomb chapels of
Theban bureaucrats. One of these, a priest named Keneben who worked in

the temple of Tuthmosis IV, shows what the colouring artists could do entirely on their own account. The tomb was set low down in the nobles' cemeteries and, as is usual in these little chapels, its walls held rows and rows of bustling figures in scenes of banquets and offerings and the funeral of the owner. One of Keneben's paintings showed the mummies of the priest and his wife standing upright in their coffins in front of his tomb chapel whilst the rituals of revivification were conducted by a mortuary priest. Behind this priest, leading a row of mourners who each carried palm branches, was the figure of draughtsman Amenhotep. He was identified by name in an inscription above his head that also called him a 'draughtsman of the noble tomb'. In his hands he held a papyrus, and written upon the roll were the rites by which the coffins and spirits of the dead priest and his wife would be revivified.

Such tomb-paintings or, at least, their remains, for they were plundered and destroyed during the last century, show all the brio and sensuality that the same artists put into painting the reliefs in the kings' tombs. But here, unhampered by the strict requirements of the state, the even-toned paint expands right across the rough surface of the wall, the dun-coloured mud plaster fusing the glowing colours together and setting-off the jewelly black and the bright white to rare advantage. Precisely the same style can be seen in the remains of the tomb of Queen Isis, made at the same time. And there, too, we can see Amenhotep's hand at work. His paintings, remarkably sophisticated essays in colours and understated outlines, shift backwards and forwards on an even-toned surface; a technique that some 3000 years later would be elaborated by some of the Post–Impressionists. It is probable that the destroyed figure in Keneben's funeral procession was a self-portrait, for an ostracon from a royal tomb bears a similar picture of a draughtsman Amenhotep praying to Thoth, and this idiosyncratic sketch – a long-limbed contented figure with the beginnings of a belly (the archetypal successful artist!) – compares closely with the surviving fragments of Keneben's tomb.

Priest Keneben's chapel paintings are the only known examples of work from the brief reign of Ramesses VIII, whose own tomb, if it was ever decorated, has never been found. Within a few years of finishing them the villagers were again painting in the private cemeteries: this time for the Priest Isiseba, a high dignitary of the temple of Amun, whose tomb was close to Keneben's. As the 'Head of the Temple Altars' and also as a senior scribe of the temple's estates, Isiseba clearly held a finger on the pipeline of the villagers' own food supplies. They made Isiseba a most impressive tomb chapel in the shell of an old tomb, for by this time the private cemeteries too were becoming almost as crowded as those by the tombmakers' village. In Isiseba's chapel the tombmakers worked in the formal style of temple wall reliefs and they painted the large scenes there with the same light golden colours. Here, alongside exotic scenes, common to the temple walls, of the King before the shrines of the gods, we see Priest Isiseba performing religious rites. Extraordinary, indeed, is the fact that in this tomb the figures of the Theban gods to whom Isiseba makes offerings are copies of those drawn on the wall of the tomb of King Ramesses IX; the central figure of Isiseba's Theban triad, the king of the gods, actually being labelled 'Amun Re of the Horizon of Eternity' [i.e. the Amun of the royal tomb]. Such figures had traditionally been worshipped by the tombmakers, and it is obvious that the artists who painted Isiseba's figure of Amun had intimate knowledge of the secret tombs of the Great Place, especially that of King Ramesses IX. Isiseba's tomb also shows that the outline artists who worked there were as familiar with the lay-out and intricate iconography of temple wall reliefs as they were with the scenes in the royal tombs.

Certainly the outline draughtsmen who first laid out the scenes on the tomb and temple walls were far more accomplished than the colouring artists. Yet today, with their work largely cut away by the relief sculptors who followed them, we can find only a few examples of their style surviving here and there upon unfinished walls and a few flakes of limestone. The outline draughtsmen painted not in modest strokes from the wrist as the colouring artists did, but straight from the shoulder using fine watery paint that floated across the dry walls in immaculate brush strokes that continued without hesitation for many feet at a time: the fluid outlines of the gods and kings. What is surprising is the precision of this draughtsmanship, for accuracy is not sacrificed to technical achievement. It is as if the artists were drawing with their minds, unhampered by bone and muscle, and with the speed of a knife through water. Seldom in history have there been such technicians, and that this skill was alive at the tombmakers' village for generation after generation is quite extraordinary: it represents a level of manual dexterity, a dancer's precision, born only of long experience. Yet paradoxically such work is, by its nature, quickly accomplished, and in the kings' tombs there are no more than ten or twelve large figures, usually around the doorways, on which these draughtsmen could practise their skills; certainly not sufficient work to keep their talents at full stretch. They must, then, have been involved in other work; and in the fragmentary records of the reigns of Ramesses II and VI, we find hints that these gang members worked outside the Great Place. Thus, the generally poor outline work in the tombs of Ramesses III and his princes may well be the result of the authorities taking the best outline draughtsmen away from the King's tomb to work on the walls of the royal temple.

We can trace the work of these outline draughtsmen in the Great Place back to the earliest days of its reorganization under Vizier Paser: in the unfinished tomb of King Horemheb, where the sculptors have only cut away half of their drawings, and in the tomb of King Seti I where there is a single chamber, made late in the reign, which was left covered in the black and white lines of the outline draughtsmen. In these scenes, the first draft of the figures was drawn in large broad strokes in a pale-ochre wash, and this was then firmed and even altered in a second, tighter, and more finished drawing in black; the final version. Few such examples have survived from later reigns but the line of the superb reliefs made in the time of the four kings show that the outline draughtsmen's art was very much alive. By Ramesses III's time, however, drawings left in the unfinished rooms of a prince's tomb in the Place of Beauty show that the outliners' skills had greatly faded; and this is also borne out by the poor quality of the work in the King's own tomb. Although the eight pretty side chambers, painted late in the reign, show the colour artists working as well as ever, with the absence of the skilled outline draughtsmen, the point of reference for the other craftsmen had gone: the large-scale reliefs in the tomb are probably the worst in the royal valley.

It is only after the involvement of the High Priests in the work at the Great Place that we find evidence of highly skilled outline draughtsmen returning to work in the royal tombs; for the High Priests, of course, had charge of the one school which could keep such artists in constant employment: the temples, though here the outline draughtsmen were usually ill-served by the sculptors who followed them. We can conjecture that the High Priests released these fine artists to work in the Great Place; sending them back briefly to layout the doorways and the first corridors of the King's tomb. Skilled outline draughtsmen were certainly working in the tomb of Ramesses IV, which already shows a vast improvement over that of his predecessor, Ramesses III. Indirect evidence of the continuing presence of these artists in the royal valley is to be found in the fine wall scenes of the later tombs: positive confirmation through a magnificent series of painted limestone ostraca, each bearing a picture of a king's face, and all drawn with such sensitivity and skill, such joy of accomplishment, that we feel the delight of a master displaying his craft before a wondering audience.

In all probability, these fine drawings made on loose slips of stone were intended to serve as guides for the sculptors and painters who followed the outliners at the work on the tomb walls, cutting away and painting over the master drawings as they went. The skills of the sculptors had fallen dramatically from the heights that they attained under Foremen Hay and Paneb, and the colour artists who followed them often covered the relief with miserable drawings of the King's face. Thus these supreme sketches by the draughtsmen not only provided a portrait of the King for all the craftsmen who would later work at the wall, but they were an exemplar for the colouring artists. In short, these particular studies were central to the artistic revival that occurred under the later Ramesside kings. And this is probably why they were so carefully carried from one king's tomb to the next, and this in turn is how the greater part of them have been preserved for us today: discovered as they were left by artists in two of the royal tombs in which they worked. The large amounts of skilled and not-so-skilled drawings of all sorts of subjects found along with these master sketches show that the tombs of Ramesses VI and Ramesses IX functioned as a school for artists and that it was there, with the encouragement of a few masters, that the small renaissance took place. In this connection, a simple inscription left in Ramesses IV's tomb by the draughtsman Amenhoteph, written some twenty years after work in the tomb had finished, takes on a special poignancy.

The final examples of the master draughtsmen's work in the royal tombs are to be seen in the cavernous monument of Ramesses XI, the last made in the Great Place, about a quarter of a century after draughtsman Amenhotep's death. Here they drew outlines on the broad high walls for paintings that were never made (colour plate 31). Where had such sleight of hand, such confident skills been nourished in the intervening decades? These preliminary drawings, just a few large figures and some hieroglyphs, were made in a few days and no draughtsman could have maintained this peak of excellence without the constant exercise of his skill. We may again find the answer in the buildings of the High Priests of Amun, for the reliefs of this period in the temple of Karnak show great similarities in detail to the work in the King's tomb. Despite the appalling quality of the relief sculpture, which must surely be some of the very worst in Egypt, these temple scenes still betray, in their mutilated outlines, the ghostly hand of the tombmakers' master draughtsmen.

That these virtuoso draughtsmen were originally from the tombmakers' village and not simply imported to the Great Place for short periods of time, is amply proven by archaeological finds at the village itself. Here fragments of their work have been found, as well as a complete master drawing of the head of a king exactly the same as those found in the two 'schoolroom' tombs in the Great Place. Although the small size of these stones cramps the artists' grand style, they still hold a precision of line and generosity of form not present in the drawings on the ostraca of Amenhotep and the other colour artists. These, though more amusing and anecdotal, are far less skilled. The walls of the village cemetery, too, hold fine examples of the line draughtsmen's work. In the burial chamber of the tomb of Foreman Anhirkawi, for example, a man who witnessed the burial of four of these Ramesside kings, we can see a master draughtsman working with unfamiliar subjects (Plate 24): domestic scenes showing the foreman sitting with his family, and the ritual combats of the afterlife. In its severe precision the line of the drawings is as masterly as one would expect, but the bright colours, though harmonious, are laid on thin and flat and have little of the close-toned richness so beloved of the colour artists.

From the evidence of some 'signed' ostraca – stones with drawings and prayers upon them that have been dedicated by a named artist – we can probably say that the fine paintings in the foreman's tomb were made by the draughtsman Hormin, the son of draughtsman Hori, one of Scribe Amennakht's brothers. This draughtsman Hori also painted a stela bearing a prayer for his sons which he set up in the Great Place. And there three young men pray together, hopeful, wide-eyed and delicately androgynous – Hormin, Nakhtamun and Nebnefer – three outline draughtsmen who worked right through the time of the little renaissance of the Great Place. As a member of the great family of Scribe Amennakht, Hormin knew that his father's voice would obtain a full hearing at the village council. On one occasion he wrote: 'To my father, draughtsman Hori: you should press the chiefs so that they will promote this servant of yours [an unspecified person] to help me with the drawing. I am alone, for my brother is ill.' Nor was it just his relationship to Amennakht that would have given Hori's case extra weight in the village council, for the colour artist Amenhotep, Scribe Amennakht's son, was a 'chief of the gang' in his own right, not only a painter but a man who on occasion would 'busy himself with drawing the plan of the King's tomb', as a work-journal records. The title of 'chief' had previously been held only by foremen and scribes. Now a painter held the office and this shows not only the status that artists now enjoyed inside the community, but also the authority of this single family, which held within its ranks two of the 'chiefs' and many of the great painters, both colour artists and line draughtsmen.

Surprisingly, the village artists' greatest work during this period is not found inside a king's tomb, nor amongst tombs in the private cemeteries, nor even in the temples, but in the tomb of a royal prince, Montuhirkhopeshef (Plate 30). Today no one knows much about this man, who is celebrated in a light-filled gallery cut in the southern cliff of the Great Place, but there the tombmakers produced the epitome of their final style. The whole of the tomb consists of a single sloping passage with the steps of an incompleted excavation across its end. Perhaps it had originally been intended for the tomb of Ramesses VIII, who ruled for less than a year, for the fine architecture is of royal proportions. The painters worked, on the high walls of this one corridor, first preparing them with a bright white wash and then covering them with simple scenes showing the Prince worshipping the gods, such as you may see in temples all over Egypt. Here, in keeping with the large scale of the work, the colours are not applied in the rich-textured manner of Amenhotep and his colour artists, but laid thin, their harmonies carefully balanced, coolly controlled. Sometimes the line around these flat tones is breathtaking in its immediacy; flashing ochres on the white wall telling of the strength and calmness of a master. And with this great skill is a meditative observation: the line encompasses the texture of shiny gold, crisp linens and woolly wigs, and the fey young man on whom fashion sits: an unknown prince in an age of transient kings. We can observe here how, although the subject-matter and style of Egyptian art had hardly altered in some 2000 years, the aesthetic was in constant flux: though the poses of this prince and his gods recall in their style the earliest monuments of ancient Egypt, the young man stands in his amber tomb fixed in a precise moment of time; a graceful balance between an icon and a living moment that is amongst the tombmakers' most profound achievements.

PART THREE
ENDING

20

TOMB-ROBBERS

Whilst the gangs made fine monuments for their northern kings, conditions at the village were becoming increasingly unsettled. Typical of many entries in the work-journal of this time is one that records: 'Year one, first month of winter, day three [probably 7 October 1141 BC, the first year of Ramesses VI's reign]. No work for fear of the enemy.' The detritus of Egypt's foreign wars – mercenaries from disbanded armies, Saharan bedouin and even bands of dispossessed Egyptians – were roving the Nile valley, attacking its towns and villages. With their bizarre cloaks, metal helmets, barbaric tattoos and penis sheaths, and a fierce variety of weapons – long swords, daggers and the like – they must have struck deep fear into the Thebans, confirming all the traditional antipathies of the householder for the nomad. Yet with the King and his army settled in the delta there was little at Thebes to control such fearsome *condottieri*. The old city, its temples and tombs piled with gold and fine things, was virtually defenceless.

In 'Year one, in the first month of winter' the work-journal reported that 'those who are enemies have reached Pernabi [presumably a town north of Thebes] and destroyed all that was there and burned its people', and that the High Priest of Amun, Ramessesnakht, had taken control of the defence of the royal valley: 'Bring the medjay of Pernabi and those who are in the south and those of the [kings'] tombs, and have them stay here to watch the [kings'] tombs.' Western Thebes held its breath, the tombmakers stayed in their houses. Would the brigands come or not? Medjay Mentmose, now well into his seventies, was still responsible for the villagers' safety and he advised them not to go to the Great Place 'Until you see what will happen. I will hurry and hear what they say. It is I [alone] who will come to tell you to go up [i.e. to the royal valley].' That the loyal old medjay was suspicious enough to believe that the tombmakers might be lured into a trap suggests the 'enemies' were people to some extent familiar with the villagers. In any event, the danger passed and the gangs were soon back at work. Such alarms would continue throughout the era of the last Ramesside kings to add an edge of danger to a febrile age.

In addition to this harassment, which continued throughout the next two decades, delivery of the village rations again became erratic and insubstantial. Sometimes Scribe Harshire presented gifts to well-placed members of the Vizier's staff, several of whom demanded such payments as their due, but by the ninth year of the ninth Ramesses even this did not succeed in opening the granary doors, and the two gangs went on strike in protest. Four years later only the arguments of a different scribe, Pabes, stopped another protest. Except for the eloquent testimony of the fine tombs, there are few records of this agitated age other than these notices of strikes and the like. What is certain is that life was becoming increasingly hard in the Southern City and the standard of living at the village was falling fast. At such times, with government slack and foreigners raiding close to Thebes, the necropolis was at especial risk. Just as in the dangerous days of the four kings, when Heria had robbed her fellow-villagers and the village gods, so once again the rich monuments of the western bank began to attract the attentions not only of foreign raiders but of some Thebans too.

The authorities had been concerned about the plundering of the Theban cemeteries for some years, and as the protectors of the royal ancestors, they had kept an especially sharp eye on the kings' tombs. Several of them were re-opened for inspection, and in Ramesses IX's ninth year, a disturbing time for the village, draughtsman Amenhotep revisited the tomb of Ramesses VI as part of one of these tours of inspection. Twenty years before he had helped to paint some of the immense ceilings in this tomb: richly-detailed star charts, pictures of the celestial voyages of the dead King and the sun through the night sky. Now he was able to show his son Amennakht, whom he had taken with him, the masterworks that he and the other colour artists had created. They left a small inked inscription on the wall of the burial chamber as a record of their visit. The King's burial, apparently, was still safe and sound. Four years later, however, whilst gangs of Libyans and mercenaries roamed the west bank once more, when there was hunger in the city and the tombmakers were again sending letters and presents north to the Vizier and his staff asking for their rations, one of the High Priest's stonemasons, a man named Amenpenefer, was arrested and held in the offices of the Mayor of Thebes, accused by the district officers of the necropolis of robbing tombs. Times were hard, and Amenpenefer had a great deal of gold; when he gave it to a well-placed official he was quietly released. Then, as he recalled some four years later: 'I rejoined my companions who compensated me with another portion of the loot. So together with other thieves who are with me, I have continued to this day the practice of robbing the tombs of the nobles and the people of the land who rest in the west. And a large number of other people rob them as well....'

A few months after the stonemason's gentle brush with authority three men were arrested for trespassing in the royal cemetery of the Place of

Beauty. As close relatives of the King were buried there, this incident was potentially far more serious, and an enquiry, headed by the Vizier himself and Paser, the Mayor of Thebes, was set up to investigate. To the accompaniment of a great deal of beating and limb-twisting, as was the custom of these tribunals, one of the men admitted to stealing objects from the tomb of the wife of Ramesses III, Queen Isis. As the mother of both Ramesses IV and VI, the Queen's tomb had received special attention, the painter Amenhotep decorating some of its corridors. It was the last large tomb to have been made in the Place of Beauty and at the time of the inquiry, the Queen had been buried in it about twenty years. Details of the robbers' punishments are not preserved, but other court records show that the men were still being held by the Theban administration many years later.

At the time of this investigation gangs of tomb-robbers had been plundering the private cemeteries of Thebes on a large scale for a decade. They operated in groups of seven or eight, possessing between them the expert knowledge and equipment necessary for such work, usually two or three stonemasons or coppersmiths with water-carriers to support them in the work of digging and of tunnelling, a smith who melted down the plundered metals in his furnace, and a boatman who ferried both the gang and their loot from the necropolis to the city. Armed with such special skills, many gangs now roamed up and down the Nile plundering cemeteries all along the river. Only by a constant round of inspections could the necropolis authorities check on the safety of the monuments under their charge. As the gangs usually broke into the tombs from the rear, leaving the tomb doors intact and their seals unbroken, a proper inspection would require a commission of officials actually to enter each one of the multitudes of tombs in the necropolis and reseal each of the doors after checking that the contents were still intact.

Once inside the tombs and undetected in their progress, the robbers smashed the burials to pieces, breaking open the stone sarcophagi, hacking the gilding from the coffins, tearing the mummies apart in a search for their jewellery, then carrying off the linens, oils and furniture that had been left with the dead. Sometimes they would simply set fire to the dense-packed burial chambers and return later to the blackened vaults to scrape the small hard pools of gold from beneath the ash. One robber recalled just such an excursion before another tribunal:

We went to the tomb of Tjanefer, who had been the third priest of Amun. We opened it and brought out his inner coffins and took his mummy and left it in a corner of his tomb. The inner coffins we took in the boat, along with the rest, to the Island of Amenhotep [a silt bar in the river], and we set fire to them in the night and made off with the gold which we found on them; four *kite* fell to the lot of each man.

Four *kite* of gold, a little over one and a quarter ounces, was roughly equivalent to a third of a year's grain supply for a royal tombworker; a good night's work indeed, and often the hauls were far larger than that. The constant flood of precious metals and fine things on to the markets of Thebes must have been terrific, and could hardly have passed unnoticed. An immediate effect of this new-found wealth was that traditional 'prices' – that is, the rates at which goods were bartered against each other in the market-place – changed dramatically, grain almost doubling in its value against copper and silver. In an economy where 'wages' were paid in kind, it was a quite unprecedented shift of values. For fifty years or more, the tombmakers' full grain ration had been about five and a half sacks a month. Thus, the 'prices' of goods at barter in private exchanges at the village had remained equally constant, though always with enough variation to underline the fact that such scales of value are never as precise as those of money-based economies. Obviously one effect of the rise in grain price at Thebes was that the village 'wages' rose in their market value. Conversely, grain had now become a far more expensive commodity to obtain on the Theban market when the royal ration failed. Little wonder then that, when serious shortages did occur, the tombmakers themselves were tempted to rob the cemeteries surrounding their village. In an age when the processes of central government could no longer gather the tithes to feed the people of Thebes, the tombs of the ancestors would become the city's gold mines.

By the end of the first decade of King Ramesses IX, the proceeds of tomb-robbery seem to have become an important part of the Theban economy. The higher grain prices certainly encouraged more farm produce back into the city markets, and of course it was not only the robbers who could afford to buy; for, along with the officials who were in direct collusion, they were merely the tip of a scandalous iceberg. Just as the flood of grave goods changed the values of the Theban market-place, so eventually many people in urban Thebes – priests, medjay, craftsmen (surprisingly, perhaps, people were still interested in obtaining better grave goods for themselves), shopkeepers and travelling merchants – indirectly benefited from the robbed tombs. As Theban society was an enormous web of relationships, so the scandal of the robbed tombs must have quickly become embedded in textures of city life. At this time, two families had controlled Thebes for more than a century. They had held a succession of high priesthoods and mayoralities and had often intermarried, and branches of their families controlled many of the other towns and cities of Upper Egypt. In the reign of Ramesses IX, the High Priest of Amun was Amenhotep, son of the High

31 King Ramesses XI, from the doorway to his tomb. This, the finest picture of the king that survives, was the outline draughtsmen's last work in the royal valley.

Overleaf 32 Western Thebes, the evening breeze blows down the river Nile.

Above 33 Evening at the tombmakers' village, looking north.

Opposite above 34 This most elegant coffin, made for a young prince, was probably one of the many gathered from the royal tombs by Butehamun and the villagers. It was found in the villagers' own cemetery.

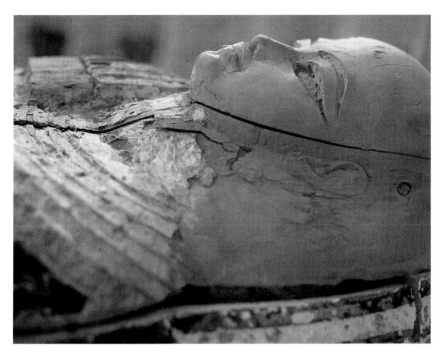

Below 35 The funeral papyrus of Nebhepet, Butehamun's son. He is shown working in the fields of Illalu, the Egyptian Elysium. Nebhepet was the third generation of his family to have farmed the land; the ploughing and reaping, drawn here with such a pastoral delight, record real experiences.

Above 36 The fortress of Ramesses III at Medinet Habu, the great compound that sheltered the tombmakers after they had abandoned their village.

Below 37 The house of Butehamun and, in all probability, of his father Djutmose, built under the western walls of the fortress of Ramesses III. The four columns which bear Butehamun's name and titles supported the roof of the house's main room where the scribes sat in public session.

Opposite 38 Wadi Sikkat el Agala, one of the remote desert valleys that were visited by the tombmakers in the time of Herihor.

39 Scribe Butehamun at prayer, drawn upon the side of one of his coffins. The scribe himself painted some of the inscriptions on these coffins and it is possible that this is a self-portrait, one of the last known works of this gifted family.

Priest Ramessesnakht; the Mayor of Thebes was Paser. It was their government that had been infiltrated and, indeed, was to some extent subsidized, by the tomb-robber's produce. At the same time they were also responsible to the King for the safety of the tombs of his ancestors, and could hardly be seen to fail in this pious duty. Yet it was their state officials, their temple staff and granary supervisors and the rest who handled the stolen grave goods. So deep did the illicit wealth now run inside the bureaucracy that to have attacked the entire network of thievery would have been to attack the fabric of Theban society itself.

The three arrests in the Place of Beauty, upon which the Vizier himself had held an enquiry, would alone have shown the northern court that the royal ancestors were now endangered in their Theban tombs. There was evidence too that the thieves were graduating from the private cemeteries to those of ancient kings and queens. Something had to be done, and the rulers of Thebes created the most masterly of compromises by which they disgorged a series of scapegoats for the crimes of the city. As far as is known today, the first significant steps to curb the tomb-robberies were taken by the senior civil authority at Thebes, Mayor Paser, 'The Prince who reports to the Ruler', as he described himself. In the sixteenth year of Ramesses IX he quietly informed the Vizier that he had received a report that some royal tombs had been robbed. Properly, the jurisdiction over the west bank cemeteries was in the hands of the Mayor of the west bank, Pawero, but Paser could hardly have ignored a denunciation involving such a sensitive issue. After all the withholding of knowledge of 'evil done in this place of Pharaoh' was as much a crime as tomb-robbing itself, a fact that at least one very junior bureaucrat, the stonemason Paneb, had used in the past to great effect.

The tomb-robbers' accusers had been two scribes of the Great Place: Harshire and Pabes. Both elders in the tombmakers' village – Harshire was now aged about fifty – were bound by the same oath of loyalty as others working in the Great Place. But there were also other, less pious motives for their action: it was essential if there was to be an enquiry into tomb-robbing at Thebes, that the tombmakers should exert influence upon the direction of that enquiry, for a gang from the tombmakers' own village had robbed the tomb of Queen Isis. So Harshire and Pabes gave Mayor Paser the names of the members of other gangs of tomb-robbers who had been plundering the cemeteries, and trusted that the investigation would stop there; for rumours of a robbed royal tomb had become widespread and the two scribes had to act to forestall unwanted developments. Wisely they made their report not to the west bank Mayor, who would have had more knowledge of the true situation, but confidentially to a much more eminent official on the other side of the river.

It was a cunning course of action, but one not without its risks for, as Mayor Paser later remarked, the two scribes faced mutilation and death for perjury if their sworn statement was found to be untrue. The great gamble now took its course; the Vizier was coming to Thebes and had convened a commission to examine the condition of the royal cemeteries. The scribes' hare was off and running. This commission was composed of representatives of the most powerful elements of Egyptian society. Along with the Vizier sat a commander of the army, another of the navy and also, from the north of Egypt, two high court officials, friends and advisors of the King. To balance these northerners there were an equal number of Thebans on the commission: High Priest Amenhotep and his brother the second priest of Amun, the manager of the Amun temple estates and Mayor Paser. In their turn, the eight worthies and the Vizier appointed a team to examine the tombs on the spot, and it was this little group, the 'controllers of the Great and Noble Necropolis' that crossed the river on 12 August 1092 BC in the sixteenth year of King Ramesses IX.

The official record of this outing has survived intact; four of the commissioner's personal scribes, a temple official, Pawero the Mayor of West Thebes, and his two chief medjay, all trudged across the west bank fields to the desert beyond that held the tombs of the nobles and some of the ancient Theban kings. What went through the minds of these 'controllers' may well be imagined. The three scribes had come from the north, and they must have found the Theban sun hot in August, the north wind agitating, and, apparently, the southerners devious. For the Thebans, of course, the commission was to some extent an act of theatre, at the conclusion of which premeditated sentences would be handed down for long-suspected crimes. However, the Theban officials must have been anxious to see the examination go well, especially Mayor Pawero and the two chief medjay, in whose bailiwick the crimes had been committed and who, presumably, knew more about the real state of affairs in the necropolis than the rest of the committee, yet had no precise information of the charges concerning the robbed tombs or who had made them. Solemnly the august body plodded along the footpaths threading through the low line of desert hills on the northern half of the necropolis; past the elaborate tomb chapels of the previous hundred years, past the rock-cut tomb chapels of the old dynasty, past the 500-year-old tombs of ancient kings who lay under brightly decorated pyramids of brick and whose portraits on stelae still stood firm in the bright sun. Some of these tombs were so old and dilapidated that, as the commission reported, the 'royal pyramid has been removed from it although its stela is still fixed in front of it and the figure of the King stands on the stela with his god, called Behhek, between his feet. Examined this day: it was found intact.'

Junior scribes kept a close record of the inspection which was limited largely to this ancient royal cemetery:

> The pyramids, graves and tombs exmined this day by the inspectors: the tomb of King Amenhotep I — which the Mayor of Thebes Paser had reported to the — commissioners ... saying 'The thieves had violated it'. Examined this day; it was found intact — .
> The pyramid tomb of King Inyotef VI — it was found intact.
> The pyramid tomb of King Inyotef VII: the thieves had not succeeded in penetrating it. [Though, the scribe noted, they were half-way in, engaged in cutting a tunnel through to the rear of the tomb.]
> The pyramid tomb of King Inyotef VI: the thieves had not succeeded in penetrating it. [But, the scribe again noted, this tomb too was in the process of being tunnelled into.]
> The pyramid tomb of Sebekemsaf II: the burial chamber was found empty of its lord, likewise the chamber of the great royal wife ... the thieves had laid their hands upon them — .
> The pyramid tomb of King Sekhenenre I: — it was found intact.
> The pyramid tomb of King Sekhenenre II: — it was found intact.
> The pyramid tomb of King Kamose: — it was found intact.
> The pyramid tomb of Prince Ahmose: — it was found intact.
> The pyramid tomb of Montuhotep: — it was found intact.
> Total pyramid tombs of the kings of old examined this day and found to be intact, nine pyramid tombs; found to have been violated, one tomb, total ten.

The situation in the private tombs which lay all around the ancient royal cemetery, and through which the inspectors had passed on their tour, was even less encouraging:

> The tombs and chambers in which rest the blessed ones of old, the citizens on the west of Thebes. It was found that the thieves had violated them all, dragging their owners from their coffins so that they were left on the desert, and stealing their funerary goods which had been given to them together with the gold and silver and the fittings which were in their coffins.

That same day, after meeting with his security officers, Pawero, Mayor of the west bank and chief of the medjay of the necropolis, placed a written list of thieves before the Vizier and his commissioners, and 'They [the thieves] were seized and imprisoned, they were examined, they told what had occurred.' How well things seemed to be going! Two royal robberies had been stopped in the nick of time. Thanks to the vigilance of the loyal Thebans only one king had been disturbed in the entire cemetery. And if the nobles' tombs had suffered a worse fate, why, the medjay had suspicions as to who had done these terrible things They were not the commissioners' first consideration and, in any case, a list of names had been produced with impressive speed. Better than that, the thieves themselves had been produced. Such efficiency was highly commendable. Yet the Vizier seems to have become suspicious and even to have caught wind of the recent robbery of a royal tomb. The next day he went himself, with one of the courtiers, to the Place of Beauty to oversee the investigation of some of the self-confessed tomb-robbers that the Thebans had produced. One individual was one of the three men who had been arrested in the Great Place two years earlier, and had already undergone an investigation by Mayor Paser and the High Priest of Amun, during which he had confessed. Now, bound and blindfolded, he was taken again into the centre of the cemetery where he was released and told to walk to the tomb which he said he had robbed – that of Queen Isis. But the poor man, a coppersmith named Pekharu, could only lead the commissioners to an open and unfinished tomb where there had never been a burial, then to an old hut built by a friend of Scribe Ramose. 'These are the places where I was,' claimed the hapless copper-smith, and so they tortured him again and he was made to swear a terrible oath on pain of mutilation that he knew no more than he had said. Still all he did was repeat: 'I know of no place here except this tomb which is open and this house which I pointed out to you.' Then the commissioners themselves examined all the tomb seals and 'they found they were intact'. The Vizier seemed satisfied.

Everyone in the necropolis must have waited anxiously for the moment when the commission finally finished its investigations on the west bank and the Vizier and his entourage walked down the white winding track that led out of the Place of Beauty, past the fortress-temple of Ramesses III, to the river-landing to cross to the city of Thebes. The news of his progress must have run from house to house, from settlement to settlement across the little desert plain and its temples. And in the tombmakers' village, just a short walk from the Place of Beauty, many households must have breathed a little easier. The commission's work was done, the suspense broke and on this evening, the last of the working week in the Great Place, 'the chiefs of the medjay and the tombmakers went round the west bank in a great demonstration '.

Once across the river, the courtier who had accompanied the Vizier went straight to Mayor Paser's house to report the day's events. Mayor Paser lived to the north of the temple of Amun, close to the old temple of the god Ptah of Memphis, at the centre of the administrative complex of the temples. A short distance away, built into the rear of the temple of Ma'at, the goddess who personified truth, was the High Priest's court of justice. A large number of the tombmakers and other people from the west bank had also crossed the river with the Vizier's party and now made their way in a great mass to Mayor Paser's house. Amongst them was the Mayor of the west bank, Pawero, the young acting foreman Userkhepeshef, and even the great painter, draughtsman Amenhotep. They danced at Mayor Paser's discomfiture, for his accusations had largely proved unfounded and he had been made to look a fool. And, on top of everything, the royal courtier was still standing with Paser on their arrival and witnessed his embarrassment at the hands of this raucus mob. Angrily, the Mayor turned on the tomb-makers: 'As for this demonstration which you made today, what you were making was no demonstration but a song of exultation — You have rejoiced over me at the very door of my house. What do you mean by it? For I am the prince who reports to the ruler. If you are rejoicing concerning the tomb — yet King Sebekemsaf II has been violated.' The angry Mayor went on to describe the crime, only to be taunted by Foreman Userkhepeshef who cried triumphantly that: 'All the kings, their royal wives and royal mothers and royal children who rest in the Great and Noble Necropolis together with those who rest in the Place of Beauty are intact; protected and ensured for eternity. The wise council of Pharaoh, their child, guards and examines them strictly.'

In the heat of the moment, the young man had first exaggerated, then lied, then finally insulted Paser; both the Mayor and the foreman must have known deep in their hearts that such claims were foolish. The fragile, unspoken collusion that had existed between the Theban officials now broke down. Mayor Paser addressed the assembly once again in what one may imagine was an icy voice. 'Your deeds belie your words,' he said, then in precise bureaucratic recitation he told how the two village scribes had come to him and made their deposition about the robberies in the west bank cemeteries. He explained how once this report had been made officially he had had to act, 'for it would have been a crime to conceal it', and that it was this statement that had led to the establishment of the commission. He finished by saying that the two scribes had made five charges between them and if these were found to be untrue they could expect the most severe punishments. Now it was the turn of the Mayor of the west bank, Pawero, to be alarmed, for the two village scribes lived, after all, under his authority. He replied: 'It was an offence on the part of these two scribes — that they should go to the Mayor of Thebes because their predecessors had never reported to him but to the Vizier when he was in Upper Egypt or, if he chanced to be in the delta — servants of the necropolis went downstream to where the Vizier was, carrying their document.' All these irregularities of procedure, including the public charges that Mayor Paser had made, Pawero now asked an attending scribe to list and send immediately to the Vizier. Never before, puffed the official, had such a thing been done. So the whole issue of the robbed tombs and the villagers' culpability become lost in a dispute between rival halls of government. One may imagine the two Mayors arguing about such rules of procedure whilst robber gangs rowed off again to cross the river in the evening light.

Two days later, at the beginning of the new week, all the commissioners met in session in the huge hypostyle hall of the temple of Amun. The three men who had been found trespassing in the Place of Beauty two years before were brought before them, and the commission was addressed by the Vizier, who, it seems, had read the west bank Mayor Pawero's report concerning his dispute with Mayor Paser:

> The Mayor Paser made certain charges to the inspectors and the workmen of the necropolis two days ago — about the great tombs which are in the Place of Beauty. Yet when I was there myself as Vizier of the land — we examined the tombs which the Mayor has said had been attacked — and found them intact and all that he had said was found to be false. Now behold, the coppersmiths stand before you; let them tell all that has happened.

Then the three men were questioned again and this time they were found not to have broken into a tomb in the Place of Beauty; Mayor Paser 'was placed in the wrong concerning it', and 'a report was drawn up; it is deposited in the archives of the Vizier'. At the end of the day, Mayor Paser was found to have bungled things. On the other hand the west bank Mayor Pawero had been vindicated as an honest and efficient official. Before he left the Southern City, the Vizier sentenced the two gangs of tomb-robbers that his officials had produced. A simple bunch, they had first confessed to their crimes then endured such dire punishments that their sufferings would be remembered at Thebes thirty years later. Such wretched Theban politicking, the Vizier must have thought to himself as his boat sailed out of the Theban harbour to drift on the stream to Memphis and the palaces of the green delta.

As the Vizier's boat zigzagged through the silt bars, then rounded the Nile's bend to disappear from view, it might have seemed to Harshire and Pabes that their plan had been successful. After all, two gangs of thieves had been arrested for robbing tombs, yet the villagers' own crimes remained undetected. But in its most vital aspect - the attempt to burden the three trespassers arrested in the Place of Beauty with the crime of robbing the tomb of Queen Isis - their plan had failed completely. Behind the intact doorway and seals that the Vizier himself had examined, the burial was destroyed, smashed and plundered by a village gang who had entered the Queen's tomb from the rear. And even as the Vizier sailed away, the stolen goods were circulating in the city. It would only be a matter of time before the plundering of the tomb of the King's step-mother would come publicly to light. And now who would stand the blame for it? For such a recent royal tomb to have been robbed required inside knowledge and many men of the gangs who had made Queen Isis's tomb were still working, including, indeed, Scribe Harshire and his brother, the painter Amenhotep. By reporting the information that had been given to them by the two scribes, Mayor Paser and his Theban colleagues had been made to appear very foolish in the eyes of the Vizier. And the village workmen, who had not known of the actions or intentions of the two scribes, had compounded the situation by publicly celebrating Mayor Paser's embarrassment. The village scribes had attempted to manipulate the rulers of Thebes and had been found out, but now these officials had had their suspicions aroused – not only that there might have been more royal robberies on the west bank than the Vizier had ever imagined, but that, because of their attempt to cover up such crimes, the tombmakers themselves might be involved. The ultimate effect of the scribes' intervention, then, was to alert the Theban authorities, to make them sensitive to the villagers' every move.

21

SCRIBE HARSHIRE

For a while nothing much happened. The records of the first months of the King's seventeenth year, 1107 BC, tell us only that supplies of fish and vegetables arrived regularly at the village, that the work in the Great Place continued – some plastering in the King's tomb took place throughout early May – and that Scribe Harshire collected the village grain ration without undue problems. Yet the experienced scribe knew that things were awry, and those actions of his which have come down to us, as terse entries in a papyrus day-book, suggest that he was trying hard to mend the rift between the villagers and the rulers of Thebes.

For several years past, it had not been unusual for Harshire to give presents on the villagers' behalf to high-placed Theban officials to obtain the release of the grain rations that had been sent from the office of the Vizier and stored in the temple of Amun. Temple officials like Scribe Pentahetnakht, himself the son of a scribe from the tombmakers' village, helped place these gifts, usually pieces of expensive furniture or even, on occasion, a pair of oxen, in the ranks of the High Priest's staff, and a levy was made throughout the village to pay for them. Scribe Harshire would make checklists of all the contributors and the two deputies of the gangs, his cousins Pa'aken and Amenhotep, would help in the collection. The scribe also spent considerable time in the temple of Amun, making a variety of deals with officials there: sometimes arranging the village presents, even, on occasion, taking an order for the villagers to make a lavish set of coffins, with the design and quality specified in the contract in some detail. 'The hair of the inner coffin's head [should be] cut in relief.' These coffins were for a priestess of Amun and she paid for them with a grand assortment of goods, from fine linens and grain to sweet oils and used clothes, each item being carefully valued in copper *deben* and set against the total amount of the order, some 395 *deben*, three years' full rations for a man of the gangs. Despite the tomb-robbers' activities there was at least one Theban still determined to go to her underworld in style. But Harshire's careful cultivation of the officials of the temple of Amun was to no avail. The High Priest Amenhotep and Mayor Paser meant to bring the tombmakers to book.

It was the deputies of the two gangs and their families on whom the axe finally fell; a stratum of village society related to both the foremen and the senior scribes, but not of the rank of village elders. In a list of the men of the two gangs who had received ten days' grain ration in the first month of winter, the word 'prisoner' appears beside some of the names. Since these 'prisoners' had been travelling freely about Thebes on the eleventh day of that month yet were arrested and taken to the temple of Ma'at as prisoners on the fourteenth, we may assume that this grain list dates from between these two events, that is 5 or 6 October 1107 BC, in the seventeenth year of King Ramesses IX. Other documents tell us that were this 'prisoner' list a complete one, its papyrus sheet less damaged, it would have comprised eight names: two deputies, their fathers and four brothers. A catch so neat, so symmetrical, that it must surely have been the result of a deliberate decision that these eight people should stand as the chosen representatives of the village tomb-robbers. Inside the small community everyone would have known something of the robbery and many different houses must have shared in the disposal of the loot.

A cloud of apprehension had hung over the whole community for some time and nerves now started to fray. One young workman had already run away. Then a meeting of the men of the two gangs was called at which the foremen were made to swear publicly that they would not permit any of the villagers to leave the west of Thebes. Any tomb loot that was in the village, therefore, could not be taken across the river to find its way into the Theban markets. From a roll of papyrus eight names were read out, six of which corresponded to the workmen labelled 'prisoner' on the grain lists, whilst the two other were brothers of the same men. The papyrus that reports these events has been badly damaged and, of the next act of the tragedy, only half, a most eloquent half, of the text has survived, the bottom of a single sheet: '... the eight men ... found, silver and gold ... year seventeen, first month of winter, day fourteen'. Other documents recording the investigation that followed give us a better grasp of what had happened. The treasures of Queen Isis' tomb had been found with eight of the tomb-makers, probably in a house-to-house search at the village. They had been taken over the river with their loot to the law courts of the temple of Ma'at, to be imprisoned in the grain magazine at its side. Of these eight, one name is lost, but six of the others are those whose names were read before the village assembly, the other is a relative. Scribe Harshire went to see the men after their arrest and sat near them outside their grain-store prison before returning across the river to the desert village in the evening. One of the prisoners, Pentaweret, a tomb-painter, was his brother; he had been arrested together with three of his sons, one of whom was the deputy Pa'aken. Another cousin of Harshire's, Amenwa, was also in prison, and he too had been arrested with three of his sons, including the deputy Amenhotep – named after his uncle, the great painter. Amenwa was a son of artist Hori; three of the village's finest outline draftsmen were his brothers.

The arrest of the eight men had been ordered by Mayor Pawero. It seems that they were first taken to the temple-fortress of Ramesses III while the High Priest and the Vizier, who was not at Thebes, were informed, before being transferred across the river. The next day a careful list of the tomb loot was drawn up: 'the gold, the silver, the copper and everything which the thieving workmen of the necropolis were found to have stolen when they were discovered to have violated the Place of Beauty', and this too was taken across. Each man's portion was weighed and listed; four of the eight men, the two deputies, a father and a brother, had received twice as much as the others. In all there was just over one and three quarter pounds of pure gold, nearly eight pounds of electrum – a gold and silver mix – and thirty-seven and a half pounds of silver; along with these precious metals were quantities of fine linens and clothes, oils (which might be the most precious extractions of rare seeds and berries, and very highly valued) vases of bronze and ebony, even fragments of Queen Isis' coffins. And more of the loot had already been traded or given away. The authorities moved very quickly after the arrests for they wanted to retrieve the plunder that the tomb-robbers had already disposed of. Though large in numbers, Theban society moved in closed circles and there was a strong possibility that most of the stolen grave goods could be recovered. This now became the main preoccupation of the authorities, and they set about extracting from the eight prisoners the names of those who had received some of Queen Isis' treasure.

All the while the village waited. At the temple of Ma'at the Vizier, newly arrived in Thebes, and Amenhotep, the High Priest of Amun, headed the court which questioned the eight men. Since such investigations usually took place to the accompaniment of limb-twisting and beating, the criminals were soon telling the court their stories in incriminating detail. At the same time, a commission was sent across the river to inspect the security arrangements for the necropolis, and a village house list was drawn up. Now, for the first time, the villagers started to complain of hunger: though fish and vegetables were still sent to the village by its own servants, the grain ration had stopped for more than thirty days. Work ceased at the royal tomb. Marking time, the village scribes carefully noted the grain arrears in their journals. The High Priest and the Vizier now held the village tightly in their grasp. Day by day, the scribes recorded: 'the tombmakers do not work, they are hungry and debilitated; eight prisoners remain in the temple of Ma'at.' On the west bank the recovery of the tomb's loot was placed in the hands of the 'Mayor of western Thebes, Pawero, his scribe Wennenefer, the foreman Userkhepeshef ... and the doorkeeper Khonsmose, of the necropolis'. The authorities had deliberately enlisted two senior men of the village, the argumentative foreman and a doorkeeper, to help in the search, doubtless because they would be especially eager to regain the property whilst there were no rations for the village and eight of their relatives were under interrogation.

The list that the inquisitors extracted from the eight men is one of the very few ancient documents whose date we may legitimately mistrust, for the scribe seems to have dated his fine copy of it to the eighth day of the first month of winter when, as we know from other documents, the eight thieves were still free men, not yet called 'prisoners' on the grain lists. Indeed, at precisely that time, Amenwa and his son, deputy Amenhotep, had gone to Thebes as free men to attend a law court in session in the hypostyle hall at the Amun temple, where they had heard a judgement against them in a dispute about the value of some linen and a sack of grain. If, however, we add another single stroke to the scribe's date, to make it the second month of winter – the eighth day being 31 October 1107 BC – we will arrive at a date that finds the eight villagers imprisoned in the grain store of the Ma'at temple for some twenty-four days: exactly the right point in their inquisition for the list to have been completed – the final fair copy of the thieves' loot drawn up just a week before the first lists of returned goods start to be made and dated.

Both the lists of the robbers' dealings with their loot and the later lists of the goods recovered show just how deeply the tomb-robbers' trade had penetrated Theban society: from the wife of the Fourth Prophet of Amun, the Lady Tami, a member of the first family of Thebes, who was given ten *deben* of copper by Hori, the son of Amenwa, to 'a cripple who lived in the temple of Ramesses I' who was given six *deben* of copper by the same man. In all, the eight robbers made thirty-six payments to officials of the temple of Amun, and many others to officials of the five royal temples on the west bank, including the fortress-temple of Ramesses III. Fourteen further payments were made to priests of temples in towns outside Thebes, several, from different members of the robbers' gang, were made to a boat-captain, Efenamun, who presumably had taken them up and down the river. Fourteen villagers were named by the robbers as receiving plunder and as well as members of the robbers' own families, there were close relatives of Foreman Userkhepeshef who was helping the Vizier's commission to collect up the loot, and even one of the grandchildren of Naunakht who had been the child-wife of the scribe Kenhirkhopeshef almost a century earlier. Many small payments had been made to the servants and slaves of priests and officials; to barbers, washerwomen and water-carriers.

What did you do at Thebes in the eleventh century before Christ if you suddenly had some twenty-five years' salary to spend? – and the gang leaders had double that amount. If you came from a village as hungry as that of the robbers you bought food and, as one would expect, payments to food merchants figure strongly in the lists, though as food was generally cheaper than luxury goods it represents only a relatively small proportion of the total amount of the loot they spent. Some fourteen payments were made directly for purchases of food and drink, although others to brewers, oil-refiners, bakers, fishermen and shepherds were probably also concerned with buying food. There were other payments too, to granary guards, and we may imagine that the fifty-odd *deben* distributed to various officials were bribes to allow the robbers to take grain from the state storerooms; a common enough confession at several later trials at Thebes.

Each of the robbers' confessions are similar in their contents and their amounts: no one man had spent more of his loot than the others, all had bought more or less the same services and goods. To us their ambitions seem modest – fine clothes, new sandals, meat flavoured with tasty oils to eat, and good beer to drink – and in their dealings to obtain these things their contacts ranged from the very top of Theban society to the bottom levels of government. No Theban peasants or farmers appear in the lists: it was only the urban population of the huge city that absorbed the tomb loot from the great necropolis. There was, however, one other category of people who dealt with them, and these were the merchants from the north of Egypt who, in fact, obtained the largest percentage of the haul. These merchants not only traded in copper, but in small amounts of stolen gold and silver too; in this way they differed from the Thebans. Unfortunately, the court lists do not tell us precisely what goods the tomb-robbers obtained from these travelling fences, with whom they had traded some 214 *deben* of copper alone, nearly a fifth of their haul. So thorough were the efforts of the investigators engaged in retrieving the loot that eventually they managed to amass somewhat larger amounts of gold, silver and copper than the robbers had ever admitted to trading. We may imagine that whilst many of the robbers' clients had returned their share to the commissioners of their own free will, some private hoards had been seized in house-to-house searches.

Finally, some thirty-seven days after their arrest, the last confessions had been heard at the court of justice and the metals, fine clothes and furnishings of Queen Isis had all been retrieved. The Vizier and the High Priest sent notice to the Mayor Pawero that he and his officials should come to the hypostyle hall of the temple of Amun. There, amidst the shadowed columns of the vast dark hall, stood the Vizier, the sorry figures of the eight prisoners, the glittering treasures from Queen Isis's tomb and the inquisitors from the temple of Ma'at. The Vizier addressed Pawero directly: 'Here are the prisoners, I give them into your hands, all eight of them.' And referring to the silver, the gold, the clothes, the copper, the oils and

everything else that had been found in the thieves' possession or seized by
the court's inspectors, the High Priest Amenhotep told Pawero and his men
to 'Take it to the fortress-temple of Ramesses III, and close it in a storeroom
with your seal.' So the eight men were taken back across the river to the
fortress-temple, from whose battlements they could see, once again, their
village and its hillside cemetery. There, after three days, further interroga-
tions took place, this time the robbers' wives being brought before the
inquisitors to be subjected to examinations no less stringent, we may
imagine, than those their husbands had undergone. And there, too, the
final lists of all the loot were prepared for the temple records: 'Received
from the temple of Ma'at at Thebes, the gold and silver recovered from the
thieving workmen — .' 'Recovered from the traders — .' 'Recovered from
the people of Thebes and western Thebes.' By the end of the enquiry,
every merchant had been found, every oil-refiner, every temple weaver
tracked down and his house searched: slowly but surely everything stolen
had been retrieved. The commission of recovery had performed its work
fast and efficiently, though with two senior tombworkers amongst their
number the spur must have been great: for now the village was very hungry,
more than forty days having passed since a grain ration delivery.

Now, apparently without rescinding the order to stop the village grain
supplies, the Vizier left Thebes, and the starvation that had accompanied
the house-searches and the trial of the eight continued. It was not until
three weeks later that the Vizier returned to the Southern City. Desperate,
the tombmakers crossed the river to see him. ' "Let us go, my Lord", they
begged him.' His answer has disappeared in a break in the text, but we
do know that they were granted rations for the Vizier's staff told them to
board their boat and take 1,000 temple offering loaves that had been stored
there. It was the first bread the villagers had seen in almost a month and a
half. But the Vizier had not yet finished teaching the tombmakers a lesson,
and even after this audience rations were still not sent to the village and
the gangs remained unable to work at the Great Place. Then, a week later,
the villagers were all summoned to the Place of Beauty, where the Vizier,
the Mayor of Thebes and a high court official oversaw the breaking of the
seals on the doorway of Queen Isis' tomb. Now it was at last opened to
view. Inside, the rose-granite sarcophagus had been smashed to pieces, the
burial chamber broken and plundered. The Vizier's reactions to this scene
have not survived. One can imagine that merely the sight of the wrecked tomb
was rebuke enough for the tombmakers: even today the black and broken
corridor and the smashed sarcophagus that still lies in the small burial
chamber at its end are dismal enough evidence of this ferocious desecration.

The thief Nakhtamun, Scribe Harshire's cousin, says in his confession
that the two fathers among the robbers told their six sons: 'go up and

excavate the face of the cliff [above the tomb] so they said to us, and we climbed down into the tomb.' They used the old trick of entering the burial chamber from the rear and leaving the outside door seals quite intact. This ruse had fooled the Vizier's personal inspection of the year before and, indeed, it was a trick that Theban administration would be slow to learn and slower still to prevent. Official responsibility for the safety of the Theban tombs seldom extended beyond the inspection of carefully-sealed doorways, although perhaps behind them in the darkness of the tomb lay 'the breaking of all that was inside'.

The next day, the Vizier sent for Foreman Nekhenmut, and told him that the villagers would receive, on just this one occasion, a double ration of grain. Then he asked to see the attendance registers for the work in the Great Place: after reaffirming his grip on the village the Vizier intended to put the delinquent workmen straight back to work. But Nekhenmut, though still nominally the senior foreman, had long retired and his son, Userkhepeshef, managed his work at the royal tomb; the records, Nekhenmut told the Vizier, were with the foremen and the draughtsman Amenhotep, who were already at work in the Great Place. But the promised rations still did not arrive at the village and two days later the workmen again appealed to the Vizier for food. And this time, finally, the Vizier seems to have relented and pardoned the village for its crime: 'You are right, you workmen of the Necropolis; I do not say that you are wrong, Oh my brothers.' Again the text is broken, but we can deduce that order now returned to village life.

Nothing, however, could be quite the same again. One thing remained constant: the King's need for a tomb, and two years after the trials Ramesses IX died before his tomb was finished. Once again the gangs put up their scaffolds, plastered over the rough rock of a small unfinished chamber and prepared it for the royal burial. The paintings there have an eerie quality. The great outline draughtsmen were no longer working in the King's tomb; at least one, the painter Amenhotep, being too old. At all events the scenes that the gangs made, though no masterpieces in themselves, seem to reflect the awful days of the trials and starvation: brittle, gaudy pictures of a sinister resurrection, the King rising from a thin and tortured hell to join eternally with the gods of the morning sunrise.

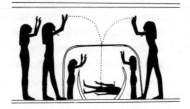

22

THEBES II

Not one of the stolen treasures that the authorities recovered was ever returned to the tomb from which it had been taken. Wrecked burials were simply tidied up, damaged mummies rewrapped, perhaps piously placed in wooden coffins, and laid again at the centre of their tombs with small offerings of flowers and fruit at their feet. All the gold and silver, the copper ewers, the fine clothes and furniture, placed with the dead at the time of their burial, was never returned to them. Tomb-robbing was controlled rather than eliminated and the authorities of Thebes took the tomb loot from the thieves and kept it in their own exchequers.

In the surviving records of the tomb-robbers' trial there is only one clear reference to the way in which honest Thebans regarded their royal dead: when Mayor Paser was taunted by the villagers after his unsuccessful denunciation of tomb-robbing on the west bank, he replied in an outburst of indignation that the commission had found the tomb of one ancient King, Sebekemsaf II, to have been robbed, 'a great ruler who made ten important monuments for Amun Re, king of the gods'. In other words it was bad that the King's tomb had been robbed because he had been a pious man who made monuments for the Theban gods. The King was seen to have suffered an indignity through the despoilation of his tomb; precisely the same sentiment as would be voiced today if the tomb of a modern king or president was desecrated. Little thought seems to have been given by the Thebans to the notion that the dead kings' continuous journeys through the underworld would be interrupted by the desecration of their graves. Once the Pharaohs had been established in their tombs, with due rites and ceremonial, they had been established in the underworld with the other gods for all eternity. Though physical intrusions into their burials were considered as state crimes to be personally investigated by the highest officials of the king, the royal robberies held none of the cosmic implications of the royal funeral. Indeed, uppermost in the minds of those who investigated the robberies was the recovery of the stolen property: robbing the dead was the same as robbing the living.

No one knows the fate of the eight tombmakers. Certainly, they disappeared from village life after their imprisonment in the temple fortress of Ramesses III and are never found again in the village records. It is probable that their punishment was not immediate, nor did it necessarily include the death-penalty. The three men who were originally believed to have robbed Queen Isis' tomb were still alive, though possibly imprisoned, at least two years after their confession. But there is no reason to assume that the penalty for tomb-robbing, or any other crime, was fixed, for there seems to have been no scale of punishment at Thebes, no set legal code. Only the process of ancient law, curiously modern in its appearance, remained constant. Nevertheless, thirty years after the robbery of Queen Isis' tomb, another man accused of tomb-robbing began his defence by recalling the fate of earlier tomb-robbers: 'I saw the punishment that was inflicted upon the thieves in the time of Vizier Khaemwase. Is it likely then that I would risk incurring such a death?' The statement implies that there was a death-sentence, but we do not know the method of execution. Forty years earlier the would-be killers of Ramesses III had been invited to commit suicide, but these were queens and courtiers not mere painters and stonemasons. The vague phrase 'on the wood' that, along with threats of mutilation and beating, was commonly used during oath-taking as a deterrent to perjury, may well have referred to the victim being tied to a post and either starved or stoned to death. For the most part, however, the Thebans were not violent people, nor were they given to brutal public display.

One thing is certain: the eight thieves never returned to their homes or the Great Place. The cauterization of the village may well have been more extensive. For all the village chiefs disappear from the records at this time: Scribe Harshire, both the foremen, Hormose and old Nekhenmut and Nekhenmut's son, the acting foreman Userkhepeshef, who just a year before had laughed in the face of Mayor Paser. Just as there was confusion over the promotion of the village chiefs after the fall of Paneb some sixty years earlier, so now the two foremanships were taken by shadowy figures. Yet so strong was the conviction that positions of authority were properly inherited, that not only did the two posts return to the old foremen's families after just one generation, but the posts of the two deputies also returned to the families of the tomb-robbers. Likewise, Scribe Harshire's son, Khaemhedjet, succeeded to his father's job of senior scribe; though as he had already taken over some of his father's work at the tomb before the tomb-robbery scandal, it is probable that the old scribe had not suffered a grisly fate but had simply died of old age and anxiety.

He had left an impoverished village behind him, and life at Thebes, too, remained very hard. Virtually no new buildings were made in the temples at this time; always a good index of the Theban economy. Even High Priest Amenhotep's house was a mean affair of mud walls set amidst a group of ancient buildings by the side of the temple's sacred lake. Indeed some of its accommodation was contained inside a chapel of alabaster and sandstone that 500 years before had housed the great god himself during the festivals of Thebes. On one of these ancient walls High Priest Amenhotep had a relief cut into the sandstone showing him receiving golden collars from King Ramesses IX, a high state honour. Along with two little scenes cut into the almost equally ancient walls of the court of the temple of Ma'at these are almost the sole memorials of his priesthood.

The villagers quickly began work on the tomb of Ramesses IX's successor: his son Ramesses X. As the architectural traditions of the valley demanded, the proportions of each king's tomb were a little bigger – about 5 per cent – than its predecessors, and by this time the royal tombs had become very large indeed. Yet the gangs, now numbering about twenty men on each side, worked at the same rate as before and progress on the huge monument was slow. By the third year of the reign the plasterers, sculptors and painters were at work again, the two walls leading up to the tomb's door having been built. The great doorway, some twenty-five feet from the ground to the top of its frieze, was decorated in bright-painted relief with the traditional scenes. Inside the tomb, the outline draughtsmen completed the work of the first corridors and the sculptors were cutting the figures of the kings and gods. The work-register of the two gangs has survived intact for a period of some five months in this third year and it tells us that out of those 150 days, the gangs worked thirty-six: a drop in the work-load from the time of Ramesses III of more than 10 per cent. It is possible of course that an unusual run of festivals may have accounted for some of these absences but it is also true that these five sparkling months, from mid-November until early April, are the best months for work at Thebes, cooler and fresher than the hard summer. Rather ominously, most of the gangs' work was performed during the first half of each month, following the delivery of the grain ration. Even more ominously, a preoccupation with food and grain deliveries beats steadily through this work-journal like a deep drum, its acquisition and delivery taking more space in the registers than the descriptions of the work at the tomb.

True, the grain rations are recorded as arriving regularly in the last two or three days of each month, but, each and every time, there was anxiety that they would not, and often the tombmakers crossed the river to visit the temple of Amun and ask for them in person: 'The fourth month of winter, day twenty-seven. The men did not work. Two doorkeepers were sent to Thebes to search for provisions.' Sometimes, all the workmen would go and sleep overnight by the temple of Amun, waiting for the grain magazines to be opened for them in the morning: 'Second month of summer, day twenty-eight — . The workers went to Thebes in a boat and passed the night there — "Our rations have not come [they said to High Priest Amen-hotep] and we have passed the night here ...".' On this occasion the High Priest's supplies were so low that he had no grain to spare for the men, and he told them so. Then the Vizier's representative at Thebes was brought to the High Priest's court and he authorized the tombmakers to draw their rations directly from the King's grain stores. On another occasion, just two days after they had received their rations, we find the gang working not in the Great Place but on the tomb of Scribe Pentahetnakht, the village boy who now worked as a scribe in the temple of Amun and who had tried to help the villagers at the time of the trials of the eight robbers. Another time, after the Vizier's representative had again helped them obtain their grain ration, the villagers promised some presents to his scribe: two decor-ated boxes and a set of writing equipment. Cabinet-makers were employed to carpenter the boxes, the small amounts of gold and silver needed for their inlays were bought from a metal-worker and on the twenty-seventh day of the month, three days before the next ration was due, the presents were sent across the river. That month, the villagers received their rations on the very first day; on the second they were back in Thebes for a two-day festival celebration.

As well as the grain ration, there were four deliveries of fish every month from the village's own fishermen. As there were almost similarly-spaced rations of firewood sent up to the village we might be tempted to imagine the tombmakers sitting in the evening light, chatting, drinking and grilling their fresh Nile fish on sticks over a round pottery brazier. But this is probably a false picture, for without their fish, carefully rationed by weight to each of the village households, the tombmakers would surely have starved; the grain rations seem to have dwindled to the point where each month's delivery was awaited with the bright-eyed intensity of the truly hungry. Perhaps it was due to the small amounts of rations supplied to the villagers that they did not work the last two months of winter and half of the first month of spring – from mid-November 1103 BC until January of the following year. For at that time, the village fishermen delivered only very small amounts of fish, and this may have been due to the condition of their fishing-boats which, the village record reports, were inspected by the High Priest at this point. By the beginning of the first month of summer, just four days after their rations had been delivered, the villagers were on strike again. Like Medjay Mentmose in more prosperous times, a medjay incited the men to protest, and they walked together into one of the temples. Apparently, the High Priest was furious: 'It is I who tell them to work', he is reported as saying in answer to the protesters – and it is clear from this remark who now held sway over the villagers.

Ramesses x died after a nine-year reign and was, presumably, buried in the huge tomb that the villagers had made for him. Today it is in ruins, filled with flood sediment, and no one has ever seen its burial chamber. This broken corridor is the sole monument of the reign, and the artists who made it were so unused to spelling the King's names in monumental hieroglyphs that before they drew them on the tomb walls they had first to experiment with the arrangement of the signs so as to achieve a proper balance.

This new poverty of the practised arts made itself obvious in the village where even a decade before Scribe Khaemhedjet had simply placed the coffin of his father Harshire in the old family vault, made by his grandfather Amennakht. And to serve as a mortuary chapel for the cults of both his father and himself, he had scribbled their two names amidst the formal decorations of an old chapel in the village cemetery; one of two that had been made by a villager, a workman at the King's tomb, living in the days of Ramesses the Great. By Khaemhedjet's day no one made private tomb chapels any more.

The poverty of the Southern City was the climax of a process of attrition so slow as to be almost indiscernable. For two centuries past, the lakes that stood deep in Africa at the head of the Nile had slowly dwindled. Each year the Nile flood was slightly reduced and the area of cultivated land diminished. Little by little the annual harvest yielded less and less. One of the first obvious signs of this process occurred as early as the time of Merneptah – a period of abundant harvests, when a delta palace built on a branch of the river had been left high and dry and another on a deeper waterway was built to replace it. A hundred years later, in the time of Ramesses x, the entire region of Lower Nubia, the southern province long settled by Egyptians and a source of great wealth for Thebes, was desiccating, the prelude to a thousand-year drought in that region. Though Thebes appeared to be as verdant as ever, its grain reserves, the legendary cushions against a bad harvest – the 'corn as the sand of the sea' described in the Book of Genesis – were gone. Now the population lived from year to year and any hitch in the food supply in the distribution system or as a result of a poor Nile flood, spelled hardship for the people of the Southern City.

To the priests of the temples and the officers of the administration, it must have seemed that the gods were squeezing the city hard, that times were waxing late indeed. Then, in about the ninth year of King Ramesses XI, High Priest Amenhotep lost all authority as a sudden wave of anarchy broke through the city.

In such ferocious times, people do not usually sit down to write about what is happening and the archaeological evidence, either the ruin of destruction or, more usually, a vacuum of nothing at all, cannot show us the heart of the matter. But the Thebans shared a powerful memory of these terrible months and their briefly recorded recollections speak volumes: some ten years later, for example, a woman said that, at the time of anarchy at Thebes, she had exchanged blocks of dried dates from the family palm grove for silver; whilst another woman told how she had earned silver enough to buy slaves in 'exchange for barley in the Year of the Hyenas, when there was a famine'. Similarly, a gang of robbers who operated at this time were called 'men who have found something that can be sold for bread'. In the *argot* of such thieves, too, loot was sometimes called 'bread'; the apparent modernity of the term should not be allowed to obscure the directness of its Theban usage.

Despite such signs of encroaching chaos, some still believed that there would be a pious remedy for the terror, that the order of the gods and the Pharaoh would soon prevail in the Southern City. The current value of such sentiments, when voiced by a father protesting to some robbers that by taking his young son into their number they would fashion a 'noose — which you have laid on the neck of the lad' received a brutally dimissive assessment by the gang's leader, one Amenkhau. In one sentence he tells us of the reality of the age: 'Oh doddering old man, evil in your old age; if you are killed and thrown into the water who will look after you?' Amenkhau and his gang had been tomb-robbing and, as the widow of one of his men later recalled, the thieves had fallen out:

They divided a mass of treasure and made it into four parts — and I took the share of my husband and put it aside in my storeroom and took some silver and bought grain with it. And when some days had passed Amenkhau — came with the scribe of the divine record Nesamun and they said to me, 'Give up this treasure.' [And they] were with — my own brother! But I said to them with an air of boldness 'My brother will not let me be interfered with', and Amenkhau gave me a blow with a spear on one of my arms and I fell. Then I got up and entered the storeroom, brought the silver and handed it over to him together with two *deben* of gold and the two seals, one of real lapis lazuli and one of turquoise; there was a weight of six *kite* of fine gold in them, in mounting and setting.

Hunger visited the Southern City, and unable to control the Thebans, unable, probably even to provision his own staff, the power of the High Priest in Upper Egypt had disappeared. From his house by Amun's temple, Amenhotep appealed to the King for help. But Ramesses XI was either reluctant or unable to move troops south to Thebes from the delta garrisons; the royal remedy for the situation was to direct the Viceroy of Nubia, Panhesi, to bring his troops north and establish order in Upper Egypt once again. Years later, a herdsman who had been sold into slavery at this time remembered the arrival of the Viceroy and his Nubian regiments on the west bank: 'The foreigners came and seized the fortress-temple of Ramesses III while I was in charge of some donkeys that belonged to my father, and Peheti, a foreigner, seized me and took me — [this] when Amenhotep, who was High Priest of Amun, had been suppressed for six months.' Along with many others, the donkey-herd had been captured by the Nubian army and taken north up the Nile valley on a three-month campaign of pacification.

Before the arrival of Panhesi's troops, Mayor Pawero's officials on the west bank had had to stand by helpless whilst gangs of looters burst into the ancient buildings, stripping gold from their walls, copper from their doors and statues and gilding from the gods' shrines. Then, when the bare wood of the temples' fittings stood exposed, others cut the precious cedar into planks and firewood and carried them away. If ever there could be said to be a time when ancient Egypt came to an end, it would be this year, 1088 BC, when in a short space of time the temples of Thebes lost their treasures. For although they continued to be used as sacred buildings, seats of reverence, for a thousand years and more, their very skin - the gold given them by their builder kings - had been torn away from them, and this by the god's own priests.

This time the tombmakers and their families do not appear to have joined in the pillage, which seems to have taken place over a relatively brief period. True, one villager was murdered by a gang of robbers after he showed them how to enter a tomb undetected and leave the door seal intact, and two others had given similar information to another gang, then joined them in robbing three queens' tombs in the Great Place; but for the most part they did not co-operate. Though reduced in numbers, they had even desultorily continued to work in the royal tomb. Indeed, just a short while before the famine the outline draughtsmen had returned to the King's tomb to draw, in superb brush strokes on the fine yellow plaster of its high walls, a skeleton plan of the tomb's decorations. But when the Viceroy of Nubia's army finally appeared on the west bank, the masons laid down their tools, the workmen dropped their baskets of chippings on the floor, and the tomb was abandoned. Most of the villagers then seem to have waited for the rule of law to be re-established and the ration delivery restored so that they might return to their work in the Great Place. Meanwhile, they managed as best as they could.

Scribe Khaemhedjet died at about the same time that Panhesi and his Nubian troops came to Thebes. Though he had lived through a terrible era of the village's history, he had not only continued his father's work in the Great Place but also the family tradition of coffin-painting, which he passed on to the family's fifth generation of artists. Now his only son, Djutmose, succeeded him as a scribe of the tomb. Like others in his family he had worked in the gangs since the days of the village tomb-robbers, living alone in one of the village houses before marrying Baketamun. And like his father Djutmose had but two children, a son, Butehamun, and a daughter, Hatia. When he succeeded his father as scribe of the tomb, Djutmose's children were aged about thirteen or fourteen; their father about thirty-three. Scribe Djutmose was a most unusual man. Possessed of a full measure of the family wit and understanding, enough indeed, to lead the villagers through their greatest trials, he also left us a great number of letters: one of the most moving records in ancient life still in existence. He was a careful man who worried about his family and his possessions in difficult times; today he even seems to have a strange modernity about him, in which timorousness and ambition run uneasily side by side.

When Viceroy Panhesi first arrived at Thebes he employed several local officials to help in the re-establishment of law and order. High Priest Amenhotep was excluded from this process however and some of his officials were taken away from the temple of Amun to work elsewhere. As a king's scribe with wide local knowledge and a firm loyalty to the crown, Djutmose was enlisted by Panhesi to investigate the looting that had occurred on the west bank of Thebes and to recover the stolen treasures. So Djutmose was suddenly promoted from supervising the desultory work upon the royal tomb to the post of a Theban official serving on a governor's commission of investigation: a promotion that put him close to the new centre of power at Thebes.

Scribe Djutmose was faced with a gigantic task in his new capacity, for the looting of the west bank had been extensive. Ramesses II's temple had suffered the worst, more than eighty pounds of gold and silver having been stripped from the temple doorways alone – a far larger haul than the eight tomb-robbers of a generation before had extracted from the tomb of Queen Isis. And at the fortress-temple of Ramesses III not only had some of the sanctuaries' furnishings been cut into pieces and melted down, but the royal palace in the compound had been looted as well. Though as a later inquiry noted, the palace guards claimed that they had deserted the 'House of Pharaoh' only when the Nubian Viceroy had arrived in Thebes, and we can speculate that the 540 pounds of copper recorded as having been stripped from the palace and the temple's doors had been taken by the Nubian armourers and used to tip spears and arrows for Panhesi's campaign in the north. By far the greater part of the robberies had been committed before this time, however, by the temples' staffs and gangs of humbler, often hungry men from the temple of Amun, who had raided the rich compounds on the west bank for the loot that they called 'bread'. Often these gangs had not entered the interiors of the temple or despoiled the gods' shrines as the temples' own staffs had done, but simply scratched up the remaining grain from the long temple warehouses where 200 years earlier Scribe Ramose and his fellows had stacked and counted the bounty of an empire. Djutmose's commission found these same magazines empty of food and stripped even of their fittings. As well as the temple robberies at least two gangs had been at work in the tombs of Thebes in this Year of the Hyenas. Like earlier tomb-robbers, they too, had used boatmen to aid their getaway from the cemeteries, and they had worked with some stealth, as if they knew that order would return one day to the city and they would stand accountable if their names became known. But then, as order broke down completely, they worried less about the future and took to roving up and down the Nile outside the Theban province, plundering the cemeteries of other towns. Similarly, provincial robbers visited Thebes to work in the cemeteries of the huge city.

Threatened, perhaps, by the prospect of a house-to-house search across the west bank - for part of the work of Panhesi's commissioners was the compilation of a detailed list of west bank houses and their occupants - more than twenty people handed over tiny hoards of cloth and metals to Scribe Djutmose and the other commissioners. Everything was listed: the chief porter at the fortress-temple of Ramesses III gave them a third of an ounce of gold, three ounces of copper and a red cloth; a bee-keeper, who also lived inside the fortress, gave similar small amounts; two fishermen, who lived in houses in front of the fortress, gave their small pieces of gold and copper to the scribe Pentahetnakht, who had now left the staff of the temple of Amun to live on the west bank. Ironically, similarly tiny amounts were surrendered to an army scribe, Kashuti, who had himself stolen some twenty pounds of silver from a huge ornamented stand, one of the fittings in the sanctuaries of the temple of Ramesses III; but it was a decade before he and other high-placed thieves were brought to account. During Djutmose's initial investigations most of them simply incriminated junior members of their own staff and escaped scot-free.

Nevertheless, Panhesi's perfunctory justice - even before the commission had begun its work, the Viceroy's troop captains had killed some suspected thieves with their own hands - had restored a sort of order to Thebes. And as if in response, the gods devoted themselves again to balancing the cosmic order, and the Nile's flood and Egypt's fruitful harvests returned. Far more than the delta lowlands, which needed only a gentle flood to water their fields, Upper Egypt always suffered badly from the effects of a poor flood: just one-seventh below normal flooding levels, merely a yard short, and the harvest was cut by more than half. In the decades before Viceroy Panhesi arrived in Thebes the city's grain reserves had been whittled away to a fraction of their former levels, and consequently grain prices had risen and fallen with the annual variations of the flood. The effect of a lean harvest on the hand-to-mouth economy was savage: in the Year of the Hyenas people had starved within six months of the low flood, and the rule of the High Priest had ended as civil chaos engulfed his state. With the return of a full flood and, with Panhesi, the rule of law, Theban grain prices regained their levels of fifty years before. The Nubian Viceroy found that he and his army had left the desiccated southlands for a paradise. As King Ramesses XI had commanded, Panhesi restored Amenhotep to the high priesthood, but he had not restored Amenhotep's temporal authority, and he now ruled Upper Egypt himself.

Two years after Panhesi's arrival at Thebes, Scribe Djutmose, having completed the work of the Viceroy's commission into the looting of the west bank, was working as an official in the new Theban government, collecting copious quantities of grain from the temple estates of Upper Egypt. On 6 September 1085 BC he set sail in the boat of Captain Djutweshbi for Esna, a town in the province of the Double Plume some forty miles south of Thebes, to collect the tithes from the holdings of the temple of Khnum. For amongst all temples' holdings, certain fields were designated as royal land, whose produce was intended for the royal exchequer. Before Panhesi's arrival at Thebes these tithes had not been collected, and indeed, even the wood of the Amun temple's grain-collection boats had been plundered. Now, under Panhesi's authority and the supervision of the west bank Mayor, Pawero, these tithes, previously used to feed the people of the west bank and the tombmakers' village, were once again gathered in.

As Djutmose left Thebes the annual flood covered the summer-hot land like a quicksilver lake. The shining water and the cool north breeze that always came to blow against the flood – traditional reasons for relief and celebration in the Southern City – made sailing an especial delight. The river swelled on its bed, the shadow of the square sail, luminous and blue, passed over the sitting scribe and the boat creaked against the heavy stream. A second, smaller vessel sailed along behind them: a fishing-boat from the Theban fleet to carry the temple grain, for boats were still scarce at Thebes. It was Djutmose's sixth river trip in as many months, though now he would be collecting much more grain than before: the last of the crop of Ramesses's eleventh year. High floods sometimes threatened grain stores with a soaking, and Djutmose's trip on the swollen river might well have been planned in order to take endangered supplies back to the dry store-rooms of Thebes, for the flood was now just days away from its full height. It was good to sail away from the tired dry city and, unlike the scribe's earlier voyages on a slow river in a slack wind, the big boat was running fast in the wind, hard against the current. Silt-browned water splashing against the hull reflected on to the curving sail.

The city and all its temples were cut off by the river's bend, and the scribe turned his head to continue with the affairs of his village:

What is the matter with you? You do not listen and are idle — . As for the men — there has been no work, and there is now work for them. Now I said to you, 'Dispatch your scribe. Make him go with the doorkeeper - fetch the grain [and you] have not obeyed me' — let them go and fetch the grain lest the men hunger and become idle in performing Pharaoh's work and blame is fixed upon you. I write to you through the watchman Wenamun.

The inked reed runs neatly across the fresh papyrus sheet while the sail shades the scribe. The boat moves right and left into the stream, avoiding the silt bars and the low islands in the river. Despite the high flood the river's banks stand green with life on either side, the water filtering into the broad low basins of the cultivated fields.

At the desert's edge a few miles away peasants are pushing the flood-black mud out on to the sand to extend their fields by a yard or two. Now as the east bank desert turns to green fields, the boat sails out of the province of the Plumed Sceptre, the province of Thebes, into a richer more-densely populated area of the valley. Towns, villages and ancient dykes still stand above the water: the skeleton of Egypt. The hills, houses and palm trees give grave, heraldic reflections in the flood. When the river had first risen, the animals - the cows, sheep and goats - had been led to the high ground along the river's edge or to the tops of the levees that stand above the flood. Now they low and bray at the passing boats, while drowned carcasses bob inflated at the river's edge, vultures stripping them of their flesh. Cranes and herons fish the shallow shoals. Loose reeds and papyrus float down with the stream. Children riding cows along the river's edge wave at the two boats. White birds wade jerkily through the water prodding the silt with their beaks. Farmers carefully inspect the banks of the dykes and channels that have sent the flood into their fields and now protect their towns and grain stores from the water. Scribe Djutmose holds the papyrus down against the hard breeze, and folds the letter into a narrow strip, then doubles it over to tie the two open ends together with a string.

This he seals with a pellet of clay that he has moistened with river water. A hand trailing in the sunlit stream. On one face of the fat strip he writes his name, on the other, where scribes write the name and the office of the person to whom they have written, he puts the name of his son. When they arrive at the temple of Khnum at Esna, his assistant will give the letter to the temple scribe there, who will see that it is sent overland to Thebes the same day.

The sail moves in the rigging again, the boat bobs and the scribe sits dazzled by the sun. The boat passes in the lee of a long island and a cloud of pelicans rises noisily from a hidden shaded shore. A sailor holding the high steering oar at the stern sings quietly, the sails ripple, tremors pass through the loose wooden boat, which grates together like an old door opening at night. 'A wife blind in one eye had been in the house of a man for twenty years; and when he found another, he said to her, "I divorce you, for you are blind in one eye." She said to him: "Is this what you have discovered in these twenty years that I have spent in your house?"' The chief taxing-master of the west bank enjoys a good tale, so Djutmose has been told, and he writes down the old village saw for the taxing-master's amusement in another letter.

Coming out into the river again, from behind the island, amidst the rising water-birds, the boat sets straight against the central stream once more. Clouds run fast across the sky in broad landscapes, the speckled pattern of a falcon's plumage. A hot breeze passes quickly over the boat, the sail flaps. They have sailed into dusk and the captain looks for a landing, for the river's sandbanks are especially hazardous at night. They close into the shore by an island half sunk in the flood; a sailor jumps down into the water and runs across the fine lawn, pulling a heavy rope with him, which he stakes to the ground. The boat grates against a flood beach of green-drowned vegetation; the little fishing boat comes in behind them and both are moored. The sailors do not like to go further ashore than these gaps in the papyrus beds, little stages set along the river banks; the shore-dwellers, the fishermen in reed huts and the lean peasant families who quickly plant the silty banks for a scavenged crop, are equally apprehensive of boatmen, who bring them nothing but menace. Djutmose unrolls a squashy mat of loose-bunched rushes on the deck and lies there in the low evening light, as copper-hot, it seems to him, as noon. He hears the water slapping between the two boats, and when he turns his head sideways, pressing his cheek hard against the scented wooden planking, he sees a village on a mound, its hearths sending up bright streams of smoke, pink-blue between the deepening flood and the fading sky.

The boatmen have tied the sail and the captain now arranges for the cooking of the evening meal. The scribe smells their fire. Once upon a time,

Djutmose considers, his neighbours would sit and 'joke with me, and I would take [it]' but, he wonders, '[can] I take it now that I am a scribe who is working as a great official?' The boat moves at its mooring, rising on a sudden swell, pitches and settles again. 'You do not know the concern in my heart for you, my desire to have your soul remembered daily for your sake — I was in the house when you were born.' The slow smoke rises into the low-starred sky, but the village scribe, the great official, sees his own family, his own village. The evening's scent and the damp air touch the scribe's face as he jumps down from the side of the boat on to the grass bank and walks over to the captain sitting by a small fire of roots and twigs with two of the village doorkeepers, Djutmose's staff for his journey. 'Every day I tell Seth the Ombite, who is before the Universal Lord in the solar boat, the Great God of Creation, to give you life, prosperity and health, and very many favours before Amun Re, King of the Gods.'

The night came as the men ate. They slept; then, rising before sunrise, they sailed to Esna, bright and high on its ancient hill, and docked on the flood close to the temple granaries. Now the water is at its full height and the walls and embankments are watched anxiously by town officials. It is a good flood, a proper year; Djutmose and his village will have grain and the priests of Khnum of Esna will harvest more from their fields within months.

Received in the town of Esna in year twelve [of Ramesses XI, 8 September 1084 BC], by the scribe of the necropolis, Djutmose, and the two doorkeepers: of the 402 *khar* of corn assessed as the tithes of the house of Khnum and Nebu, from the hand of the deputy-superintendent and the temple scribe in the granary of Khnum and Nebu at Esna, 337 *Khar*.

Labourers shovel the grain into hundredweight – one *khar* – sacks which they carry out of the granary along the dust path to the river bank, where it is stacked on to the two boats. Flocks of pigeons peck at the loose grain as it falls from the swollen sacks. The boats set sail on the fast stream back to Thebes, the deep-piled craft riding the river like castle towers. The bright patterned sails move slowly past the sunken fields, showing the villages of the Double Plume and the Plumed Sceptre that, along with the cool flood, the affairs of Pharaoh move through the land once more. Sitting atop his grain sacks in the sharp breeze, Djutmose reckons his accounts: he has brought enough wheat from the Khnum temple farms to keep his village for months; and wheat, too, for the other people of the west bank. Mayor Pawero and his staff will check all these supplies into the great granary called, 'The Harvest Overflows'.

Scribe Djutmose sails around the river bend to Thebes on the full flood; temple pennants wave in the sun and the western mountains on the city's skyline have a silver light around their edges. Then the two boats turn away

175

from the river and are pulled home along the canal that runs through the shallow glittering flood to the gate of the fortress-temple. Here Mayor Pawero and Scribe Nesamenopet come to receive them and labourers carry the grain sacks through the stone High Gate and into the granary. Djutmose is pleased to be home, to move through the blue smoke and the golden dust of his city and to see his family again. 'Received in year twelve [12 September 1085 BC] by the Mayor of the west, Pawero; the corn brought by the scribe of the necropolis Djutmose and the two doorkeepers, in the boat of Captain Djutweshbi and the boat of the fisherman Kadore, from the town of Esna, 337 *khar*.'

23

RENAISSANCE

A sort of calm returned to Thebes during Panhesi's rule. Scribe Djutmose continued to sail the river collecting grain and supplies and the Viceroy even started to settle some of his southern troops on land around the city, probably in areas to its north which were still partly wild. Up in the delta, King Ramesses XI and his court were content to leave the government of Upper Egypt to the Nubian Viceroy, merely demanding the usual displays of vassalage: that Panhesi ran occasional errands for the royal administration, kept the Theban temples in good order, and sent token tribute.

> Royal command to the King's son of Nubia — Panhesi, leader of the King's archers — you will seek the [courtier] of Pharaoh and make him proceed with the royal business which he was sent to the south to perform — You shall look to the shrine of the Great Goddess and you shall finish it and have it brought by boat to where I live — [precious] stones and flowers of the *katha* plants and blue flowers — in order to supply the craftsmen. Do not neglect this business which I send you, I write so that a proper record is made of this request. The letter [also] informs you of the King's well-being. Year seventeen, fourth month of the inundation, day fifteen [3 September 1080 BC].

Whether the delta King ever received his Theban tribute we do not know; probably not, for that same year Panhesi was on the march again, moving north from Thebes with an army composed of his Nubian soldiers, some impressed Thebans and even medjay from the west bank. Three hundred miles north of Thebes, just south of Tajoy, they fought a battle and sacked a town, then advanced into the delta. But though he won a battle, Panhesi had lost the war, and soon he was marching south down the Nile valley, through Thebes and back into Nubia. From this time on government records always link Panhesi's name with a sign derived from the hieroglyph signifying 'enemy' and 'death': Panhesi was now an enemy of the state.

Two years after Panhesi's retreat the King came back to Thebes, and there he would have seen the ruin of the Southern City. Indeed, inside the enclosure of the Amun temple Ramesses would have seen evidence not only of the looting of the previous decades but also of the poverty of the city and the decline of the priesthood. The temple of the god Khonsu, Amun's son, built from stone that the High Priest Amenhotep and his predecessors had taken from several of the royal temples, was still unfinished, the sandstone walls of its outer courts blank and undecorated. Even the great ceremonial bark of Amun, the huge gilded barge on which the god journeyed during the Theban festivals, lay stripped of its gilding and most of its timbers. Doubtless the King also visited the Great Place where his vast yellow cavern of a tomb stood open and unfinished, its wall-plaster dented and scratched, the outline draughtsmen's drawings old and faded. Twenty years earlier it had been planned as an impressive monument, massive and wide, the largest tomb ever cut in the Great Place, with high, well-carved doorways and a dark elegant interior. But in the course of that impoverished epoch the traditional design had been attenuated and so many rooms and passages omitted from the royal plan that sunlight shone down into the centre of the burial chamber itself.

Ancient Thebes needed a ruler with a firm hand. Ramesses XI returned to his delta palace, but he left one of his generals, Herihor, a professional soldier and, probably, a Libyan mercenary, to control the Southern City. Now that Amenhotep was either dead or dismissed, he gave this new ruler of Thebes the titles of Southern Vizier and High Priest of Amun. With the villainous Viceroy driven back to Nubia and Herihor awarded all the highest Theban offices, with the return of high flood and good government to the Southern City, Ramesses XI decided that a new era, a new reckoning of dates would be initiated: the nineteenth year of his reign would be 'Year One of the Era of Rebirth'. It was decreed that there would be a renaissance at Thebes, and to affirm these sentiments – destined to be repeated so often in other periods of history and on other continents – the King ordered that Herihor, the High Priest-General, should straightaway see to the completion of Khonsu's temple. Soon outline draughtsmen were drawing again on the temple's walls: filling them with rows of scenes showing General Herihor and the King offering to the gods, and inscriptions telling of Ramesses XI's orders to his new High Priest. A few years later, with the King back in the delta, the temple's outer court was decorated with scenes that showed Herihor himself dressed and named as Pharaoh; in Upper Egypt Herihor was now ruler of a province extending as far as the town of Tajoy, now a border fortress in the middle of Egypt. But the High Priest-General still owed ultimate allegiance to his delta King. Similarly, at Thebes he bowed to the state god, and every major decision of state was made with the nodding consent of the oracle. In Khonsu's temple the General had a prayer cut on to the wall asking for a long life; it is reported that the 'gods agreed exceedingly' to his request. Whilst Herihor's artists carved reliefs showing the High Priest celebrating the Theban festivals once again, a temple official set sail for the Lebanon to obtain fresh cedarwood for the refurbishing of Amun's bark.

An important psychological step in this renaissance, a method by which all the bad things of the past could be recorded and then put away for ever, was a royal investigation to arrest and try the pillagers of the city's tombs and temples. Thebes may have spun and fallen, but now the King and his officers would put the disaster in its proper context: a mere pause in the eternal progress of the state and its gods. Even before Ramesses had left Thebes the commission was underway and members of a gang who admitted robbing tombs in the Place of Beauty were taken to 'the place where Pharaoh was' where at least one of them was cross-examined by the King himself. After the King's departure, evidence was heard in front of a commission composed of members of the royal court: a vizier, a treasurer and an honoured courtier. Not a single Theban, neither mayor nor priest, would serve on this commission; Herihor and his family had replaced the old order; the influence of the ancient Theban families had been swept away for ever.

For the delicate task of investigation the two leading scribes of the tomb-makers' village, Djutmose and Nesamenopet, were appointed as officers of the commission. Men long in the direct service of the King, from old-established Theban families, yet ones quite separate from the discredited clans that had long ruled the city, the village scribes were ideal lieutenants for the new rulers of Thebes. Almost immediately, they presented the commission with the most disquieting evidence: 'There was brought the servant Penuferahy, and it was said that he had washed a long heavy cloak of fine Upper Egyptian linen; they said that it belonged to Pharaoh. ' This, then, was plunder from a royal tomb.

It must have been common knowledge amongst the people of Thebes that not only the temples and private cemeteries had suffered heavy despoilation during the two previous decades – the royal tombs in the Great Place had been robbed too. Before the time of the Year of the Hyenas such plundering of royal tombs seems to have taken place either during or shortly after the kings' burials, but by Herihor's time most of the kings' tombs, old and recent alike, had been entered and robbed; the royal mummies stripped of their jewels, the tomb chambers looted of their grave goods. Such events could only have happened during the Year of the Hyenas or, during the brief period of Panhesi's retreat through Thebes to Nubia.

Unfortunately, most of the evidence the commission heard concerning these crimes has perished; though one undated fragment of the trial of the robbers of Ramesses vi's tomb has survived, and this, by strong circumstantial evidence, may be dated to the time of Herihor's royal commission. The text suggests that the robbers – a mixed band of foreigners and Theban metalsmiths – probably used the old trick of breaking into the tomb through a small tunnel, thus leaving the sealed doorway intact and the robbery undetectable by simple external inspection. Indeed, there is still a small secondary entrance to Ramesses VI's tomb today, through a hole in the floor of an older tomb which passes over the corridor. Thus the robbers must have raided the royal valley with the aid of an informant, and indeed a villager, who probably knew of this tomb's Achilles' heel, had been in their gang, though by the time they set out to rob the tomb he was dead:

> We went up in a single body. The foreigner Nesamun showed us the tomb of Ramesses VI, the Great God. We said to him, 'Where is the tombmaker [i.e. the villager] who was with you?' And he said to us 'The cemetery worker was killed — ', so he said to us. And I spent four days breaking into it [the tomb] there being five of us present. We opened the tomb and we entered it. We found a basket lying on sixty ... chests ... We opened it and found a ... of bronze and [a list of a quantity of metal goods follows; bowls, vases, even beds]. We weighed the copper of these objects and found it to be 500 *deben*, 100 falling to the share of each man. We opened two chests full of clothes; we found good quality Upper Egyptian cloth — a basket of clothes ... twenty-five garments of coloured cloth.

Djutmose and Nesamenopet went all over Thebes asking questions, checking on gossip, observing the thieves that were still living on their loot; it was obviously impossible to keep such terrible secrets now that order had returned. Quickly, more than 100 people were rounded up, and limb-twisting and beating brought the pith of truth out of their lengthy statements. If some of the thieves and their accomplices had died of old age or been killed in Panhesi's campaign in the delta, or even murdered by fellow-thieves, then their wives were found and questioned in their stead. Even an elderly fisherman who had been prosecuted some thirty years before, in a trial preceding that of the village's tomb-robbers, was brought before the commission and made to tell his story once again. As Djutmose and Nesamenopet brought in their witnesses one by one, accusers and accused, the Vizier and the other commissioners listened impassively to the long parade of reminiscences and protestations: 'There was brought Seka'atiamun the servant of the merchant Pesyenwase. The Vizier said to him, "What is the story of your going to raid the Great Tombs?" He said "Far be it from me! The Great Tombs! Put me to death for the tombs of Imiotru [a town just south of Thebes] for they are the tombs in which I was." He was examined further with a stick.' With such cruel inducements many of the thieves confessed, and only once do we find a man later refuting his statement by saying that he had made it only 'out of fear'.

Not all the commission's evidence was obtained by confession and torture however, for Djutmose and Nesamenopet had done a great deal of research and often interrupted witnesses to provoke exchanges as fast as those in a modern courtroom: 'The Vizier said to her, "What is the story of this silver which your husband took from the Great Tombs?" She replied, "I did not see it"; then the scribe Djutmose asked, "How then did you buy the servants?" And she said, "I bought them in exchange for blocks of dates from my palm grove".' Another witness received a beating during his interrogation.

'Stop,' he exclaimed, 'I will tell you. [We] took a silver mummy-covering from the tomb and broke it up and put it into a basket and divided it up — .' The scribe Djutmose said, 'The tomb from which you brought away the silver vases is one tomb but the tomb from which you brought away this mummy-covering is another, making two tombs.' — He said, 'It is false, the silver vases belong to the main treasure of which I have told you already; one tomb and one only was what we opened.' He was examined again with the birch, the stick and the screw.

Recognizing that self-confessed robbers might well attempt to implicate innocent people in their crimes, the two scribes treated confessions with due scepticism. For, as Scribe Nesamenopet put it: 'If I went and stole a goatskin from a cattleshed and someone went [there] after me, would I not inform against him to make the punishment fall on him as well as me?'

Members of virtually all classes of Theban society, from priests to peasants, were called before the commission. Even the army scribe, Kashuti, who, in the course of Panhesi's cursury enquiry ten years before had himself been a member of an investigating body and had accepted a few ounces of precious metal from frightened villagers, now found himself brought before the Vizier and commissioners: 'The matter of this vase stand of eighty-six *deben* [over seventeen pounds] of silver which had been stolen — Kashuti said "I did not see what happened to it. How could I? Listen to my story — Hori the priest came — and had the vase stand brought and appropriated it".' Kashuti's prevarications run on and on. There were even moments of humour in the Vizier's hall, as when a much-travelled foreign mercenary who had been accused of 'robbing the west' pointed out that the oath the commission required of all its witnesses 'not to speak falsehood on pain of being sent to Nubia' had especial poignancy in his case, for 'am I, who comes from Syria, to be sent to Nubia?' Records of sentencing are rare and we do not know if the mercenary did in fact end his days in the land of the villainous Viceroy.

The commission seems to have finished its work by the end of the second year of the Era of Rebirth, though its staff did not finish with their records until some four years later, when all the witnesses' statements were placed haphazardly, together with the records of the trials of earlier tomb-robbers, in two large earthenware pots and deposited, in all probability, in the archives of the fortress-temple on the west bank. Each jar held six or eight rolls of papyrus and was carefully labelled with its contents: 'The records of the men of old — concerning the thieves ... records of the gold and silver which the tombmakers were found to have stolen — the examination of the pyramid tombs ... the list of thieves.' For the Theban bureaucracy this store of records probably represented the listing, labelling and putting away of all the city's misadventures; for us, the scrolls tell of ordinary people struggling against the hunger and crime that had engulfed their lives.

My father ferried [the thieves] over to the island of Amenemopet — [and they] said to him, 'This inner coffin is ours. It belonged to some great person. We were hungry and we went and brought it away, but you be silent and we will give you a loincloth.' So they said to him. And they gave him a loincloth. But my mother said to him, 'You are a silly old man; what you have done is stealing.'

Whilst Djutmose and Nesamenopet conducted the King's investigation and sometimes sailed the river collecting the royal grain, the villagers continued, sporadically, to work in the Great Place, though one may imagine that their labours were as much concerned with tidying the robbed burials as they were with preparing the tomb of Ramesses XI. Increasingly, life on the west bank was focused on the fortress-temple, the area between its elephantine fortifications and the royal temple being transformed from the well-spaced storerooms and dwellings of the royal priests into a warren of small alleys, tight streets and rows of little houses. Scribe Djutmose built a large house at the western end of the enclosure behind the temple and there he lived with his wife and two children whilst his son Butehamun learnt his father's profession.

Their old village was less than half a mile away from this new house, a mere step across the desert plain out of the high stone gate at the southern end of the fortress. Scribe Djutmose must have gone there often, either to the old family houses now used as storerooms or to supervise the delivery of rations and supplies to those families who still remained in the village, though in smaller numbers than before. The cemeteries around the village still accommodated new generations of village dead, and the temples, now jumbled full of stelae and statues, still held the village gods and goddesses. Just as his forefathers had done in their time, Scribe Djutmose would walk out of the village and up the gentle sloping path running through the temples, then out along the base of the quiet cliffs that looked over to the Southern City. And there, on 6 October 1079 BC, he scratched on the yellow rocks his name and those of his scribal forebears: 'Year eighteen, first month of winter, day eighteen. The King's Scribe Djutmose, son of the King's Scribe Khaemhedjet, son of the King's Scribe Harshire, son of the King's Scribe Amennakht.' This was exactly the time of Ramesses xi's last visit to Thebes, when Herihor was installed as the ruler of the Southern City and the Era of Rebirth was initiated. Looking back, Djutmose could reflect on the difficulties that his village had survived.

Their exploits as grain-tax officials and investigators for the royal commission had made Djutmose and Nesamenopet prominent figures in the Theban hierarchy. Now the administration of Herihor and his general Piankh used Djutmose as both scribe and personal advisor. Loyal to the King, and separate from the discredited Theban bureaucracy, the villagers were becoming valuable agents of the new administration. Thus, in the very first years of Herihor's office a move was made to establish the tombmakers and their families as a self-sufficient branch of the new bureaucracy. Grants of land were made to the two scribes and, with the aid of field labourers and, perhaps the tombmakers themselves, they began to farm. In effect, the scribes had become squires; for the first time in the village's history, some of its members were land managers at the top of the Theban establishment. Now even the highest officials of the city, the Mayor of Thebes and the dignitaries of the temple of Amun, treated the two scribes as equals or, at least, as personages to whom the full weight of their office needed to be displayed. Accordingly the Mayor of Thebes wrote directly to Scribe Djutmose about a quarrel between their respective servants, and a senior scribe of the treasury of Amun corresponded with him about another dispute, attempting to intercede on the behalf of someone whom Djutmose had taken into custody: 'Let him go,' he asks. 'This man is [like] a brother of mine — Yield! Do not make a claim against him in opposition to me.'

Not all contacts with the east bank were so unfriendly. Once when the young men of the gangs, on their return from a spell of working away from Thebes, had seized the opportunity of their return to the Southern City to sample its delights, the east bank authorities had been enlisted to send the truants back home:

[To] the Deputy of the Estate of Amun Re ... [from] the scribe of the necropolis Djutmose — and the scribe of the army Pentahetnakht — we have heard that you have returned and reached the city; that Amun has received you well and has done every good thing for you. We are dwelling here in the fortress-temple; you know how we live. Now, the young men of the tomb have returned and are staying in the city whilst I am here with the scribe of the army Pentahetnakht. Please have the men of the tomb that are in the city assembled and sent to this side. A list of them for you — . Place them under the supervision of the scribe Butehamun. Send them quickly.

Butehamun, Scribe Djutmose's son, was about twenty-five when his father wrote that letter - it is the first example we have of him being given a commission as village scribe. From this time onwards, however, Butehamun plays an increasing role in his father's work, especially as Djutmose spent much time away from Thebes running the affairs of his family and the village in correspondence with his son and the two foremen:

> The scribe of the Great and Noble Necropolis Djutmose to the chief workmen — the guardians — and all the workmen of the necropolis — . How are you, how are your men? Indeed, I am alive today; tomorrow is in god's hands — . What is the good of my sending several letters if you have not sent one? What have I done against you? — Please tell Amun of the Thrones of the Two Lands and the men who are in the fields to prevent someone from doing wrong to them. Another matter; for the ladies — and all the men. Please tell Amun to bring me back. Indeed, I was ill when I arrived [in the] north and I am not at all in my [normal] condition. Do not set your minds to anything else; as soon as my letter arrives go to the open court of Amun of the Thrones of the Two Lands, taking the children along with you, and coax him and tell him to save me.

This letter was probably written during the first or second year of the Era of Rebirth whilst Djutmose was at Tajoy, the stronghold on the border between Herihor's domain and that of General Smendes, who was ruling the north of Egypt for the King. Occasionally Ramesses XI himself would come to Tajoy to meet representatives of the southern kingdom or adjudicate in legal disputes, as was the ancient royal prerogative. Indeed, it may have been in this court that the father of Scribe Nesamenopet obtained a favourable judgement for the King in a lawsuit - a victory joyfully reported to the scribe in a letter from his wife Hennutawi whilst he was travelling south from Thebes on the city's business.

Such trips away from Thebes not only dislocated the affairs of the village but also the scribes' attempts to farm the land recently ceded to them. Quite unused to cultivating, the tombmakers appear to have started this enterprise sensibly by copying their neighbours - and in a nation of farmers there could have been little shortage either of skilled workpeople or of agricultural advice. Caught away from Thebes in the crucial month before the high flood, Scribe Nesamenopet sent long and detailed instructions to Hennutawi about the establishment of an orchard which included the most basic of farming information: 'As soon as my letter reaches you, you shall dispatch Sobeksankh — and give him ten measures of fruit [for seed] — and they shall plant it before the flood has soaked it so that after it is planted the flood will enter it — . You are to tell Sobeksankh — proceed with clearing the land which is in your charge.' Orchards were planted on the high ground in the village, not usually covered by the annual flooding.

Djutmose wrote to Butehamun about similar plots which he had been given on levees bordering the banks of the low-water level of the Nile, and these too were planted with trees: 'And you shall look after these three riverside fields of ours and cause the trees which are on their mounds to be cleared, just as on the holding that Esmontu used to cultivate.' In the same letter, written during the month before the flood's full height and probably in the same year as Scribe Nesamenopet's, we find Djutmose concerning himself with oxen for ploughing and grain transportation, the collection of which had probably caused the scribe to leave Thebes and his fieldhands. He also tells us that Medjay Sermont, an old village worker who had served with Viceroy Panhesi during his raid on the delta, now farms on his own account – and he sends Butehamun a little boat: 'and take care of it,' he says, 'for you shall find it useful'.

Djutmose's letters worry and cajole, threaten and grumble and show a loving concern for the welfare of his family and of the village community that he regarded as being in his care. They also reveal the extent of his new household at the fortress-temple: in one letter Butehamun is instructed to 'look after the men that are in the house and give them clothing' as well as attend to some conscripted soldiers; in yet another he is told to attend to the construction of the new home, whose large upper room was being finished in stone, a rare luxury in Theban domestic architecture. 'And', Djutmose invariably concludes, 'you shall take water to Amun of the Thrones of the Two Lands and tell him to save me. — And you shall give attention to my orders. Do not neglect them. And you shall tell Amun to remove this illness from me.' There had been a lot of illness and death amongst the villagers for some time past. Djutmose's wife, Butehamun's mother, Baketamun, had died young, before the inauguration of the Era of Rebirth, and Butehamun too had buried, and grieved over, a wife. As he travelled around Egypt, Djutmose grumbled about his health in almost every letter he wrote home. This was no mere out-of-sorts out-of-town grumbling, for other village correspondents also took the trouble to report on the scribe's health; whilst letters from Djutmose's own family always tell him to be careful and go to great pains to reassure him about life in the fortress-temple. The middle-aged Djutmose was always inclined to worry, and regularly needed such reassurance:

As for your having told us to look after the scribe Butehamun, Shemdemdua and the children — they are all right, do not worry about them. They are alive today; tomorrow is in god's hands. You are the one they wish to see. I tell Amun Re, King of the Gods, to give you favour before the General your Lord and may Amun bring you back prospering — . May your health be good. Do not stop writing to me through whatever people shall come south, so that our hearts may be happy.

Now, the Thebans say 'Tomorrow is in god's hands'. The tremendous self-confidence with which Scribe Ramose had addressed the gods in the inscriptions in his temples and tomb chapels, the assurance with which a villager of the previous century had argued with the village oracle, all this had gone, people's outlook had changed. Amun had become more inscrutable; true faith a matter for each individual. As the ancient city grew more worldly and corrupt, individuals like Djutmose took firm control of their own lives; 'Tomorrow is in god's hands' he commented fatalistically, but before this phrase he always wrote 'I am alive today!' Though the world was now harder for the villagers, and its people were more superstitious, they appear kinder and more approachable.

By the first years of the Era of Rebirth both Djutmose and his son had remarried. Both loved their new families and Djutmose was as close to his son's family as he was to his own. A new generation of scribes of the necropolis was planned, for Djutmose instituted a scribal school inside the walls of the fortress-temple. The correspondence between Djutmose and his villagers shows, perhaps for the first time, something of the role of the village women inside the community, those rows of well-dressed wives and daughters who for the previous 300 years had sat silently beside their fathers and husbands in so many of the reliefs and sculptures of village funerary chapels. They had nothing to do with tombmaking, nor, indeed, in normal times, with the village administration. Seldom do we find a woman in the village documents who is anything more than a name. Only very rarely do they desert their household role and use their status of civic equality to make a mark on village affairs. However, when Scribe Nesamenopet was away from Thebes it was his wife Hennutawi who took charge of dispensing the village grain rations, and later made a series of pointed observations about the short weight of one of the village's measures in her correspondence with her husband. Djutmose's letters show that although the traditional village division of labour between the sexes was observed in his family, all its voices carried equal weight.

Nowhere, perhaps, may we sense the potential of the emotional relationships between village men and women as clearly as in the remarkable letter that Butehamun wrote to the spirit of his dead first wife, Akhtay. Even the scribes' usual epistolary formulas, hieratic and repetitious to modern tastes, here bend under the weight of the young man's emotions as, speaking simply and directly to his wife, he inadvertently allows us to come as close as we may ever come to such ancient lives. Butehamun wrote his letter on a chip of stone which he left at the foot of Akhtay's coffin, doubtless originally placed in the family vault in the village cemetery. Butehamun speaks to his wife through the medium of her coffin, which in the absence of a tomb chapel, was the link between this world and the next:

Oh noble chest of Osiris, the songstress of Amun Akhtay, who rests in you. Listen to me and give her this message: ask her, since you are next to her, 'How do you fare? How are you?' Tell her that her lover, her companion, says 'Woe that you do not prosper. Woe you beautiful one, who has no equal — Good to me are my mother and father, brother and sister; they have come, but you have been taken from me ... Woe, that you do not prosper, you who brought the cattle home — who attended to our fields ... while you were loaded with all kinds of heavy loads, though there were no carrying poles for them, no resting place to put them down — Oh Akhtay, you gracious one as woman.'

Under the new administration Thebes was more settled than it had been for generations and, after some ten years of the Era of Rebirth, prosperous enough to support a southbound expedition under General Piankh - who had succeeded Herihor - in pursuit of Viceroy Panhesi, to beard the wicked traitor in his lair. There is some suggestion that Piankh's expedition was prompted by the re-emergence of the former Viceroy; at any rate, he certainly left Thebes in a hurry, in such a hurry that he left some of his army's supplies and even his own clothes, behind. A curt note from Piankh's personal scribe to Djutmose at Thebes tells him to send rags and cloth so that the army can make dressings for their wounded, whilst another asks him to send gold and supplies for the expedition. A whole series of similar notes, always short and to the point, continued to guide Djutmose and the other officials on the west bank in their government of the area. Another letter from Piankh's expedition, sent by a close friend of Djutmose's who was taking advantage of the General's efficient courier system, tells the Theban that he is well but, inevitably, that 'tomorrow is in god's hands'.

Before he left Thebes, Piankh had installed Djutmose not only as controller of the west bank, but also as his eyes and ears about the Southern City and shortly after his departure the scribe reported the seditious gossip of two Theban medjay. Characteristically, the General's response was blunt: 'Take these men to my house,' he said, 'get to the bottom of what they say quickly, and if you find out that [their gossip] has foundation, put them in two sacks and throw them in the river without anyone in the land finding out about it.' With this order, in seemingly inadvertent explanation, Piankh asks Djutmose rhetorically, 'As for Pharaoh, how shall he reach [i.e. rule] this land, of whom he is master still?' Thebes's masters now ruled according to their own devices. Always a thorough administrator, Piankh sought to help the scribe in his murderous mission by writing two similarly worded orders, one to his deputy at Thebes and another to his mother; the latter with a codicil, probably in the General's own scrawling hand, asking her to write to him about her health, which concerned him. Of these three correspondents, the deputy seems to have been the most junior, for Piankh ordered him alone to take charge of the killings, advising him to work at night. At a later date all three of these sinister letters were collected together and placed in a linen bag. 'I belong to Amun, the breath of life', reads the impression on the bag's seal – doubtless it was once part of the secret state archives.

As he and his army prepared to leave the border of Egypt for Nubia, Piankh discovered that he had greater need of experienced Djutmose by his side than at Thebes, and ordered him south to join the army. At Esna, where sixteen years earlier Djutmose had collected the grain from the warehouses of the temple of Khnum, he found one of Piankh's war boats standing by to take him to Elephantine. This ancient town stood on a granite outcrop in the centre of the Nile, the southern border of Egypt. There Djutmose met his general, finding him in a genial, if somethat martial, frame of mind. Together, Piankh told him (and here you can almost feel the General's arm clasping the shoulders of his timorous scribe) they would go down into Nubia and attack the traitorous Panhesi. Elephantine would serve as their base camp and from there Piankh's wife later attended to the affairs of the village, ordering the issue of rations and pursuing those who did not deliver them in time with a series of written orders.

Poor Djutmose! Never in good health at the best of times and now well over fifty, he was to sail south into Nubia and fight a desert war. No Egyptian actively enjoyed foreign travel at the best of times, and though Djutmose was not to voyage more than forty miles into Nubia, he felt that he might as well be setting off for the moon. None the less, in his letters to his family, he puts on a brave face: 'Now do not worry about me, my chief has done very good things for me'. But in a more sober moment he also asks some of the villagers by name to pray for him in the fortress-temple and to beg the gods to bring him back to Thebes alive. Djutmose's family and many of the other villagers were clearly worried about him. First they wrote to Djutmose's friend in Piankh's court telling him to look after the scribe who, after all, was 'a man who has no strength and has never made such a journey before', and help and comfort him on the long voyage south. Then one of Djutmose's friends at Thebes, a senior villager, named Amenhotep, wrote a fond letter directly to him telling him to be careful, and to avoid the fighting, for he had not been pressed into the military but was accompanying Piankh so that the General could benefit from his advice. 'Stay in the boat where you can protect yourself from arrows and spears!' he begs. 'You are not to abandon us all, for you are our father.' Finally Amenhotep tells Djutmose that the workmen are all well and praying for his return. Butehamun added a paragraph to the letter informing his father that he too was praying for him, that his 'eye is blind since it does not see you' and that no harm has come to any of the villagers – from 'young to old'.

Even Piankh seems to have felt the flurry of apprehension that greeted his order for Scribe Djutmose to join him on the expedition, for now when he sends orders to the villagers through Scribe Butehamun his curt notes reassure them about the old man's safety before rapping out his list of army needs, chariots, spears and the like. Gracefully, even, he also grants the tombmakers some village servants once again, five people who, he says, are to be the property of all the gangs 'from the foremen down to all the workmen'. For his part, Djutmose sought further to allay village fears by relating how Piankh had told him that he was quite indispensable and made him the honoured recipient of special rations of bread and beer. His letters home are still filled with the minutiae of village business; the fussing scribe snows Butehamun under with orders, requests and observations. By early January, mid-winter, Djutmose had reached the southernmost point of his journey and was writing to his family from Yar – the 'hellhole', as it has been translated – deep in Nubia near the fortress of Kuban, which once guarded the entrance to the empire's gold mines. From this dry and ancient world deep in the desert, the long lists of errands to be run and prayers to be recited that Djutmose sends to Butehamun and the villagers read more like a nostalgic conjuring up of his beloved Thebes than anything else. He particularly asks the men to go up to the little shrine of Amun of the Good Encounter near the tombmakers' settlement above the Valley of the Kings, and there offer water to the god and ask for his safe return; a pleasant walk that the scribe could recapture in his mind's eye as he wrote his letter. One by one, Djutmose lists the names of the villagers for whom he is offering prayers in the temple of Horus outside the walls of the ancient desert fort.

Djutmose was very homesick. By mid-February he was also ill and Piankh was giving him augmented rations to help him regain his strength. Letters flowed backwards and forwards between the scribe and his village. Some asked about the fate of other members of the expedition, others from subordinates inquired politely into the health of the scribe, but only the letters of his son Butehamun helped him shake off his illness. Although he felt 'abandoned in this far-off land' Djutmose would revive sufficiently to 'open my eyes and raise my head' before launching into lengthy discourses on the simplest village matters. In one letter alone his family is told to 'look after Nofreti's ass' and 'train it', to 'attend to the fowler's daughter' and 'ask her to pray that I might return', to command the coppersmith to make spears, to pay attention to the medjay, to instruct Butehamun to go to all the villagers' favourite shrines and pray for his father's return, to speak confidentially about 'a certain matter' to Piankh's officer at Thebes, to send Medjay Hednakht to Nubia – and oh, he wishes his wife was with him ...

Dutifully, Butehamun and the villagers seem to have done their best to keep pace with the orders of both Djutmose and Piankh. One letter informs the General that his clothes have been forwarded to him (this when Scribe Djutmose was journeying south to join the expedition), others describe how the villagers are maintaining the supply of weapons for the army. The storekeepers of the Great Place, who once supplied tools and chisels for the work on the kings' tombs, were now armourers; the copper once used for quarrying points and engraving chisels was now fashioned into spears and daggers. All in all, Piankh was as well-supplied as he could expect from the impoverished city.

For all their efforts, though, the Thebans did not catch Panhesi, and later the *ci-devant* Viceroy went to his grave in Nubia with a full burial, the decorations and inscriptions in his tomb chapel quite untouched by any revenging Theban army. Piankh seems to have returned to Thebes within a year of his departure, and died a short while later. As for Scribe Djutmose, we really do not know if he returned from the southlands alive or embalmed and ready for his burial, but like his General, he does seem to have come home to Thebes. In a prayer scribbled on a rock close by the tomb of the village's patron king, Butehamun prayed to Amun: 'Guard my limbs and let me reach old age. Do not do as you have done to my father, The King's Scribe in the Place of Truth, Djutmose.' This short epitaph is Djutmose's last memorial.

24

KINGS AND WADIS

Whilst Scribe Djutmose was away from Thebes, there was a gradual drift away from the old village. Some families moved with Butehamun into the enclosure of the fortress-temple, others, a junior scribe amongst them, went to live in houses down by the fields where they would keep an eye on the village crops. But there were still sufficient people for Scribe Djutmose to continue to worry about the distribution of their water rations when he was at Thebes and there was still a skilled labour force at the scribes' disposal. And that was just as well, for there was a great deal to be done in the royal necropolis at this time: although King Ramesses xi's tomb had been abandoned – the Pharaoh was hardly seen to rule now and never visited Thebes – Herihor and his successors were concerned that the burials of the old kings should be restored.

The entrances to some of the tombs of the Great Place were still visible at this time, their doorways and walls standing high above the rubble of the valley floor, but for the most part the tombs of the kings of the old dynasty had been buried by the floods of the past 300 years. These tombs too were to be searched out and opened; everyone at Thebes, living and dead alike, was to share in the high priests' renaissance. In between his river trips even Scribe Djutmose ventured down into some of the deep old tombs which the gangs were digging out, and occasionally he left inscriptions recording these visits. In another of these old tombs, that of Tuthmosis III, Amenhotep – probably the same man who later wrote a fond letter to Djutmose in Nubia advising him to keep his head down – wrote a graffito in the wall-plaster of the burial chamber declaring that a painting there was very good, that 'the figure on the right is a thousand times beautiful'.

The villagers found the mummy of Tuthmosis III, the crusty old warrior who had established the royal cemetery of the Great Place almost half a millennium before, still in his tomb and contained in his coffins, but badly damaged by jewel-thieves. Many of the kings of the old dynasty were discovered in a similar condition, some of them having been discreetly plundered hundreds of years before, even, perhaps, at the time of their funerals. But although both kings and tombs were badly smashed, none of them had been burnt and there was still much of value and use lying in them, and even about the mummies themselves.

Butehamun and his men would locate the stairway of an old tomb, dig it out, and then pass down through the narrow corridors and across deep pits to the royal burial chamber. There they would lift the lid of the king's sarcophagus, many of which had already been displaced by thieves, and stack the brittle stone sheet carefully against a wall or column, or even against some of the broken funeral equipment in the tomb. Then the royal mummy, often still encased inside its original coffins, would be carried out into the daylight. For the most part, the kings would never return to their own tombs again. Once these tombs were opened up, bats soon took up residence in them; small chattering creatures that flew down into the fields each evening for their food. Most, however, were covered by rubble once again and lost; before this happened a few were visited in the course of the following centuries by poor Thebans, who, after sweeping away the robbers' debris and accumulated bat-droppings, would leave simple family burials in the empty rooms.

Not only the monarchs of the old dynasty were taken from their tombs, but also those kings the villagers themselves had entombed during the last three centuries. Most of these too had been robbed and now needed restoration and a ritual rewrapping in new burial shrouds. So the broken kings were gathered up, tied back together and wrapped in fine fresh linens, as they were at their funerals. At the rewrapping of Ramesses II one of the senior workmen, another of Djutmose's friends who went to Nubia with Piankh, seized the opportunity to link himself to the legendary monarch by writing his name on the royal shroud: the kings themselves had become sacred monuments. But once the Pharaohs had been exposed to public view they were gently relieved of most of what the robbers had left: their tombs being denuded even of their cedarwood door lintels and wooden statues, only fragments of wood and faience, of pottery, cloth and leather remaining. As for the royal coffins, the gold foil that covered many of them was now scraped off – though precisely and literately so that the royal names and titles were left intact and their occupants identifiable. So careful were the restorations and rewrappings, and so scrupulous the removal of any precious thing from mummies and tombs alike, that both these processes seem to have been simultaneous; like a fee exacted by the high priests for their pious attentions. In fact, this scouring of the royal coffins and corpses, this reduction of the broken kings in all their plundered finery to the skin and bone of sacred relics, proved to be their salvation, for throughout all of ancient history they were never molested again.

For part, if not all, of this melancholy process, the kings were taken to the unfinished tomb of Ramesses XI along with pieces of their broken tomb furniture, statues, chests and some of the ritual trappings of their funerals. There it was that these fragments were finally stripped of the last of their finery, then chopped into small pieces of wood, as neat as kindling. There it was too, that some of the coffins' gold foil was chopped off carefully and methodically with the sharpest of adzes, the yellow metal intended, perhaps, for the royal coffers of the delta or the impoverished treasury of the high priests across the river at Thebes. At the back of the huge tomb, now a veritable workshop, a deep rectangular shaft was excavated into the floor of the unfinished burial chamber. Originally this was intended to be the entrance to a royal tomb, a new doorway into the underworld, and to emphasize this fresh beginning in the Era of Rebirth four ritual deposits were placed in four small pits cut into the floor at the corners of the shaft: caches of gold and faience plaques bearing King Ramesses XI's name, models of the four monkeys that, according to the 'Book of the Dead', guarded the rectangular fiery lake forming an entrance to the underworld, and a fine statue group of the King worshipping Ma'at, the goddess of truth. Although the Theban exchequers could only find a few ounces of gold for the deposits, and this mixed unevenly with silver and copper, although the little statues that were to have been cast in coppery-bronze were simply left as beeswax models, the sentiments of the ritual were those of the days of the old, grander, kings. And the priests who carefully placed all these fragile things under chips of stone were careful enough to ensure that the magical hoards stayed hidden and protected inside the rough tomb for thousands of years.

Similar care was taken with the excavation of the shaft, dug just slightly askew from the old axis of the tomb, but dead precise in its own measurements and finely worked: the last of the tombmakers' traditional labours in the Great Place. And that this work too was done under the authority of the temple of Amun and, doubtless, of its High Priest, may be seen in the design of a seal impression that was buried in one of the deposits: a tiny pellet of clay that had probably come from the bag in which the priests brought the ritual objects to the tomb. Though indistinct, and less than an inch high, it shows the King worshipping a male and female god – the male either Min or, more probably, the ipthyphallic Amun. With the wisdom of hindsight, we may now deduce that this shaft was intended to have corridors and chambers running from its bottom, possibly even to hold a cache of the royal mummies, for a similarly-sized shaft made elsewhere almost at the same time served just that purpose. But the quarrymen hit a stratum of shale so soft that it was impossible to excavate the corridors and rooms in which the kings would have laid; accordingly the shaft was abandoned and used only as a dark hole into which many of the stripped and broken fragments of royal tomb furniture could be thrown.

Not surprisingly the High Priests took a keen interest in the villagers' work. Piankh himself wrote from Nubia instructing Butehamun to dig out another tomb in the Great Place, and received in return the splendidly transparent reply that although work was indeed continuing in the royal cemetery, Scribe Butehamun (then aged about thirty) did not know 'where to put his feet' but that if only his father Djutmose could be returned to him, work could proceed at a proper pace. None the less, Butehamun and his men did continue to gather up the royal mummies from their tombs and rewrap the shattered corpses – 'osirifying' the dead kings, as the scribes' notations sometimes describe it. One particular tomb, a peculiar archaic grave deep at the bottom of a shaft under a rock in the foothills of the Great Place, must have held the villagers' interest more than most, for there they found the burials of the village's patrons, King Amenhotep I and his mother Queen Nefertari. Amenhotep, whose oracle was still the most revered of all the village's gods. The King had been hacked by the axes used to cut the burial jewellery, hard-set in the dried resins, from the corpse: both of his shoulder-blades had been torn off, along with his feet and a hand. Similarly, Queen Nefertari's hands and wrists, which must have been heavy with rings and bracelets, were also missing, snapped from her thin arms. But the old embalmers' treatment of the royal corpses had resulted in their partial petrification and although all the kings were damaged the bulk of them – their heads, rib-cages, pelvises and thighs – remained as resinous skin-covered boulders, difficult and unprofitable to demolish. In some shape or form then, most of the ancient kings survived their ordeal.

By the end of Butehamun's work, more than a decade after his father's death, most of the kings were gathered together into a few tombs at the centre of the Great Place. Ramesses II was moved, along with his royal grandfather, into the tomb of Seti I, whilst in the ancient tomb of Amenhotep II, where the old King had been replaced in his sarcophagus inside a brand-new set of coffins, a whole clutch of kings was placed in a nearby side chamber. Eight monarchs and numerous queens and princes lay there, side by side, in a motley collection of coffins culled from all over the Theban necropolis. One of these kings was Merneptah, in whose tomb Scribe Kenhirkhopeshef had worked so long and hard more than 100 years before.

When Piankh's son Pinejem became High Priest on his father's death he continued the refurbishing of Thebes and the ancient kings, initiating at the fortress-temple the restoration of the palace of King Ramesses III, destroyed long ago by Viceroy Panhesi's armourers, and ordering Butehamun to attend to the osirification of that king's mummy. Probably the scribe put the old warrior in the tomb of Seti I, along with other kings and Queen Nefertari; for his mummy was eventually found, crammed against that of a woman's, inside a huge coffin that had been made for the great Queen.

Shadowy Ramesses XI finally died, after a reign of some twenty-seven years, in the same year that Pinejem succeeded to the high priesthood. This time, however, Pharaoh was not brought to Thebes for burial, his half-finished tomb continued to be used as a funerary workshop. Some fifteen years later, Pinejem would even order the restoration of some of the inscriptions on the tomb's walls, broken away by a rock fall. But though the High Priest restored the King's text, his own names and titles were inscribed in place of Ramesses XI's. Some idea of the high sentiments involved in such restorations may be understood when it is realized that some seventy years later, when many of the royal mummies had still not found their permanent resting places, the daughters of noble families wove new linen shrouds for the old kings with their own hands; recording their devotion in long inscriptions painted directly on to the raw gauzy sheets. Pinejem himself displayed a positively archaeological passion for the ancient kings and their trappings, even taking over the 500-year-old coffins of an ancient king and having them refurbished for his own use, covering their pocked surfaces with fresh gilding and a blaze of carnelian and glass inlays. But Pinejem's attempt to clothe himself in the legend of the god kings was ultimately unsuccessful: during a later reburial, Butehamun's successors restored the ancient King to his rightful coffin and put the mummy of the High Priest into a simple anonymous box.

The kings of the Great Place were not the only ones to receive the attentions of Butehamun and his men. All the cemeteries of Thebes were visited, from the little pyramids of ancient kings to the tombs of queens and princes scattered throughout the cliffs and hills of western Thebes. Many of these tombs, too, had been plundered, and these were usually cleared up, their burials stripped and carefully restored. One boy-prince, an ephemeral co-regent of a distant age, was especially carefully restored and reburied in a new grave in the cliffs by the village.

In their travels the scribes and their men visited even the most remote of all the Theban cemeteries in the long golden wadis to the south-west of the village, miles into the desert. There they inspected the tombs of ancient queens and courtiers and, on the smooth cliffs and the great rocks strewn down these valley floors like dice, they scratched texts recording the names of the expedition's members; lines sometimes six or eight feet long that dance over the limestone's yellow patina like cotton threads. Here too, in these isolated, pitiless places, Butehamun and his friends recorded the names of the high priests and raised prayers to Amun, the hidden one, the king of the gods. So remote from the fortress-temple were some of these valleys that each expedition took several days, and the scribe and his men would camp out under the warm cliffs, sheltered by overhanging rocks. The oldest of Butehamun's graffiti in these lonely southern valleys, written when his father Djutmose was still in Nubia, records an expedition to a wadi which, unbeknown to the scribe and his five companions, held at its head the golden burials of three women of an ancient harem. Ten years later Butehamun was back in these same valleys, now as a senior scribe heading a larger expedition, with some of his many sons to keep him company.

Butehamun continued to inspect these distant wadis and the cliffs running along the edge of western Thebes until the year of his death. One of his graffiti records that on a particular expedition he found some coffins from a plundered tomb lying out in the sunlight of a distant valley; most, however, simply celebrate his dead father and other members of his family. (One of these even claims that Scribe Ramose, that straightlaced individual of an earlier age, was his ancestor, which he certainly was not.) Another graffito records a trip into the mountains after a visit to the west bank by the High Priest Pinejem himself. Pinejem could well have been on the west bank inspecting the progress of the work – not only on the tombs of the ancient kings, but on his own funeral vault. For the high priests too had tombs prepared for them, and a few years earlier, in the sixth year of the Era of Rebirth, just such an inspection 'of the tomb of the great General' had taken place; though it is not clear whether this was the tomb of Herihor, who died in that year, or of his successor Piankh.

Many of the burials of members of the families of both Herihor and Piankh have survived, and are very fine. However, neither the tombs nor the mummies of these two High Priests have ever come to light, and as none of their funeral equipment has been found either it is probable that their graves have not been plundered and broken up but are still intact somewhere in the fastness of the Theban mountain. But where would Butehamun and his villagers have put the High Priests and their tombs? From the sad experiences of the preceding decades we can hardly believe that they would have begun new monuments amidst the ruin of the Great Place. From their graffiti and other clues in the southern wadis, however, we may assume that the High Priests were buried there, in that most remote section of the Theban mountain, in the valleys holding the ancient cemeteries of queens and princes.

In Butehamun's day, communities of men went to live in these dry valleys just as they had 500 years before. Once again the stairways that the ancient tombmakers had cut in the cliff chimneys to allow access to these valleys from the high plateau were cleared for use; once again the ancient network of paths, carefully built and designed to reach the remotest cliffs, were crossed by teams of donkeys carrying supplies. Deep in the furthermost wadi of them all – today called Wadi Gharbi, 'the southern valley' – the tombmakers built small huts and individual sleeping places for themselves underneath huge slabs of stone that had fallen from the cliffs above. Wadi Gharbi is nothing like the modest landscape of the Great Place, but is a huge semi-circle of rock some 600 feet high enclosing a tiny plateau, a valley-head less than 100 feet across that channels the rain which occasionally runs in waterfalls from the cliffs above into the narrow canyon below. It is an isolated, completely silent place, a ruined slab-filled arena that holds in it the imminence, the same sense of expectation as an empty theatre, but on a colossal scale. Long after Butehamun's day, other ancient Egyptians believed this valley to be so sacred that it became a place of pilgrimage where small offerings could be left under rocks and boulders.

On the stones and slabs that lay all around their rough huts the villagers scribbled and scrawled idle doodles of pictures and hieroglyphs: signs that might commemorate such simple emotions as the word 'beautiful', expressed, in the palaeography of the day, as a lotus flower upon a folded stem; or the sign of a man with his arms raised in adoration, the determining hieroglyph used in such words as 'high' and 'rejoice'. They drew the sign signifying 'tomb' over and over again, and often they scratched a group of signs that held the same meaning, but expressed the archaic phrase 'the house of life' – a term which was in fashion again in Butehamun's time and signified 'royal tomb'. Frequently, either in the royal name rings or simply as a group of signs, they also wrote the names and titles of the high priests.

Rather more prosaically, the men also scratched lists of the supplies brought up to them in the desolate valley. The logistics of supplying such remote locations was a serious problem and, indeed, it defeated the only modern archaeologist to work there some 3,000 years later. Unlike modern man however, the ancient villagers lacked neither the time nor the resources for such work. On the plateau above the cliffs they constructed a series of sinks and connecting canals to gather and contain the water of a flash flood or a gentle shower. Even today, in a region which is virtually rainless, you may put your hand into a crack in this high and windy place and find a dampness there against the stone. Perhaps the ancient people, too, knew of this phenomenon and were able to turn it to their advantage. Close by this elaborate water system, the villagers left several offering tables, each one carefully inscribed in the characteristic village style and cut from slabs of fine white Theban limestone that they had carried there from the valley

some six miles below. Today these individual memorials are the most far-flung of all the monuments of western Thebes. To climb to the plateau from their settlement in the wadi the villagers used a stairway running through a tall chimney in the valley cliff. Fragments of their water-jars still litter the ancient pathways on the plateau leading up to their water system, but it is no longer possible to climb down the stairway in the chimney to the wadi below as the narrow crack is blocked with rock and sand.

Where, then, are the tombs that these workmen made? As Butehamun and his men traversed these desert valleys year by year they had recognized the discretion and relative invulnerability of the ancient tombs that they inspected. Tacit acknowledgement of the security that such tombs afforded was shown when some of those closer to Thebes were enlarged on the orders of the high priests to hold the kings that Butehamun and his men had collected. Many of these ancient tombs were set high in the cliffs behind hidden doorways, hundreds of feet up sheer rock faces. Others, belonging to nobles and servants, were cut into the bottom of the same cliffs, near cracks in the limestone; their entrances disguised by the debris carried by the rainwater that occasionally poured down these cracks from the plateau above. How much more successful in protecting their occupants had these tombs been than the huge monuments of the Great Place in which generations of tombmakers spent their lives!

It seems possible then, that Herihor and Piankh lie in tombs set high in the valley cliffs, either in specially made chambers or in old vaults that the villagers appropriated for them, tombs that today may be spotted only by the swishing black crows gliding high over the cliffs. Obvious evidence of large-scale ancient quarrying in this valley are the large mounds of debris – man-made chippings like those from the work in the royal tombs still covering much of the Great Place – all over the end of the wadi close to the ancient huts. Equally intriguing is the discovery in this same valley of the bosses from a granite sarcophagus – the projections to which ropes would be tied to aid the transportation of the smooth sarcophagi – usually cut off after the huge blocks had been hauled into their final positions. So this desolate valley holds the answers to many questions: careful excavation may reveal not only tombs but rich details of ancient life and a clearer understanding of the religious cult which was practised there.

Concerned with the care of the royal dead, the business of the high priests and his village and its fields, Butehamun also took the time to provide for his own burial. And it is interesting to see what this scribe, so intimate with the rituals of death and the burial of great kings, prepared for his personal afterlife. Certainly, with his long and heavy experience of the mortality of the Pharaoh, Butehamun could hardly have expected to lie undisturbed in his own burial vault. Unusually, he did; although his burial was merely the traditional village arrangement of the time, a bright-painted coffin placed amidst the remains of generations of ancestors in a family vault.

Butehamun's coffins were all that you would expect of such a long line of family craftsmen. Three mummiform cedar shells fitting one inside the other, the innermost so small that when the old scribe came to be put into it the burial party had to cut away at the coffin to allow his shoulders to fit; even so, Butehamun's mummy must have been a tiny thing, the size of a boy. Each of these coffins, covered with scenes – of creation, of mourning gods, of the transformations of the soul, of the gods and goddesses of Thebes – that the villagers had been painting and engraving in the Theban tombs for hundreds of years, were drawn by master draughtsmen and coloured, like book illuminations, in the densest of harmonies. If Butehamun had ever suffered the royal fate of being carried from grave to grave in his coffins, he would have taken his tomb-paintings with him – the village painters having transferred some of the subjects from the walls of royal tombs to the coffins themselves. And in these scenes in place of the great kings is Scribe Butehamun himself, his worried face peering at the gods a little shortsightedly; sometimes wearing a noble's wig, sometimes bald, always in attitudes of prayer. For despite their melancholy careers as undertakers to dynasties of kings, Butehamun and his colleagues were as aware of the gods as their ancestors had been, but now they were conscious of human frailty too. They had lost an empire and found themselves.

Though the three modelled faces on his coffin lids stare rather impassively towards eternity, little of the scribe's personality can be seen in them; curiously enough, we find his most touching memorial under the coffin-shaped lid that fitted directly over his mummy in the innermost coffin. On the underside of this gesso cover, Butehamun wrote out precise prayers in texts running the entire length of the cover, verses from the Book of the Dead, keys to the next life as sure as the passes issued to the craftsmen who wanted to enter the gates of the fortress-temple. 'My mouth is opened by Ptah, the god of my city has loosened my bindings. Thoth, filled with magic, has come and loosened my bindings, even those that fasten my mouth, Atum has freed my hands.' Butehamun has checked each short prayer against an original version, and placed it in the correct order. At the end of every line is the scribe's red check-mark, the precise dot that had skipped through the tombmakers' records for 300 years or more, as generations of pens followed the writing with an accountant's careful eye. In Butehamun's coffin, for the last time, the same small red mark slips quickly through the careful list of requests for the afterlife, ensuring that each one is set in its proper place.

Butehamun died about 1056 BC and was placed in his fine coffins inside the family vault in the village; just before he died he had attended to the final osirification of King Ramesses III, the monarch in whose reign his great-great-grandfather Amennakht had founded a family of scribes and artists. Butehamun was buried by his eldest son, Ankhefenamun, who, in the now traditional way, recorded his father's passing in an inked graffito, written on a wall in one of the village tomb chapels, that of the workmen Nu and Nakhtmin, made almost three centuries before: 'Yours is the west, that has been made ready for you, where the blessed are hidden and sinners do not enter. The Scribe Butehamun has come to it in old age, his body being in good health. Written by the scribe of the tomb, Ankhefenamun.'

Ankhefenamun continued his father's work, aided by numerous relatives, for gangs of villagers were still required to go up to the royal valley and assemble in the Great Place to dig for ancient kings. Some of Ankhefenamun's brothers even made a trip into the cavernous tomb of Ramesses II, and viewed the scenes on which their forefathers had worked so long and hard. Trips were still made to the southern wadis, where the tombs of queens and princes were regularly inspected. In all probability, Ankhefenamun and his brother were born and lived all their lives in the family house at the fortress-temple. But their real home was still in the little desert valley across the plain, where members of their family would make requests to the ancient oracle of King Amenhotep amidst the old houses and the cemeteries holding the village's past generations. These houses now had some twenty coats of whitewash on their walls, and elaborate shrines half-filled the rooms where once the villagers had sat and talked and made music in the evening light.

In the end the old village was abandoned a short while after Butehamun's death. We can imagine how the donkeys of the few families that had remained carried their possessions out through the village walls, down the gentle valley and across the white plain to the enclosure of the fortress-temple. Here they would have delivered their loads to new homes set in the shaded maze of streets surrounding the royal temple. And as the village had died slowly, so do its records cease. Not as the result of a catastrophe, a consuming fire or a ruinous earthquake, but as a stream gently dries during a long summer. We know nothing about Ankhefenamun's house-hold, or his brothers, or their descendants: the entire family disappears: how tenuous our connection with these people, how valuable the ancient fragments of their lives.

EPILOGUE: DEIR EL MEDINA

Already half-ruined, the little village soon filled with windblown sand, and loose rubble and tomb-chippings tumbled down from the hillsides all around. Sometimes poor Thebans would come to the quiet valley to use the villager's tombs and occasionally even the house cellars for their family graves. But the identity and professions of the people who had lived in the dry valley was soon completely forgotten.

The villagers' shrines and temples fared rather better, local memories of the sacredness of the site persisting to such an extent that during the resurgence of stone-building at Thebes under the Ptolemaic dynasty some 800 years later, a brand-new temple was built in their midst. Though some of the villagers' monuments, such as Ramose's little temple to Hathor, were demolished during this work, others, including some of the most sacred shrines, were enclosed inside the high brick walls of the new temple's compound, which was especially planned to protect them. And even when Christianity overwhelmed Thebes some five centuries later, the area still retained something of its sanctity, for a monastery was built close by and some of the monks lived in the stone temple and established their own cemetery along its northern wall. The priests of the Ptolemaic temple left us records and documents of their community, similar in many ways to those of the ancient villagers. The Christian monks, on the other hand, have bequeathed to us the name – Deir el Medina, 'the monastery of the town' – that, for better or for worse, the ancient village bears in modern scholarship.

In the nineteenth century, however, Deir el Medina meant little more than the elegant little stone temple which was greatly celebrated for its fine architectural detail and was much visited by foreign travellers to Thebes in consequence. At that time all the ancient sites were attracting ever larger numbers of sightseers and with this growing interest came a taste and a demand for portable antiquities. To supply this new market, the modern villagers, living in a scattering of houses to the north of the valley, began rummaging through the ancient cemeteries, especially those at Deir el Medina, which had long held out the promise of buried treasure.

Even in the 1820s such desultory digging had already uncovered a re-markable archive of papyrus documents which included all of Scribe Djut-mose's letters to his son Butehamun and the correspondence of General Piankh, sent from Nubia when he was fighting Viceroy Panhesi. It is prob-able that the same ancient store also held the papyrus map of the gold mines and the plan of Ramesses vi's tomb which bears upon its reverse the document recounting the settlement of the estate of Scribe Amennakht after his death. Indeed the so-called 'Erotic Papyrus' and many other celebrated documents without provenance were found at this time and may also have come from the same source. Never again would such a rich mixture of ancient scholarship and mundane documentation come from ancient Egypt; the papyri were collected by a small number of Europeans and most found their way into the manuscript rooms of numerous museums to await scho-lars of a later generation. Many of these documents had been stored by Butehamun in his family tomb. For while Djutmose was in Nubia with Piankh, the roof of grandfather Harshire's house, which held the family's archives, collapsed in a rainstorm and Djutmose told his son to remove the scrolls and letters to the safety of the family vault. (As Butehamun's own coffins came to Europe at the same time as many of the documents it seems that Djutmose's instructions were followed.) Before Butehamun moved the soaked scrolls and letters to the tomb he laid them in the sun to dry; today, on many of these precious documents, now stored in European museums, you may see the grains of sand which stuck to them at that time.

Along with these hoards of papyri also came a rich *raccolta* of antiquities that, due to the tenacity of the French Consul in Egypt, went principally to the court of Savoy and subsequently to the great museum of Turin. Stelae made by the villagers, even the door-frames and column bases of their houses and tombs, were dug from the preserving sands that covered the village along with a large collection of household objects. But such digging was haphazard in the extreme. No one understood what it was under the sand and rubble that the modern villagers were attacking with their mat-tocks and iron probes, and certainly no one ever thought to dig out an ancient village in that dry place.

About 1850, the two document-jars that the vizier's officials had filled with the records of both the tomb-robbers' trials and the investigations into the events of the Year of the Hyenas were dug up, either at Deir el Medina or in the compound of the fortress-temple, today no one quite knows where. Bought and sold for many years, most of these too eventually made their way into the collections of the state museums. But although the egyptolo-gists of the day could read most of their hieroglyphs, the special terms with which these texts were filled rendered many of them virtually unintelligible, and those that did not contain gems of lively detail, little snippets of ancient life, were often relegated, unpublished and unconsidered, to museum storerooms.

Such esoteric concerns as the translation of ancient papyrus were as nothing compared with the sensational discovery at Thebes in 1881 of a whole tombful of kings, kings that Butehamun and his villagers had so carefully collected and restored 3,000 years before. A public that was already enchanted by the vivid, if European, visions of ancient oriental splendours could now gaze upon the faces of the most famous Pharaohs of all. The ancient scribes' rough notations on these kings' coffins told the extraordinary tale of their survival. How, some seventy years after Butehamun's death, they had been gathered together at the order of a Theban oracle (some taken from the tomb of Seti I) and carried from the Great Place back over the horizon of Thebes, there to be lowered into the tomb of an ancient queen especially enlarged to hold them. And there the Pharaohs had all lain until a modern villager noticed the tomb's shaft in the cliffs and, under duress some ten years later, revealed his treasure trove to the authorities.

These kings were soon joined in the Cairo Museum by another group, this time of the eight monarchs that Butehamun's villagers had cached in the tomb of Amenhotep II. In this same period a third great vaultful of priests was discovered and shared by museums in the West, whilst in the Valley of the Kings many of the royal tombs were disencumbered of their rubble – quantities of the finest drawings of the outline draughtsmen being found in the process – and shipped off to the museum at Cairo. It must have seemed as if old Thebes was being rapidly emptied.

In 1886 the antiquary Eduardo Toda described the valley of Deir el Medina simply as the 'ruin of the cemetery of the immense city'. A *memento mori* of a landscape where broken vases and amphorae, fragments of stelae and statues, mummy-cloths, even fragments of the villagers themselves, lay scattered about the heaps of debris raised by the diggings of the previous eighty years. Toda visited the valley to witness the dismantling of the tomb of Sennejem – a senior workman of the gangs, an old man when Scribe Ramose came to live in the village – and he saw Sennejem still lying in the friendly vault whose glowing paintings are now one of the sights of modern Thebes. Scholars could read from the tomb's inscriptions that Sennejem was a 'worker in the Place of Truth', but the general and somewhat poetic opinion at the time was that this was the title of a judge in a court of law. Sennejem had been accompanied in his tomb by his wife and generations of his family. One by one they were all packed off, along with their bright-painted grave goods, for exhibition in many different museums.

In 1905 the village cemeteries were excavated by the archaeologist Ernesto Schiaparelli who, as the director of the museum in Turin, was doubtless attracted to the site from which so many of his museum's finest objects had been found. High on the western hillside he uncovered the tomb of an architect of the old dynasty which held the perfectly preserved furnishings of a village house; a unique discovery that was sent in its entirety to join so many other of the village records and furnishings in the Turin Museum. Schiaparelli also excavated parts of five houses in the village and presumably it was in one of these that he found a column base from Scribe Ramose's home – evidence that the scribe had lived with Wia in this north-eastern section of the village.

In the end, of course, the villagers were not re-discovered by such piece-meal excavations but in the museums of Europe where, since the turn of the century, a handful of scholars had increasingly devoted their time to the decipherment and understanding of many of the papyri collected at Thebes. One of these, a young Englishman, T. Eric Peet, focused his attention on the texts found in the two document-jars. In 1920 he published two of the papyri, dealing with the despoilation of the temples and the robbing of a royal tomb in the time of Viceroy Panhesi. Over the next ten years he published all the other documents from the archive that were then known, along with a considerable amount of supporting material including large fragments of the village work-diaries – this in a huge volume in co-operation with the Torinese egyptologist Guiseppe Botti. So the life and times of Scribe Harshire and the investigations of Scribe Djutmose and his contemporaries were brought to light, not as unknown actors in a series of unrelated anecdotes, but as characters in a continuing story. In 1930 Peet published his *magnum opus, The Great Tomb-Robberies of the Twentieth Egyptian Dynasty.* Four years later, at the age of fifty-two, he was dead.

While Peet was investigating the doings of Scribe Harshire and grandson Djutmose, an American expedition was excavating the compound of the fortress-temple of Ramesses III – Medinet Habu as it is now known. There, in the ruins of the temple compound where the remains of the doorways of Djutmose's house had already been found, they discovered several rooms of a large house – in all probability the same family dwelling – in which lay four fallen columns cut with small reliefs showing Scribe Butehamun praying to the gods and honouring King Amenhotep I. The excavators re-erected the columns, but were not rewarded in their efforts by the discovery of any more papyri-filled jars.

A year after Peet's death a missing half of one of the papyri that he had studied unexpectedly came to light, pulled out of a cavity in the back of an unprepossessing statue, where it had been placed by a modern dealer who had hoped to increase this relic's value. Imagine the delight of the surprised egyptologist who first matched the newly-unwrapped scroll directly to a facsimile of the other much celebrated half; it was the final link in the long story of the investigations in the sixteenth year of King Ramesses IX; of the plots of Harshire and the dismal fate of his brother and cousins.

During his work, Peet had often collaborated with a young Czech scholar, Jaroslav Černý, who had been interested in the tombmakers of the Theban necropolis from the very beginning of his studies. Like Peet, he worked with the papyri and was a brilliant interpreter of the rapid handwriting of the ancient scribes, but from the outset his approach to the material was different: for Černý had long sensed that the people buried in the cemetery at Deir el Medina were the men who had made the tombs of the Theban kings. Once this essential fact had been grasped, all the elaborate titles in the tombs and upon the papyri, statues and village stelae were transformed into coherent records from the life of a single village that had existed for one purpose for some 300 years. Although Černý did not publish his crucial paper about the relationship of the title 'servant in the Place of Truth' to the workmen of the royal Theban necropolis until 1929, long before that he was working with this understanding and encouraging other scholars to study some of the mass of material stored in European museums. Thus, along with Černý's account of the cult of Amenhotep I amongst the necropolis workers, an English egyptologist, Aylward Blackman, published the texts describing Scribe Amennakht's archaeological sorties in the village cemetery and his adventures with the drunken Foreman Khonsu. In Blackman's accounts of these village wrangles, the first coherent versions of these difficult texts, was a nugget of history, for one of the villagers' legal depositions gave the information that the village had first been reformed in 1313 BC, in the reign of King Horemheb; this was proof that the village was the same one later transformed by Vizier Paser into the community of scribes and workmen who made the elaborate tombs of the new dynasty kings.

At Thebes too, things had changed for the better, for just when it seemed that the village was doomed to piecemeal excavation - at one point no less than four archaeological excavations worked there in one ten-year period - it found its saviour. Just as Černý's studies would breathe life into the village people, so Bernard Bruyère from the French Archaeological Institute of Cairo would take their ruined and plundered valley, excavate it (in the process leaving a shelf-full of reports), and transform the ancient houses and cemeteries into one of the prettiest archaeological sites in the world. The story of these excavations contains few dramas - no more grand tombs were found - but is rather a chronicle of slow realization. Right from the start Bruyère found much of the substance of the same villagers that Černý encountered in his texts. In the first year of work, Bruyère discovered fragments of Scribe Ramose's coffin and funeral papyrus, and the fragile tomb of the scribe's harem was cleared out, studied and recorded in line-drawings and photographs. Paneb's tomb too was excavated and there Bruyère found a courtyard that could once have held the stone blocks that the foreman was accused of stealing from the Great Place.

After the first three seasons Bruyère was joined at Deir el Medina by Černý, who was to work with the excavations until they finished some thirty years later, deciphering and publishing the thousands upon thousands of inscriptions that were discovered. In the long process, Černý got to know the individual ancient villagers, and learned to sift through the very dust of their lives like no one else; this experience, perhaps, helped to give the sensitivity and humanity to his writings that still fires young scholars today. During his first years at the village Černý also published the so-called 'Salt Papyrus' (named after the British Consul of the previous century who had collected it for the British Museum), the denunciation of Paneb by Amennakht, Foreman Neferhotep's brother. To this day it remains the most vivid of all the village's myriad documents and Černý's elucidation of its intricacies, aided by his own copies of unpublished inscriptions at the village and in the museums of Europe, was masterly.

As Černý grappled with the intricacies of the village feud, an English egyptologist, Alan (later Sir Alan) Gardiner, also turned his attentions to the village. Gardiner had long been interested in the hieratic texts in which so much of village life was recorded, and as early as 1913 he had published an article about the three letters in which Piankh arranged for the liquidation of the two talkative medjay. Now he studied some of the village poetry and the part of Kenhirkhopeshef's library that held the 'Dream Book' and the 'Description of the Followers of Seth'. For Gardiner's publication of this difficult text Černý was able to supply his friend with a list of references of ostraca, papyri and graffiti that encompassed all of Kenhirkhopeshef's life. At this time, too, Černý could recognize the scribe's own handwriting.

In the winter of 1934-5 Bruyère turned his attention away from the cemeteries towards the village itself, which still lay under heaps of rubble left by earlier excavators. Hand-pushed light railway wagons carried immense amounts of debris away from the valley, and these were carefully graded so that the tips would not disfigure the landscape. Underneath this debris Bruyère found the village remarkably well-preserved, and was able to assemble a complete plan of it and even identify several of the houses of individual workmen. He was also able to establish the date of the village's foundation – this from the name of King Tuthmosis I stamped on the bricks of the oldest surviving walls. On the whitewashed walls of two village houses, Černý was able to read the faint inscriptions of Scribe Amennakht and Scribe Harshire, the latter in all probability inked on to the walls of Butehamun's leaky archive storeroom. Scribe Amennakht's inscription identified the house near which the statue of Amenhotep I had stopped when the oracle accused the scribe's daughter of stealing clothes. In all probability Bruyère also located the house of Foreman Neferhotep; and here the shiny-smooth lintel of the doorway would have felt the full force of an enraged young Paneb.

When he had finished with the village Bruyère transferred his excavation to the settlement high above the Valley of the Kings, where the workers had passed their evenings when they were working in the Great Place, and there he found many stone seats, some inscribed with the names of several villagers including Scribe Kenhirkhopeshef. Bruyère even uncovered a room in the scribe's hut that seemed to have served as his office, with a stack of unused white ostraca still lying on the paved stone floor. If proof was still required that the villagers of Deir el Medina had made the royal tombs, Bruyère found it here. By the late 1930s he was at the village again, starting to clear the shrines, a task that he would not finish until after the Second World War. There he found many of the works of Ramose, including the limestone phallus that the scribe had dedicated to Hathor, Golden Lady of the Western Mountains, with a prayer asking for children for himself and his wife.

And all this while Černý and Gardiner continued to study the most important of the village records. In 1939 Černý published the *Late Ramesside Letters*, virtually all the correspondence from the archive found in the 1820s and now scattered through Europe and Egypt. In this same period, Černý also published the 'Will of Naunakht': documents relating to the disposal of the property of Kenhirkhopeshef's young wife and, by references to several other documents, stelae, graffiti and the like transformed a dull legal exposition into a rare piece of family history – and one of the few occasions when a village woman appears as more than a name and a pretty picture of a lady in a fine dress. A few years later, in 1948, Gardiner published an edition of the papyrus, probably written by Scribe Amennakht, describing the village strikes during the reign of Ramesses III. Included in this same book was the so-called 'Turin Taxation Papyrus': the accounts written by Scribe Djutmose during his voyage on a full flood from Thebes to the temple of Khnum at Esna to collect the village's wheat.

Bruyère finished his work at Deir el Medina with a flourish, excavating a vast mysterious pit outside the area of the village proper, to the north of the shrines. It took two seasons, the pit being so wide and deep that the archaeologist must have wondered if he would ever see the bottom. In all probability it had been dug during the Ptolemaic period to provide the water essential for temple ritual – for every temple needed its own water-supply. But after they had cut through more than 100 feet of shale the ancient quarrymen failed to find any water and abandoned their colossal enterprise. From the dry hole, Bruyère took thousands more ostraca, statues and objects of village life; evidently the priests of the stone temple had used their abortive well as a rubbish-tip when cleaning out the old shrines.

There is a story of Černý standing at the top of the Great Pit during its excavation, waiting expectantly for the archaeologists working below to send up their baskets of finds. As these were brought to him, he carefully examined each piece, peering at the numerous inscriptions through his thick round glasses and hoping to discern an ancient name there, someone whom he knew. The texts from the Great Pit fell into two types: those of the Ptolemaic temple priests were written in demotic script, whilst those of the villagers were either in hieroglyphic or the scribe's hieratic. If the text that Černý was examining proved to be the former, the object would be duly stacked in trays for transfer to the expedition house and study at a later date, but if it was written by one of his villagers, Černý would swathe it carefully in cotton wool and carry it away for translation late that same evening, after work.

Bruyère stopped his excavations in 1952. In 1965 Černý retired from the Chair of Egyptology at Oxford University, a post he had held for fifteen years, and initiated the ambitious and strenuous project of mapping and recording the graffiti of the Theban mountains, a great number of which had been written by the villagers. Like the two pioneer scholars in the field, Wilhelm Spiegelberg and Howard Carter, Černý was fascinated by these most intimate and immediate of all ancient records, and until the year of his death in 1973 he led a joint Franco-Egyptian expedition over the hills and valleys of western Thebes in search of his villagers. In the Theban cliffs he found much fresh information about, for example, Foreman Paneb and Scribes Amennakht and Butehamun. Černý and Bruyère have been celebrated at Thebes by the naming of the peak over the village as 'Mont Cernabru' but their lifetime of study is more immediately commemorated by the indissoluble link they forged between themselves and the ancient people whose lives they uncovered.

Today, a world-wide group of scholars continues to study Deir el Medina. Most prominent amongst the published works has been the sensitive translations of Černý's *Late Ramesside Letters* by Professor Edward F. Wente of the University of Chicago, the economic studies of Professor Jac. J. Janssen and the genealogical investigations of Dr Morris Bierbrier, Keeper of the Egyptian Antiquities at the British Museum. The royal tombmakers and their esoteric village are rapidly becoming the most thoroughly researched group of people in the ancient world. At the village itself, recent *sondages* by young French archaeologists have uncovered an older village under the one Bruyère cleared out, and this promises even earlier chapters of village history. The application of modern archaeological methods to these remaining areas also offers the prospect of fresh evidence concerning daily life in the village, aspects of diet and health, of methods of cooking, painting and bee-keeping; a miscellany of vulgar information which, in common with other people of their race, the ancient villagers did not bother to record in their monuments or writings.

At the end of the day, after all the research and the books and scholarly articles have been written and read, it is to the village and its valley that you must go to feel, to see, to walk through the same spaces that the ancient tombmakers inhabited. These people who worshipped images and pictures, who wrote not in abstract signs but in drawings of things, who thought largely in concrete images, moved through that same brilliant landscape of banded yellows, blues and greens, and transformed its materials into kings' tombs, shadowed jewels in the desert hills. Only at Thebes can you walk along a track that the ancient people made and still see their scribblings on the cliff, now often with an archaeologist's number pencilled alongside; suddenly you are strolling alongside a scribe and his sons, out for a walk in the timeless hills.

MAPS

Ancient Egypt showing places mentioned in the text

The tombmakers' village and its monuments

Paneb

Ramose's first tomb

Ramose and Wia

Kha

Neferhotep

Irinefer
Nu

SHRINES

to the Ramesseum

Ipy

WESTERN CEMETERY

Ramose?

Kaha

Ramose's servants

Ipy

Amennakht

Neferhotep?

Harshire

Sennejem

Kenhirkhopeshef?

Anhirkawi

Sennejem

to the fortress-temple

☐ Tombs
☐ Houses

N

| 0 | 10 | 20 | 30 | 40 | 50 yards |
| 0 | 10 | 20 | 30 | 40 | 50 metres |

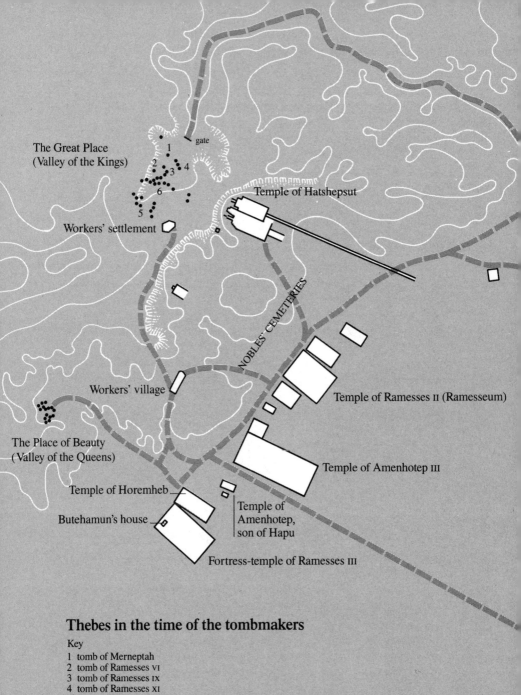

The Great Place
(Valley of the Kings)

gate

1

2
3 4

6

Workers' settlement

5

Temple of Hatshepsut

NOBLES' CEMETERIES

Workers' village

Temple of Ramesses II (Ramesseum)

The Place of Beauty
(Valley of the Queens)

Temple of Amenhotep III

Temple of Horemheb

Butehamun's house

Temple of
Amenhotep,
son of Hapu

Fortress-temple of Ramesses III

Thebes in the time of the tombmakers

Key
1 tomb of Merneptah
2 tomb of Ramesses VI
3 tomb of Ramesses IX
4 tomb of Ramesses XI
5 tomb of Seti II
6 tomb of Amenmesse

N

0   250   500 yards

0   250   500 metres

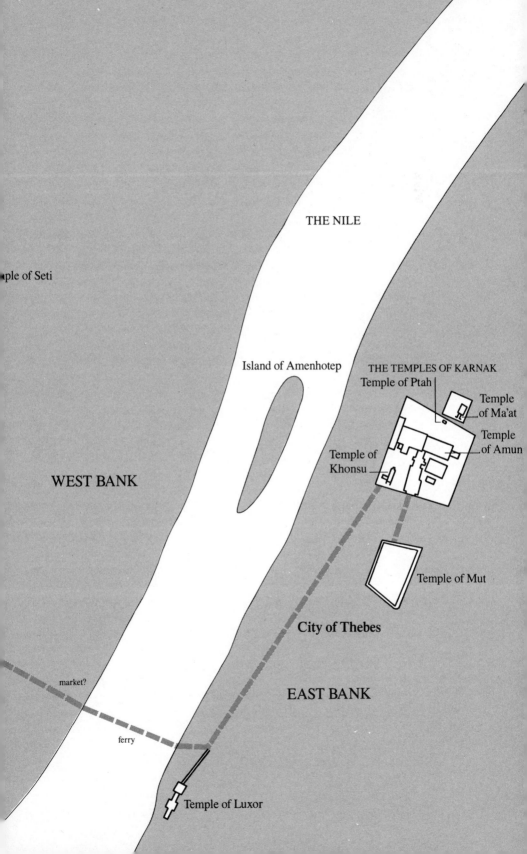

THE NILE

ple of Seti

Island of Amenhotep

THE TEMPLES OF KARNAK
Temple of Ptah

Temple
of Ma'at

Temple
of Amun

Temple of
Khonsu

WEST BANK

Temple of Mut

City of Thebes

EAST BANK

market?

ferry

Temple of Luxor

Chronology

KING	DATES	YEARS RULED
Horemheb	1320–1292	28
Ramesses I	1292–1290	2
Seti II	1290–1279	11
Ramesses II	1279–1212	67
Merneptah	1212–1199	13
Amenmesse	1199–1195	4
Seti II	1195–1189	6
Siptah	1189–1183	6
Sethakht	1183–1181	2
Ramesses III	1181–1149	32
Ramesses IV	1149–1143	6
Ramesses V	1143–1139	4
Ramesses VI	1139–1132	7
Ramesses VII	1132–1125	7
Ramesses VIII	1125–1124	1
Ramesses IX	1124–1105	19
Ramesses X	1105–1096	9
Ramesses XI	1096–1069	27

HIGH PRIEST		
Herihor	1079–1073	6
Piankh	1073–1069	4
Pinejem	1069–1054	15

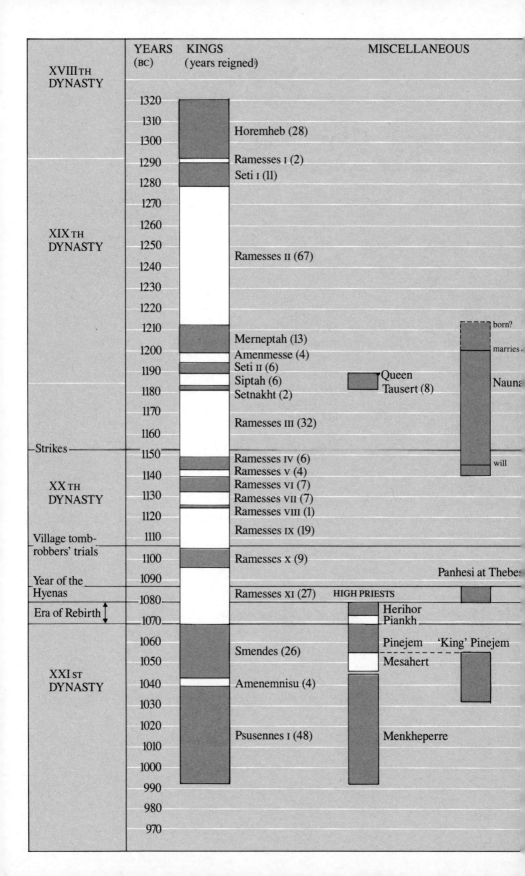

	YEARS (BC)	KINGS (years reigned)	MISCELLANEOUS	
XVIIITH DYNASTY	1320			
	1310	Horemheb (28)		
	1300			
XIXTH DYNASTY	1290	Ramesses I (2)		
	1280	Seti I (11)		
	1270			
	1260			
	1250	Ramesses II (67)		
	1240			
	1230			
	1220			
	1210	Merneptah (13)	born?	
	1200	Amenmesse (4)	marries	
	1190	Seti II (6)		
	1180	Siptah (6)	Queen Tausert (8)	Nauna
		Setnakht (2)		
	1170	Ramesses III (32)		
	1160			
Strikes	1150		will	
	1140	Ramesses IV (6)		
XXTH DYNASTY		Ramesses V (4)		
	1130	Ramesses VI (7)		
		Ramesses VII (7)		
	1120	Ramesses VIII (1)		
Village tomb-robbers' trials	1110	Ramesses IX (19)		
	1100	Ramesses X (9)		
Year of the Hyenas	1090		Panhesi at Thebes	
	1080	Ramesses XI (27)	**HIGH PRIESTS**	
Era of Rebirth	1070		Herihor	
			Piankh	
XXIST DYNASTY	1060		Pinejem 'King' Pinejem	
	1050	Smendes (26)	Mesahert	
	1040	Amenemnisu (4)		
	1030			
	1020			
	1010	Psusennes I (48)	Menkheperre	
	1000			
	990			
	980			
	970			

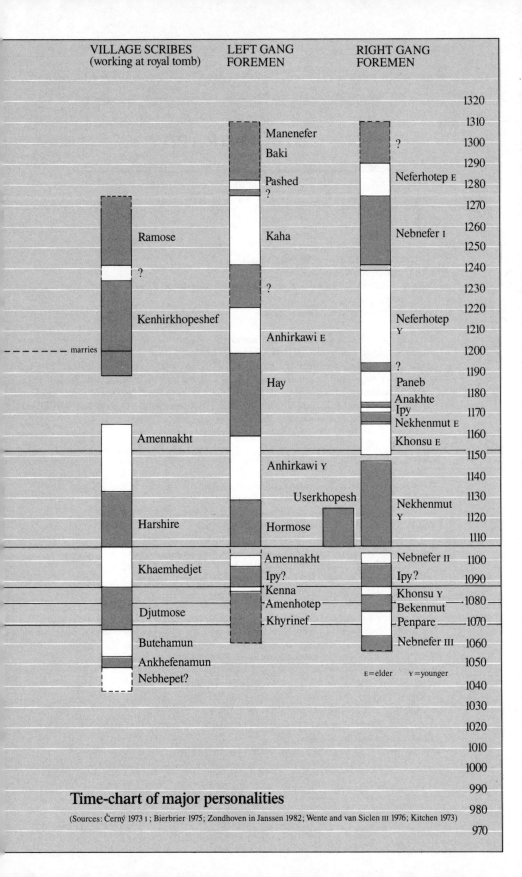

VILLAGE SCRIBES
(working at royal tomb)

LEFT GANG
FOREMEN

RIGHT GANG
FOREMEN

1320
1310
1300
1290
1280
1270
1260
1250
1240
1230
1220
1210
1200
1190
1180
1170
1160
1150
1140
1130
1120
1110
1100
1090
1080
1070
1060
1050
1040
1030
1020
1010
1000
990
980
970

Ramose

?

Kenhirkhopeshef

— — — — marries

Amennakht

Harshire

Khaemhedjet

Djutmose

Butehamun
Ankhefenamun
Nebhepet?

Manenefer
Baki
Pashed
?

Kaha

?

Anhirkawi E

Hay

Anhirkawi Y

Userkhopesh

Hormose

Amennakht
Ipy?
Kenna
Amenhotep
Khyrinef

?

Neferhotep E

Nebnefer I

Neferhotep Y

?
Paneb
Anakhte
Ipy
Nekhenmut E
Khonsu E

Nekhenmut Y

Nebnefer II
Ipy?
Khonsu Y
Bekenmut
Penpare
Nebnefer III

E=elder   Y=younger

Time-chart of major personalities

(Sources: Černý 1973 I ; Bierbrier 1975; Zondhoven in Janssen 1982; Wente and van Siclen III 1976; Kitchen 1973)

BIBLIOGRAPHY

The following abbreviations have been used:
ASAE: Annales du Service des Antiquités de l'Égypte
BIFAO: Bulletin de l'Institut français d'archéologie orientale du Caire
JEA: Journal of Egyptian Archaeology
JNES: Journal of Near Eastern Studies

Virtually all the published material concerning the village of Deir el Medina and its times was consulted during the research for this book, but it seems unnecessary to list it all here. A convenient bibliography, focussed tight upon the ancient village, yet still with more than 350 items in it, has recently been published by L.M.J. Zonhoven in Demarée and Janssen 1982. The publications listed below are either works that are mentioned specifically in this book or are fundamental studies by such scholars as Černý and Janssen without knowledge of which one could not obtain even a basic understanding of the ancient village and its people.

Aldred, C., 'More light on the Ramesside Tomb Robberies' in *Glimpses of Ancient Egypt*, Warminster, 1979
Allam, S., *Hieratische Ostraka und Papyri aus der Ramessidenzeit*, 2 vols., Tübingen, 1973
Baedeker's Egypt and the Sudan, 8th ed., Leipzig, 1929
Baer, K., 'The Oath *sdf3-tryt* in Papyrus Lee I, I', *JEA* 50, 1964
Ball, J., *Egypt in the Classical Geographers*, Cairo, 1942
Baud, M., *Les dessins ébauchés de la nécropole Thébain*, Cairo, 1935
Bierbrier, M.L., *The Late New Kingdom in Egypt*, Warminster, 1975 I
Beirbrier, M.L., 'The Length of the Reign of Ramesses x', *JEA* 61, 1975 II
Beirbrier, M.L., *The Tomb-builders of the Pharaohs*, London, 1982
Blackman, A.M., 'Oracles in Ancient Egypt II', *JEA* 12, 1926
Bonnet, C., and D. Valbelle, 'Le village de Deir el-Médineh', *BIFAO* 75, 1975
Bonnet, C., and D. Valbelle, 'Le village de Deir el-Médineh', *BIFAO* 76, 1976
Botti, G., 'Frammenti di registri di stato civile della xxa dinastia', *Rendiconti. R. Accademia Nazionale de Lincei*, 5, 31, Rome, 1922
Botti, G., and T.E. Peet, *Il giornale della necropoli di Tebe*, Turin, 1928
Breasted, J.H., *Ancient Records of Egypt*, Chicago, 1906
Breasted, J.H., *The Dawn of Conscience*, New York, 1933
Brunner-Traut, E., *Die altägyptischen Scherbenbilder*, Wiesbaden, 1956
Brunner-Traut, E., *Egyptian Artists' Sketches*, Istanbul, 1979
Bruyère, B., *Rapport sur les fouilles de Deir el-Médineh*, 17 parts (including Bruyère 1927, 1935, 1937, 1948), Cairo, 1924-53
Bruyère, B., 'Un jeune prince ramesside trouvé à Deir el-Médineh', *BIFAO* 25, 1925

Bruyère, B., *Mert Seger à Deir el-Médineh*, Cairo, 1930
Bruyère, B., *Tombes thébaines de Deir el-Médineh à decoration monochrome*, Cairo, 1952
Bruyère, B., and C. Kuentz, *La tombe de Nakht-min et la tombe d'Ari-nefer*, Cairo, 1926
Budge, E.A.W. *The Book of the Dead*, London, 1899
Butzer, K.W., *Early Hydraulic Civilisation in Egypt*, Chicago, 1976
Cambridge Ancient History, 2nd edn, Cambridge, 1964-71
Capart, J., *Thebes The Glory of a Great Past*, London, 1926
Capart, J., A.H. Gardiner and B.v.d. Walle, 'New Light on the Ramesside Tomb-Robberies', *JEA* 22, 1936
Carter, H., and A.H. Gardiner, 'The Tomb of Ramesses IV etc.', *JEA* 4, 1917
Černý, J., 'Quelques ostraca hiératiques inédits de Thèbes au Musée du Caire', *ASAE* 27, 1927 I
Černý, J., 'Le culte d'Amenophis Ier chez les ouvriers de la nécropole thébaine', *BIFAO* 27, 1927 II
Černý, J., 'Papyrus Salt 124', *JEA* 15, 1929 I
Černý, J., 'L'identité des "Serviteurs dans la Place de Vérité" et des ouvriers de la necropole royale de Thèbes', *Revue de L'Egypte ancienne* 2, 1929 II
Černý, J., 'Fluctuations in Grain Prices during the Twentieth Egyptian Dynasty', *Archiv Orientáli* 6, 1934
Černý, J., 'Questions adressées aux oracles', *BIFAO* 35, 1935 I
Černý, J., *Ostraca hiératiques*, Cairo, 1935 II
Černý, J., *Catalogue des ostraca hiératiques non-littéraires de Deir el Médineh*, 6 vols., Cairo, 1935-70
Černý, J., 'Datum des Todes Ramses' III und die Thronbesteigung Ramses' IV', *Zeitschrift für Agyptischen Sprache* 72, 1936
Černý, J., *Late Ramesside Letters*, Brussels, 1939
Černý, J., 'Nouvelle série de questions adressées aux oracles', *BIFAO* 41, 1942
Černý, J., 'The Will of Naunakhte and the Related Documents', *JEA* 31, 1945
Černý, J., *Repertoire onomastique de Deir el-Médineh*, Cairo, 1949
Černý, J., *Graffiti hiéroglyphiques et hiératiques de la nécropole thébaine*, Cairo, 1956
Černý, J., *Egyptian Stelae in the Bankes Collection*, Oxford, 1958
Černý, J., 'Egyptian Oracles' in R. Parker, *A Saite Oracle Papyrus from Thebes in the Brooklyn Museum*, Providence, Rhode Island, 1962
Černý, J., 'Troisième série de questions adressées aux oracles', *BIFAO* 72, 1972
Černý, J., *A Community of Workmen at Thebes in the Ramesside Period*, Cairo, 1973 I
Černý, J., *The Valley of the Kings. Fragments d'un manuscrit inachevé*, Cairo, 1973 II
Černý, J., *Papyrus hiératiques de Deir el-Médineh*, Cairo, 1978
Černý, J., and A.H. Gardiner, *Hieratic Ostraca*, Oxford, 1957
Černý, J., A.F. Sadek et al., *Graffiti de la montagne thébaine*, 4 vols., Cairo, 1969-74
Couyat, J., and P. Montet, *Les Inscriptions hiéroglyphiques et hiératiques du Ouâdi Hammâmât*, Cairo, 1912
Daressy, G., 'Quelques ostraca de Biban el Molouk', *ASAE* 27, 1927
Davies, N., *The Tomb of Huy*, London, 1926
Davies, N., *Picture Writing in Ancient Egypt*, London, 1958
Davies, N. de Gavis, 'A High Place in Thebes', *Melanges Maspero* I, Cairo, 1935-8
Dawson, W., 'Some observations on the Egyption calendars, etc.', *JEA* 12, 1926
Demarée, R.J., and J.J. Janssen (eds), *Gleanings from Deir el-Medina*, Leiden, 1982
Edgerton, W.G., 'The Strikes in Ramses III's Twenty-ninth Year', *JNES* 9, 1950
Edwards, I.E.S., 'Kenhikhopshef's Prophylactic Charm', *JEA* 54, 1968
Epigraphic Survey, *Medinet Habu* V, Chicago, 1957
Gardiner, A.H., 'A Political Crime in Ancient Egypt', *Journal of the Manchester Egyptian and Oriental Society*, 1912-13

Gardiner, A.H., *Theban Ostraca*, Oxford, 1913

Gardiner, A.H., *The Chester Beatty Papyri, No. 1*, London, 1931

Gardiner, A.H., *Hieratic Papyri in the British Museum. Third Series*, London, 1935

Gardiner, A.H., 'Ramesside Texts Relating to the Taxation and Transport of Corn', *JEA* 27, 1941

Gardiner, A.H., *Ramesside Administrative Documents*, Oxford, 1948

Gardiner, A.H., *Egypt of the Pharaohs*, Oxford, 1961

Goedicke, H., and E.F. Wente, *Ostraka Michaelides*, Wiesbaden, 1962

Griffith, F.L.L., *A Collection of Hieroglyphs*, London, 1898

Guilmant, F., *Le Tombeau de Ramsès* IX, Cairo, 1907

Gunn, B., *The Religion of the Poor in Ancient Egypt*, *JEA* 3, 1916

Habashi, L., 'Lids of the outer sarcophagi, etc.', *Mitteilungen aus der ägyptischen Sammlung* VIII, Berlin, 1975

Habashi, L., *Tavole d'offerta, are e bacili da libagione*, Turin, 1977

Harris, J., and E.F. Wente (eds), *An X-Ray Atlas of the Royal Mummies*, Chicago, 1980

Hayes, W.C., *The Scepter of Egypt*, part II, New York, 1959

Helck, W., *Materialien zur Wirtschaftsgeschichte des Neuen Reiches*, 6 vols. Wiesbaden, 1961–9

Janssen, J.J., 'An Unusual Donation Stela of the Twentieth Dynasty', *JEA* 49, 1963

Janssen, J.J., *Commodity Prices from the Ramesside Period*, Leiden, 1975

Janssen, J.J., 'The Water Supply of a Desert Village', *Medelhavsmuseet Bulletin* 14, 1979

Janssen, J.J., 'The Mission of the Scribe Pesiūr' (O Berlin 12654), in Demarée and Janssen 1982

Kitchen, K.A., *Ramesside Inscriptions* I, Oxford, 1975

Lichtheim, M., *Ancient Egyptian Literature*, vol. II, Berkeley, 1976

Moss, R., 'By-products of bibliography', *JEA* 54, 1968

Omlin, J., *Der Papyrus 55001 und seine Satirische-erotischen Zeichnungen und Inschriften*, Turin, 1973

Peet, T.E., *The Mayer Papyri A & B*, London, 1920

Peet, T.E., 'Fresh Light on the Tomb Robberies of the Twentieth Dynasty at Thebes', *JEA* 11, 1925

Peet, T.E., 'The Supposed Revolution of the High Priest Amenhotpe under Ramesses IX', *JEA* 12, 1926

Peet, T.E., *The Great Tomb-Robberies of the Twentieth Egyptian Dynasty*, Oxford, 1930

Peterson, B., 'Zeichnungen aus einer Totenstadt', *Medelhavsmuseet Bulletin* 7–8, 1973

Petrie, W.M.F., *A History of Egypt*, vol. III, London, 1925

Pleyte, W., and F. Rossi, *Papyrus de Turin*, 2 vols., Leiden, 1869–76

Porter, R. and B. Moss, *Topographical Bibliography of Ancient Egyptian Hieroglyphic Texts, Reliefs and Paintings*, 8 vols., Oxford, 1927–81

Romer, J., *Valley of the Kings*, London and New York, 1981

Rosellini, I., *I Monumenti dell'Egitto e della Nubia*, 3 vols., Pisa, 1832–44

Schiaparelli, E., *Relazione sui lavori della Missione Archeologica Italiana in Egitto*, vol. II: *La tomba intatta dell'architetto Cha*, Turin, 1927

Schott, S., 'The Feasts of Thebes' in Nelson and Holscher, *Work in Western Thebes 1931–3*, Chicago, 1934

Spiegelberg, W., 'Hieratic Ostraca from Thebes', *Ancient Egypt* I, 1914

Spiegelberg, W., *Aegyptische und andere graffiti aus der Thebanischen Nekropolis*, 2 vols. Heidelberg, 1921

Thomas, E., *The Royal Necropoleis of Thebes*, Princeton, 1966

Toda, E., 'La découverte et l'inventaire du tombeau de Sen-nezem', *ASAE* 20, 1920

Tosi, M., *Una stirpe di pittori a Tebe*, Turin, 1972

Tosi, M., and A. Roccati, *Stele e altre epigrafi di Deir el Medina*, Turin, 1972

Vandersleyen, C., 'La statue d'Amenophis I', *Oriens Antiquus* 19, 1980
Wente, E.F., 'A Letter of Complaint to the Vizier To', *JNES* 20, 1961
Wente, E.F., *Late Ramesside Letters*, Chicago, 1967
Wente, E.F., and C. van Siclen III, 'A chronology of the New Kingdom', in *Studies in Honor of G.R. Hughes*, Chicago, 1976
Wilkinson, Sir J.G., *The Manners and Customs of the Ancient Egyptians*, London, 1837-78
Wilson, J.A., 'The Oath in Ancient Egypt', *JNES* 7, 1948
Zonhoven, L.M.J., 'The Inspection of a Tomb at Deir el-Medîna', *JEA* 65, 1979
Zonhoven, L.M.J., 'A Systematic Bibliography on Deir el-Medîna', in Demarée and Janssen 1982

DOCUMENTS CITED

The following abbreviations have been used:

ff.: and following quotes
O: ostraca
Pap.: papyrus
Stat.: statue

QV: Valley of the Queens' tomb-number
TG: Theban Graffiti
TT: Theban Tomb

ASAE: Annales du Service des Antiquités de l'Egypte
BIFAO: Bulletin de l'Institut français d'archéologie orientale du Caire
JEA: Journal of Egyptian Archaeology
Giornale: Botti and Peet 1928
Hier. Ost.: Černý and Gardiner 1959

LRL: Černý 1939
RAD: Gardiner 1948

The village scribes wrote an esoteric form of ancient Egyptian that still requires expert translation. Over the years, the scholars engaged in this work have employed a variety of styles ranging from King James' to Henry James'. Although scientifically accurate, such translations frequently seem inappropriate to the ancient Egyptians, while using a mixture of styles can produce an absurd effect. I have, therefore, compared the available translations and rendered them into a uniform style. I hope that the result is clear, consistent and understandable.

The page number of the reference is given first, followed by the opening words of the document quoted, then the reference for the document is given. The final reference is to a translation or to a discussion of the quoted text.

10 'to whom' and ff. Stat. BM EA687 etc.; Černý 1973 I, pp. 57–8

16 'There was'. O Černý 17, 2–6; Černý 1973 I, p. 163

22 '[In] year seven'. O BM 5624; Blackman 1926

22 'The Scribe'. O MMA 14120; Tosi 1972

23 'Made scribe'. O Cairo Cat.' 671,3 + TG 1140; Černý 1973 I, pp. 223 and 317

24 'The wages'. *Hier. Ost.* 30; Janssen 1975

26 'Third month'. O Gardiner 123; Černý 1973 I, p. 179

26 'I am'. O Toronto A11, 12; Černý 1973 I, p. 265

27 'I made'. Bruyère 1948, fasc. II, p. 65 and pl. XXX; Černý 1973 I, p. 323

27 'Giving praise'. Bankes Stela 3; Černý 1958

27 'Adoration of'. Bankes Stela 4; Černý 1958

28 'Hathor, remember'. Cairo Museum $\frac{29\ 4}{26\ 3}$ (Bruyère 1935); Černý 1973 I, p. 325

29 'West', 'Beautiful Flood'. TT 212; Černý 1973, p. 325

29 'honest scribe'. Stat. Turin Cat. 1603; Černý 1973 I, p. 225

30 'May your'. Sacrophagus. Turin Mus. Sup.5153; Habashi 1975

33 'The draughtsman'. O DM 303; Černý 1973 I, p. 337

34 'Be very'. O DM 114,4; Černý 1973 I, p. 72

36 'King's Scribe'. Bruyère 1937; Černý 1973 I, p. 326

37 'in truth'. Peterson 1973 (Book of the Dead, Ch.VI)

41 'Year one'. O Cairo Cat '651, verso; Černý 1973 II, p. 18

41 'weight of'. Weight Gardiner no. 12; Černý 1973 I, p. 337

42 'The Great'. Pap.Ch.Beatty III, verso 4.1; Gardiner 1935

42 'Sitting place'. TG 1400; Černý 1956

44 'A summary'. Pap.Ch.Beatty III, pl. 11–12a; Gardiner 1935

44 'First month'. O Cairo Cat. '542; Černý 1973 II, pp. 47–8

45 'The Great'. Pap.Ch.Beatty III, pl. 11–12a; Gardiner 1935

45 'for the'. Pap.Ch.Beatty III, pl. 11–12; Gardiner 1935

46 'old writings'. Černý 1973 I; ibid. p. 18

50 'Twenty-first day'. O Cairo J. 50345; Černý 1927

51 'Pharaoh let'. O Cairo J. 51515; Černý 1927

53 'Follow your'. Pap. Harris 500 (Harper's Song); Breasted 1933

54 '... I'll pluck'. Pap. Harris 500 (Song 19); Lichtheim 1976

58 'The land'. Pap. Harris 75, 2–5; Gardiner 1961

60 'Year one [of his.' O Cairo 25560; Černý 1927

60 'Year one, first'. O MMA 14.6.217 (Hier. Ost. 64,1); Černý 1973 II, p. 16

64 'I will'. Pap. Salt 124 (=BM 10055), recto 16; Černý 1929 I

65 'by the enemy'. Pap. Salt, recto 1,2; Černý 1929 I

66 'Do not indulge'. Pap. Instructions of Ani 5,0–5,1; Lichtheim 1976

67 'The Marks'. Pap. Ch. Beatty III, pl. 8; Gardiner 1935

69 'If a man'. Pap. Ch. Beatty III, pl. 5–8a; Gardiner 1935

69 'dead'. Pap. Ch. Beatty III, 4,14; Gardiner 1935

69 'eating crocodile'. Pap.Ch.Beatty III, 2,23; Gardiner 1935

69 'with his face'. Pap.Ch.Beatty III, 7, 11; Gardiner 1935

69 'uncovering his own'. Pap. Ch.Beatty III, 9,10; Gardiner 1935

73 'shaved the head' and ff. O Gardiner 197, verso 3–6; Černý 1973 I, p. 332

75 'fed on' and ff. Pap. BM 10731; Edwards 1968

75 'Come, my stick'. Cairo J. 27310B; Černý 1973 I, pp. 55–6

76 'Scribe in'. TG 802; Beirbrier 1975

78 'I am'. Will of Naunakht 1.2,1 to 3,1; Černý 1945

78 'as a special'. Will of Naunakht 1.3,3–3,4; Černý 1945

79 'I saw Heria'. Hier. Ost. 1,46,1; Beirbrier 1982

80 'as for me'. O Cairo 25656; Černý 1927

80 'As truly as Amun'. O Cairo J49887; Černý 1927

80 'I will come'. Pap. Salt, recto 2,21; Baer 1964

81 'In the sixth'. O Cairo 25515; Černý 1973 II, p. 15

81 'upset a stone'. Pap. Salt, recto 1,16; Wilson 1948

82 'don't let.'. Pap. Salt, verso 1, 15; Baer 1964

83 'I opened'. O Michaelides 13,6–7; Černý 1973 I, pp. 164–5

84 'took them away'. Pap. Salt, recto 2,6; Černý 1929 I

84 'should the Vizier'. Pap. Salt, verso 6; Baer 1964

84 'Year one'. Hier. Ost. 25518, recto 5–6; Bierbrier 1975

84 'I cannot'. Pap. Salt 124, recto 2,1–4; Černý 1929 I

88 'I am'. Pap. Salt 124, recto 1,1; Černý 1929 I

89 'such conduct'. Pap. Salt 124, verso 2,1–4; Černý 1929 I

91 'Year two'. O U. Coll. 19614 (Kitchen 1975); Spiegelberg 1914

91 'tombs though'. Pap. Salt, recto 1,17–18; Černý 1929 I

91 'carried off'. Pap. Salt, verso 1, 1–3; Černý 1929 I

92 'Charge concerning'. Pap. Salt, verso 1,11–12; Wilson 1948

93 'Year six'. O Non. Kit.697 (Černý 1936–70); Bierbrier 1975

94 'To Scribe'. O Berlin 10627; Černý 1973I, pp. 212–13

98 'Come behind'. Pap. Turin 55001; Omlin 1973

101 'The magistrate'. O Gardiner 140,2; Černý 1973I, p. 172

101 'act, my'. O BM 5637, verso 5; Blackman 1926

102 'Is it'. O IFAO 501; Černý 1962

102 'Shall the'. O Cairo J. 59464; Černý 1962

102 'Will they'. O IFAO 692; Černý 1962

102 'Are these'. O IFAO 40; Černý 1962

102 'Shall one'. O IFAO 556; Černý 1962

103 'The procession'. Coronation inscription of Tuthmoses III; Breasted 1906

103 'and the god' and ff. Pap. BM 10335, recto 1,2-verso 1,15; Blackman 1926

104 'I am a man'. Stela BM EA589; Gunn 1916

105 'I was an'. Stela Turin 50058; Tosi and Roccati 1972

106 'Year sixteen'. TG 1111 + 1143; Černý 1973I, p. 223

108 'What do they'. O Gardiner 25,10; Černý 1973I, p. 348

108 'My Lord'. O Gardiner 4; Černý 1927

110 'he made a'. and ff. O BM 5624,0,3; Blackman 1926

111 'walk to'. O BM 5624,0,5; Blackman 1926

112 'a donkey'. O Cairo Cat. '302; Černý 1973I, p.93

112 'Whoever'. and ff. Pap. Sallier IV and Pap. BM 10474; Dawson 1926

113 'The King's'. Pap. Turin 107,17; Černý 1973I, pp. 11–12

113 'The tomb'. O Turin 5660; Černý 1973I, p.10

113 'Working in'. O Turin 5654, Černý 1973I, p.10

113 'first king's'. QV 42; Černý 1973I, p. 11

116 'I am working'. and ff. O Or. Inst. 16991; Wente 1961

117 'This day'. O Berlin 10633; Edgerton 1951

118 'Statement of'. RAD 49,4-12 (=Pap. Turin 1880); Edgerton 1950

119 'great oaths'. and ff. RAD 52, 14–53; Edgerton 1950

120 'It was because'. RAD 53, 14–54; Edgerton 1950

120 'Look, I will'. RAD 54, 5–12; Edgerton 1950

120 'By Amun'. RAD 54, 13–55; Baer 1964

120 'Tell your superiors'. RAD 55, 5–12; Edgerton 1950

121 'It was not'. RAD 55, 15–56; Edgerton 1950

122 'take the ration'. RAD 56,8-16; Edgerton 1950

122 'I have given'. RAD 56, 8-16; Edgerton 1950

123 'I will go'. RAD 51, 15–52; Edgerton 1950

123 'my superiors'. RAD 57, 6–58; Edgerton 1950

125 'I will go'. RAD 51, 15–52; Edgerton 1950

127 'Third month'. Pap. Turin Cat. 1949 + 1946, verso 1,10-15; Černý 1936

127 'The Falcon'. O DM 39.16; Černý 1973II, p. 16

127 'from Askelon'. Stela BM EA588; Janssen 1963

127 'evil done'. RAD 57, 6–58; Edgerton 1950

128 'the dead'. Wadi Hammamat Stela, yr.3, Ramesses IV; Couyat and Montet 1912

129 'And you shall'. Stela Cairo Mus. 48876; Breasted 1906

129 'a place of'. O DM 45, 16–17; Černý 1973II, p. 17

130 'Mountains of'. Turin Goldmine Pap.; Ball 1942

131 'drawn in'. Turin Tomb Plan Pap. (Pap. Turin 72); Carter and Gardiner 1917

131 'drawn in'. Turin Tomb Plan Pap. (Pap. Turin 72); Carter and Gardiner 1917

132 'Personnel that'. O Berlin 12654, verso 3; Janssen 1982

132 'a hundred'. O Berlin 12654, recto 10-11; Janssen 1982

132 'This day'. O Berlin 12654, verso 5; Janssen 1982

133 'from the.' Pap. Turin 99 + 1961; Černý 1973I, p. 344

135 'drawing with'. Turin Tomb Plan Pap. (Pap. Turin 72); Carter and Gardiner 1917

137 'draughtman of'. TT 113; Wilkinson 1837-78

138 'Head of'. TT 65; Černý 1973I, p. 78

138 'Amun Re'. TT 65; Černý 1973I, p. 78

141 'To my father'. O Gardiner 106; Černý 1973I, p. 116

141 'busy himself'. O Gardiner 70, 4; Černý 1973I, p. 12

145 'Year one' and ff. Pap. Turin Cat. 2044 II 1,5; Černý 1973I, p. 277

146 'I rejoined'. Pap. Leopold/Amherst 3,1-3; Capart and Gardiner 1936

147 'We went'. Pap. BM 10054, recto 3-7; Peet 1930

149 'evildone'. RAD 57, 6-58; Edgerton 1950

150 'royal pyramid'. Pap. Abbott (BM 10221) 2, 8-11; Peet 1930

151 'The pyramids'. Pap. Abbott 2,3-15; Peet 1930

151 'the pyramid tomb'. Pap. Abbott 2-3, 15; Peet 1930

151 'The tombs'. Pap. Abbott 2-4, 1-4; Peet 1930

151 'They [the'. Pap. Abbott 4,10; Peet 1930

152 'These are' and ff. Pap. Abbott 5,4-10; Peet 1930

153 'As for' and ff. Pap. Abbott 5,15-6,7; Peet 1930

153 'Your deeds'. Pap. Abbott 6,8-17; Peet 1930

153 'It was'. Pap. Abbott 6, 20-23; Peet 1930

154 'The Mayor'. and ff. Pap. Abbott 7,8-14; Peet 1930

156 'The hair'. Giornale, Anno 17. 8B, verso 15

157 'prisoner'. Giornale, Anno 17 1A-3A

157 'the eight men'. Giornale, Anno 17,6A, 1-3

158 'the gold'. Pap. BM 10068, recto 1,3-4; Peet 1930

158 'the tombmakers'. Giornale, Anno 17,IB, recto 17

158 'Mayor of western'. Pap. BM 10053 1,6-7; Peet 1930

159 'a cripple'. Pap. BM 10053 7,12; Peet 1930

160 'Here are'. Giornale, Anno 17.IB, recto 22-24

161 'Received from'. Pap. BM 10068, recto 4,1; Peet 1930

161 'Recovered from'. Pap. BM 10068, recto 4,18; Peet 1930

161 'Recovered from'. Pap. BM 10068, recto 4,22: Peet 1930

161 'Let us go'. Giornale, Anno 17.2B, recto 31

162 'go up and'. Giornale, Anno 17 C, recto 3-5

162 'the breaking'. Giornale, Anno 17 8B, recto 10

162 'You are'. Giornale, Anno 17 9B, recto 10-11

163 'a great'. Pap. BM 10221 6,3-4; Peet 1930

165 'The fourth month'. Giornale, Anno 3.2, recto 11

165-6 'Second month'. Giornale, Anno 3.3, recto 23

166 'It is I'. Giornale, Anno 3.2, recto 17

167 'corn as the'. Genesis 41,49

168 'exchange for.' Pap. BM 10052 11,7-8; Peet 1930

168 'men who'. Pap. BM 10052 1,9; Peet 1930

168 'noose—'. Pap. BM 10052 3, 14-17; Peet 1930

168 'They divided'. Pap. BM 10052 6, 5-13; Peet 1930

169 'The foreigners'. Pap. Mayer A., section 4 6,3; Peet 1926

173 'What is the'. LRL 68-70; Wente 1967

174 'A wife'. LRL 67-68; Wente 1967

175 'joke with'. LRL 68; Wente 1967

175 'Every day'. LRL 68; Wente 1967

175 'Received in'. RAD 39,3.10-11; Gardiner 1941

176 'Received in'. RAD 40, 4.1-3; Gardiner 1941

177 'Royal command'. Pleyte and Rossi, 1869-76, pl. LXVI-LXVII; Breasted 1906

179 'the place'. Pap. Mayer A, list B, 4.12.12; Peet 1920

179 'There was'. Pap. Mayer A, Section III 5,13; Peet 1920

180 'We went'. Pap. Mayer B, 7-14; Peet 1920

180 'There was'. Pap. BM 10052 8, 3-6; Peet 1930

181 'The Vizier' and ff. Pap. BM 10052 10, 13-15; Peet 1930

181 'Stop'. Pap. BM 10052 5, 13-17; Peet 1930

181 'If I went'. Pap. BM 10052 1, 19-21; Peet 1930

181 'The matter of'. Pap. BM 10383 1, 4-26; Peet 1930

181 'not to speak'. Pap. BM 10052; 12,8; Peet 1930

182 'The records'. Pap. Ambras (Pap. Vienna 30) 1,1; Peet 1930

182 'concerning the'. and ff. Pap. Ambras 2,1-11; Peet 1930

182 'My father'. Pap. BM 10052, 4-8; Peet 1930

182-3 'Year eighteen'. TG 1109; Černý 1973 1, p. 339

183 'Let him go'. *LRL* 42-43; Wente 1967

183 '[To] the'. *LRL* 23-24; Wente 1967

184 'The scribe'. *LRL* 1-2; Wente 1967

184 'As soon as'. *LRL* 55-56; Wente 1967

185 'And you shall'. *LRL* 11,3; Wente 1967

185 'and take'. *LRL* 10,5; Wente 1967

185 'And … you'. *LRL* 11, 12-16; Wente 1967

185 'As for your'. *LRL* 27-28; Wente 1967

186 'Tomorrow is'. and ff. *LRL* 27; Wente 1967

187 'Oh noble'. O Louvre Inv. 698; Černý 1973I, pp. 369-70

187 'Take these'. *LRL* 36,1-12; Wente 1967

188 'I belong'. Seal attached to *LRL* 36 etc.; Gardiner 1912-13

188 'a man'. *LRL* 48-49; Wente 1967

188 'Stay in'. *LRL* 29,12-16; Wente 1967

188-9 'eye is blind'. *LRL* 30; Wente 1967

189 'from the'. *LRL* 50; Wente 1967

189 'hellhole'. *LRL* 2,3; Wente 1967

189 'abandoned in'. and ff. *LRL* 17, 19-20,8; Wente 1967

190 'Guard my limbs'. TG 1574 (but not in location listed in Porter and Moss 1927-81); Černý 1973 1, p. 374

194 'where to put'. *LRL* 48,1; Wente 1967

196 'of the tomb'. Pap. Vienna 30.II, 8. Černý 1973 1, p. 9

200 'My mouth'. Coffin lid. Turin 2236 (Book of the Dead, Ch. XXIII)

200 'Yours is'. graffito in TT 291; Černý 1973 I, p. 373

204 'ruin of'. *ASAE* 20; Toda 1920

206 'Servant in'. *Revue de l'Égypte ancienne* 2; Černý 1929 II

ACKNOWLEDGEMENTS

I should like to thank the people who, in a diversity of ways have helped me in the preparation of this book: Martha Caute, Professor Hans Goedicke, Caradoc King, Donald Lowle, Nicholas Reeves and Louis Romer. I should also like to thank Professor Silvio Curto and his most friendly staff at the Museo Egizio in Turin for allowing me the use of the Museum's fine library and to photograph in the public galleries. I am in especial debt to Michael O'Mara for his help and advice over the years and also to Beth, my wife, who has not only typed my manuscript three times over and listened to me talk on and on about the ancient village whilst she endeavoured to write her own book, but who also made the thirty-seven drawings that decorate the chapters and provided the noble title as well! Half the book, at least, is hers.

JOHN ROMER

THE FILMING OF 'ANCIENT LIVES'

Words set ancient thoughts running again, but pictures alone can show us the other side of the ancient coin – especially of the ancient Egyptians, a nation of superb image-makers. It was an especial delight for me, therefore, to help to make four television films about the ancient village.

Richard Creasy of Central Independent Television first saw the possibilities of filming 'Ancient Lives' and introduced me to Peter Spry-Leverton who was to produce and direct the series with such flair and thoughtfulness. The bulk of the films were shot at Thebes in the autumn of 1983 in an atmosphere of genuine enthusiasm: Peter Greenhalgh's elegant camera-work, especially, shows Egypt as it has never been seen before on film. More than anything else, however, the four films are the result of Peter Spry-Leverton's quiet professionalism and I sincerely hope that he enjoyed their making as much as I did and that he is satisfied with the result. All the people listed below greatly contributed to the four films and also, incidentally, helped in their most modern way to further the villagers' most earnest wish: that their ancient names might 'live for ever'. Certainly, the great monuments in which the villagers spent their lives have now been seen by more people than ever they could have imagined.

Peter Spry-Leverton: Producer; Peggy Morris: Production Assistant; Peter Greenhalgh: Film Cameraman; Robin Macdonald: Camera Assistant; Mike Claydon: Sound Recordist; David Hamilton: Electrician.

Kevin Brazier: Film Editor; Jonathan Morris: Film Editor; Tony Pound: Assistant Film Editor; Bill Hopkins: Assistant Film Editor; Steve Masters: Graphics; Edward Wynne: Music.

Richard Creasy: Head of Documentaries, Central Independent Television; Carol Haslam: Commissioning Editor, Channel 4; Naomi Sargant: Senior Commissioning Editor, Channel 4.

I must also record my continuing debt to my friend Nabil Osman, Councillor and Director of the Press and Information Office of the Embassy of Egypt in London; and at Thebes, to Selim Abu Said and Ahmed Nubie, both of the Egyptian Ministry of Information, Luxor.

INDEX

Aaphate (Paneb's son), 67, 84-5, 87, 90, 93
Abydos, 9, 128, 129, 130; annual pilgrimage to, 51
Akhenaten, King, 21
Ahmose, Prince, 151
Akhtay (wife of Butehamun), 186-7
Amenemheb, messenger, 6
Amenemopet, Foreman (Ipy), 106
Amenemopet, villager, 110-11
Amenhotep I, 21, 35, 50, 120, 200, 205, 206; oracle of, 101-3, 108-9, 111, 194, 200; tomb of, 151, 194
Amenhotep II, tomb of, 194, 204
Amenhotep III, 8-9; temple of, 8
Amenhotep, Deputy, 157-8, 159
Amenhotep, Draughtsman, 136, 137, 140, 141, 142, 146, 147, 153, 155, 162
Amenhotep, High Priest of Amun, 148-50, 152, 156, 158, 161, 164-5, 166, 168, 169, 170, 172, 178
Amenhotep, Scribe, 8-9, 12, 24
Amehhotep (Harshire's cousin), 156
Amenhotep, senior villager, 188, 191
Amehkhau, leader of gang, 168
Amenmesse, King, 57, 60, 64, 112; tomb of, 57, 60, 85-6
Amenmose, Scribe, 108-9
Amennakht (Neferhotep's brother), 31, 207; accusations against Paneb, 81, 84-5, 88-93
Amennakht, Scribe (son of Ipy), 106, 107-13, 117, 118, 119, 120, 121, 122, 123, 124, 131, 133, 136, 141, 167, 183, 200, 203, 206, 207, 208, 209
Amennakht (son of Draughtsman Amenhotep), 146
Amenpenefer, stonemason, 146
Amenwa (Harshire's cousin), 157-8, 159

Amun, 8, 9, 27, 186, 196; ceremonial bark, 178; festivals, 10, 48-50; temples, 10, 35, 48, 102, 103, 156, 159, 160, 165, 170, 171, 177-8, 183, 193
Amun of the Good Encounter, shrine of, 189
Amun-Re, 27, 138, 163, 175, 185
Anhirkawi, Foreman, 31, 42, 60, 124, 127, 141
animal drawings, 96-8
Ankhefenamun, Scribe, 200, 201
Anubis, god, 47
Anupemheb, Scribe, 33, 51, 74
Apis Bull, 10
Armant, 128

bailiffs see doorkeepers
Baketamun, 170, 185
Baki, Foreman, 23
Bay, Chancellor, 58, 82, 85
Behhek, god, 150
Bes, god, 52
Bierbrier, Dr Morris, 209
Blackman, Aylward, 206
blindness, 103-5
Book of the Dead, 37, 193, 200
Botti, Giuseppe, 205
Bruyère, Bernard, 206-8, 209
Butehamun, Scribe (son of Djutmose), 170, 184, 185, 186-7, 188-9, 190, 191, 192, 194, 195-6, 197, 198, 200, 201, 203, 204, 209; coffins, 199-200

calendars, 112
Carter, Howard, 209
Černý, Jaroslav, xi, 206, 207, 208, 209
clothing of villagers, 61-2, 108
coffin-painting, 23, 83, 106, 108, 136, 170, 199
colour artists, 135-6, 137, 138, 140, 141, 142, 199

231

copper chisels, 15–16, 17, 82–3, 84, 125
Coptos, 128

Deir el Medina, xii, 202–10
Djutmose, Mayor of Thebes, 22
Djutmose, Scribe, 170, 171, 172–6, 177, 179, 180, 181, 182–3, 184, 185, 186, 187–90, 191, 194, 203, 205, 208
Djutweshbi, Captain, 172, 176
doctors, 104–5
doorkeepers (and bailiffs), 16–17, 23, 100–1, 124–5
Double Plume province, 172, 175
drawings, 95–9
Dream Book, 68–72, 207

Efenamun, boat-captain, 159
Elephantine, 46, 188
Era of Rebirth, 178, 181, 183, 184, 185, 187, 196
Erotic Papyrus, 98–9, 203
Esna, 172, 174, 175, 176, 188, 208

Feast of the Valley, 49–50, 112
festivals, 10, 21, 45, 48–54, 77, 101
fish, 25, 51, 116, 166
floods, 38–9, 40, 172, 173
Followers of Seth, 66–7, 76, 90, 92, 93, 96, 207
food and drink, 51–3; see also grain rations

Gardiner, Sir Alan, 207, 208
gold mining, 130, 203
grain (wheat) rations, 24–5, 26, 33, 108, 156, 157, 158, 161, 162, 165–6; workers' disputes over, 116–23, 125, 146
Great Pit, excavation of, 208–9
The Great Place see Valley of the Kings

Harshire, Scribe, 108, 123, 133, 136, 146, 149–50, 154, 155, 156, 157, 161, 164, 167, 183, 203, 205, 206, 207
'The Harvest Overflows', granary, 175
Hathor, goddess of the Western Mountain, 14, 73, 208; temple of, 28, 30, 202
Hatia (daughter of Djutmose), 170
Hay, Foreman, 60, 62, 73, 80–1, 83, 85, 86, 91, 101, 106, 108, 140; trial of, 80, 81
Hay, son of Siwadj, 91
Hednakht, medjay, 189

Heliopolis, 10
Hennutawi (Nesamenopet's wife), 184, 186
Henutmire, Queen, 92
Heria, 146; trial of, 79–80
Herihor, Southern Vizier and High Priest of Amun, 178, 179, 180, 181, 183, 184, 187, 191; tomb of, 196, 198–9
Hermopolis, 126
Herodotus, 127
Hesysenebef, 63, 90, 91
High Priests of Amun, Theban, 125–7, 128, 132, 133, 139, 140, 148, 193, 194
Horemheb, King, 11, 21, 22, 26, 118, 139, 206
Hori, Draughtsman, 141, 158
Hori (son of Amenwa), 159
Hori, Scribe, 125, 133
Hori, Vizier, 89, 90, 92, 93
Hormin, Draughtsman, 141
Hormose, Foreman, 164
Horus, 14, 66, 67, 93, 96, 97, 189
household furnishings, 62, 63, 108
Hunro, Lady, 84, 90–1
Huy, Scribe, 25, 26, 32, 46

Imiotru, 180
inheritance, 77–8
Inyotef VI, 151
Inyotef VII, 151
Isis, goddess, 30, 73, 160
Isis, Queen, tomb of, 137, 147, 149, 152, 154, 155, 157, 158, 161, 164, 170
Isiseba, Priest, 138
Island of Amenhotep, 147

Janssen, Professor Jac. J., 209

Kadesh, Palestinian god, 28
Kadore, fisherman, 176
Kaha, gang foreman, 19, 31
Kaha, sculptor, 108, 109
Kamose, King, 151
Karnak, temples of, 125–6, 128, 140; temple of Amun, 35, 48, 102, 103
Kashuti, Army Scribe, 171, 181
Keneben, Priest, 136–7
Kenhirkhopeshef, Scribe, 32–6, 41, 42, 44–5, 60, 66, 67, 68, 73–7, 78, 90, 91, 94, 96, 98, 109, 125, 133, 194, 208; child-bride of, 73–4, 159; death of, 77; Dream Book of, 68–72

Kenna (son of Siwadj), 91-2
Khaemhedjet, Scribe, 164, 167, 170, 183
Khaemnum (Naunakht's 2nd husband), 77
Khaemwase, Doorkeeper, 101, 118, 124-5
Khaemwase, Vizier, 164
Kha'nun, villager, 110
Khnum, temple of, 172, 174, 175, 188, 208
Khonsmose, Doorkeeper, 158
Khonsu, Foreman, 110, 111, 113, 122, 124, 129, 206
Khonsu, moon god, 27, 126, 178
Kuban fortress, 189

Lebanon, 178
litigation, 34-5, 100-1, 111
Lower Nubia, 167
Luxor, xii, 48, 102

Ma'at, goddess of truth, 193; temple of, 157, 158, 159, 160, 161, 165
marriage and divorce, 73-4
Mayor of Thebes, 11, 22, 119, 122, 123, 125, 183
Medinet Habu, xii, 205
medjay (policemen), 17-18, 19, 26, 79, 100-1, 134, 140, 166
Memphis, 9, 10, 128, 154
Menna, workman, 100, 101
Mentmose, Chief Medjay, 100, 101, 111, 119, 120, 121, 127, 145, 166
Meretseger, 35, 113
Merneptah, King, 51, 52, 53, 57, 58, 60, 62, 64, 67, 75, 95, 112, 125, 167; tomb of, 40-7, 48, 194
Merybast, Priest, 126
Min, god, 28
Mininuiy, Medjay, 26
Montuhirkhopeshef, Prince, 142
Montuhotep, 151
'Mountains of Bekhen' (papyrus map), 130
mummies, royal, 33, 45-7, 60; mummification, 13, 37, 191-4, 200
Mut, goddess, 27
Mutemwia see Wia

Nakhtamun, Draughtsman, 141
Nakhtamun (Harshire's cousin), 161-2
Naunakht (Kenhirkhopeshef's child bride), 73, 76, 77-8, 159, 208
Nebenmaat, workman, 37

Nebnefer, artist, 132
Nebnefer, Draughtsman, 141
Nebnefer, Foreman, 22, 29, 30, 31, 34, 88, 90
Nebre, Scribe, 22, 37
Neferabu, blinded painter, 103-4, 105, 106
Neferhotep, Foreman (the elder), 22, 23, 29, 30, 31
Neferhotep, Foreman, 29, 30-1, 36, 42, 60, 61-6, 76, 79, 83, 91, 100, 116, 207; feud between Paneb and, 64-6, 73, 76, 79, 81-2, 88, 90
Neferhotep, painter, 83
Neferhoteb, Scribe, 116, 129
Nefersenet (Paneb's father), 61
Nefertari, Queen (mother of Amenhotep I), 194
Nefertari, Queen (wife of Ramesses II), 21, 30
Nekhenmut, Foreman, 101, 103, 106, 110, 113, 116, 162, 164
Nekhenmut, Scribe, 94
Nesamenopet, Scribe, 176, 179, 180, 181, 182, 184, 185, 186
Nubia, 17, 30, 167, 169, 177, 179, 181, 188, 189, 190, 192, 194, 203

old age and retirement, 74-6
Opet Festival, 48-9, 51-2, 103, 112
oracles, 102-3, 108-9, 111, 194, 200, 204
Osiris, 14, 30, 37, 51, 66, 73, 129, 187
outline draughtsmen, 135, 138-41, 199

Pa'aken (Harshire's cousin), 156
Pa'anuket (son of Paneb), 123, 127-8, 129
Pabes, Scribe, 146, 149-50, 154
painters, 83, 108, 109-10, 114, 135-42
Paneb, Foreman, 61-7, 68, 80, 94, 100, 106, 120, 140, 164, 206-7, 209; feud between Neferhotep and, 64-6, 76, 79, 81-2; and Amennakt's accusations, 88-93; trial of, 89, 90, 92
Paneb, stonemason, 149
Panhesi, Viceroy of Nubia, 169, 170-1, 172, 177, 179, 181, 185, 187, 188, 190, 194, 203, 205
Panhesi, Vizier, 44-5, 46
Paser, Mayor of Thebes, 147, 149-50, 151, 152, 153, 154, 155, 156, 163, 164
Paser, Scribe, 60, 74, 86
Paser, Vizier and High Priest, 9, 10, 11-12, 21, 22, 23, 27, 32, 35, 48, 139, 206

Patwere, Scribe, 119, 122
Pawero, Mayor of West Thebes, 149–50, 151, 153, 154, 158, 160–1, 169, 172, 175, 176
Peet, T. Eric, 205, 206
Pekharu, coppersmith, 152
Pentahetnakht, Scribe, 156, 166, 171
Pentaweret, painter, 136, 157
Penuferahy, servant, 179
Pesyenwase, merchant, 180
Piankh, General, 183, 187–8, 189, 190, 192, 194, 196, 198–9, 203
Pinejem, High Priest, 194, 195, 196
Place of Beauty see Valley of the Queens
Plumed Sceptre, province, 173, 175
Poy, Draughtsman, 23
Prahirwenemef, 113
Prahoteb, draughtsman, 33–4
Ptah, god, 10, 107, 152
Pthsankh, peasant, 29
Ptolemaic dynasty, 202, 208, 209

Rahotep, 73
Ramesses I, 159
Ramesses II, 6, 10, 15, 25, 26, 29, 30, 31, 32, 38, 40, 57, 107, 119, 130, 139; tomb, 15, 23, 35, 39, 40, 43, 123, 139, 170, 192, 194, 200
Ramesses III, 58, 86–7, 89, 106–7, 108, 110, 112, 113, 114–15, 116, 117–18, 121, 123, 126, 127, 139, 164, 165, 200, 208; fortress-temple (Medinet Habu) xii, 114, 117, 126, 127, 128, 152, 159, 161, 170, 171, 194, 205
Ramesses IV, 127, 128–9, 130, 134; tomb, 129, 130–2, 133, 135, 139, 140
Ramesses VI, 139, 145; tomb, 140, 146, 179–80, 203
Ramesses VIII, 138, 142
Ramesses IX, 146, 148, 149, 150, 156, 157, 165, 206; tomb, 138, 140, 162
Ramesses X, 165, 166–7
Ramesses XI, 168, 169, 172, 175, 177–9, 183, 184, 191, 195; tomb, 140, 178, 182, 191, 193, 195
Ramessesnakht, High Priest, 128, 145, 149
Ramose, Scribe, 6–9, 12, 13, 14, 15, 16, 19–20, 22, 23–6, 27–9, 30, 31, 32, 33, 35, 39, 41, 50, 61, 76, 77, 106, 107, 108, 152, 171, 186, 196, 202, 204, 205, 206, 208
Re of Heliopolis, god, 27

Reshef, Palestinian god, 28
Roma, head of royal workshops, 48, 51

Salt Papyrus, 207
Schiaparelli, Ernesto, 204–5
scribes, scribal schools, 6–8, 12, 16, 26, 186
sculptors, 60, 135–6, 114, 128, 139, 140
Sebekemsaf II, 151, 153, 163
Seka'atiamun, servant, 180
Sekhenenre I, 151
Sekhenenre II, 151
Sennejem, tomb of, 204
Sermont, Medjay, 185
Seth, god, 58, 96, 97; Followers of, 66–7, 76, 90, 92, 96
Seti I, King, 9–11, 12, 45, 130; tomb of, 10–11, 12, 23, 25, 139, 194, 204
Seti II, King, 57, 60, 65, 79, 81; tomb of, 60–1, 62, 65, 81, 82, 84
Setnakht, King, 57–8, 85, 86, 113; tomb of, 85, 86, 112
sexual behaviour, 71, 98
Shed, god, 28
Sidwadj, 91
Siptah, King, 57, 82, 83, 85; tomb of, 82, 85
Smendes, General, 184
Southern City see Thebes
Southern Opet, Amun's temple at, 48
Spiegelberg, Wilhelm, 209
strikes, 118–23, 124, 146, 166, 208

Tajoy, 177, 178, 184
Tami, Lady, 159
Tausert, Queen, 57, 85, 95; tomb of, 82, 85, 86
Thebes (the Southern City), xi, xii, 3–5, 9, 10, 21, 48, 96, 107–8, 114, 115, 121, 122, 125, 126, 127, 130, 132, 133, 134, 146, 159, 161, 164, 165, 168, 177–8, 182, 183, 187, 202
Thoeris, god, 28
Thoth, moon god, 14, 37, 104, 137
Thothmaktef, quarryman, 25
Tjanefer, priest, 147
To, Vizier, 113, 117, 118, 121–2, 125
Toda, Eduardo, 204
tombmakers' settlement, 35–7
tomb-paintings, 135–42, 199
tomb-robbers, 65, 79–80, 145–55, 157–62, 163–4, 169, 170–1, 179–81, 191, 203, 205
'Turin Taxation Papyrus', 208

Tutankhamun, King, 39
Tuthmosis I, 21, 22, 207
Tuthmosis III, 119, 191
Tuthmosis IV, 8, 12, 31, 137

ushabtis, 26, 37
Userkhepeshef, Acting Foreman, 153, 158, 159, 162, 164

Valley of the Kings (The Great Place), xii, 11, 12, 13-18, 19, 25, 29, 32, 33, 34, 35-6, 50, 51, 57, 58, 59, 60-1, 64-5, 76, 82-4, 85, 88, 100, 113, 119, 120, 121, 125, 126-7, 130, 133, 135, 138, 139, 140, 141, 149, 162, 182, 191, 194, 195, 204, 208; flood, 38-9; Merneptah's tomb, 40-7; security system, 16-17; tombmakers' new settlement, 35-7
Valley of the Queens (Place of Beauty), xii, 24, 30, 106, 113, 116, 139, 147, 149, 152, 154, 158, 161, 179
village cemetery, 20-1, 30-1, 33, 109-11, 133, 206

village hierarchy/chiefs, 106, 124-5, 132
village houses, 20, 22
village tribunal, 100, 102, 111
village women, 186
Vizier, office of, 9, 10, 11, 124, 125, 132-3

Wa'bet (Paneb's wife), 62
Wabkhet (Neferhotep's wife), 36, 61, 90, 91
Wadi Gharbi, 197
Wadi Hammamat stone quarries, 128; map ('Mountains of Bekhen'), 130; royal expedition to, 128, 129
wadis, Theban tombs in, 195-9, 200
warehouses/storerooms, 6, 17, 100, 101
Wennenefer, Scribe, 158
Wente, Prof. Edward F., 209
Wia (Mutemwia: Ramose's wife), 26, 27-8, 30, 32, 33, 75

Yar, Nubia, 189
Year of the Hyenas, 168, 171, 179, 203
Yemyemwah, Lady, 90